한국 인권문제

민주화 관련
기타 자료 2

한국 인권문제

민주화 관련
기타 자료 2

| 머리말

일제 강점기 독립운동과 병행되었던 한국의 인권운동은 해방이 되었음에도 큰 결실을 보지 못했다. 1950년대 반공을 앞세운 이승만 정부와 한국전쟁, 역시 경제발전과 반공을 내세우다 유신 체제에 이르렀던 박정희 정권, 쿠데타로 집권한 1980년대 전두환 정권까지, 한국의 인권은 이를 보장해야 할 국가와 정부에 의해 도리어 억압받고 침해되었다. 이런 배경상 근대 한국의 인권운동은 반독재, 민주화운동과 결을 같이했고, 대체로 국외에 본부를 둔 인권 단체나 정치로부터 상대적으로 자유로운 종교 단체에 의해 주도되곤 했다. 이는 1980년 5·18광주민주화운동을 계기로 보다 근적인 변혁을 요구하는 형태로 조직화되었고, 그 활동 영역도 정치를 넘어 노동자, 농민, 빈민 등으로 확대되었다. 이들이 없었다면 한국은 1987년 군부 독재 종식하고 절차적 민주주의를 도입할 수 없었을 것이다. 민주화 이후에도 수많은 어려움이 있었지만, 한국의 인권운동은 점차 전문적이고 독립된 운동으로 분화되며 더 많은 이들의 참여를 이끌어냈고, 지금까지 많은 결실을 맺을 수 있었다.

본 총서는 1980년대 중반부터 1990년대 초반까지, 외교부에서 작성하여 30여 년간 유지했던 한국 인권문제와 관련한 국내외 자료를 담고 있다. 6월 항쟁이 일어나고 민주화 선언이 이뤄지는 등 한국 인권운동에 많은 변화가 있었던 시기다. 당시 인권문제와 관련한 국내외 사안들, 각종 사건에 대한 미국과 우방국, 유엔의 반응, 최초의 한국 인권보고서 제출과 아동의 권리에 관한 협약 과정, 유엔인권위원회 활동, 기타 민주화 관련 자료 등 총 18권으로 구성되었다. 전체 분량은 약 9천여 쪽에 이른다.

2024년 3월

한국학술정보(주)

| 일러두기

· 본 총서에 실린 자료는 2022년 4월과 2023년 4월에 각각 공개한 외교문서 4,827권, 76만 여 쪽 가운데 일부를 발췌한 것이다.

· 각 권의 제목과 순서는 공개된 원본을 최대한 반영하였으나, 주제에 따라 일부는 적절히 변경하였다.

· 원본 자료는 A4 판형에 맞게 축소하거나 원본 비율을 유지한 채 A4 페이지 안에 삽입 하였다. 또한 현재 시점에선 공개되지 않아 '공란'이란 표기만 있는 페이지 역시 그대로 실었다.

· 외교부가 공개한 문서 각 권의 첫 페이지에는 '정리 보존 문서 목록'이란 이름으로 기록물 종류, 일자, 명칭, 간단한 내용 등의 정보가 수록되어 있으며, 이를 기준으로 0001번부터 번호가 매겨져 있다. 이는 삭제하지 않고 총서에 그대로 수록하였다.

· 보고서 내용에 관한 더 자세한 정보가 필요하다면, 외교부가 온라인상에 제공하는 『대한 민국 외교사료요약집』 1991년과 1992년 자료를 참조할 수 있다.

| 차례

정/리/보/존/문/서/목/록

기록물종류	문서-일반공문서철	등록번호	10038		등록일자	91-11-28
분류번호	701	국가코드	AU		주제	
문서철명	한국 정세 및 인권문제에 대한 호주 반응, 1987					
생산과	동남아과	생산년도	1987 ~ 1987		보존기간	영구
담당과(그룹)	아주	동남아.서남아.대양주		서가번호	--	
참조분류						
권차명						
내용목차						

마/이/크/로/필/름/사/항

촬영연도	*롤 번호	화일 번호	후레임 번호	보관함 번호

0001

주 호 주 대 사 관

호주(정)2000- 01   1987. 1. 9.

수신 장관

참조 아주국장

제목 인권문제 관련진정

    1. 아래와 같이 주재국 인사로부터 인권관련 진정이 있었음을 보고합니다.

       가. 양동화, 김성만 사형 감형요구

          Mrs.M.Beaufremez
          185 Dover St
          Richmond, 3121

          Lynn Dugay
          16 Devlow Dr.
          East Doncaster, VIC 3109

          Ms.Megan Adams, Ms.Saskia Adams,Mr.Chris Middendorp
          9 Kildare St.
          East Hawthorne, VIC 3123

          V.C.Mitchell
          413 Wellington Street
          CLIFTON HILL VIC 3068

       나. 조정식, 이민용, 이동엽, 천원하 외 11명 옥중 대우관심표명

          Mr.Noel S.Havenhand
          1 Hillingdon Cres.
          Kiama, NSW 2533

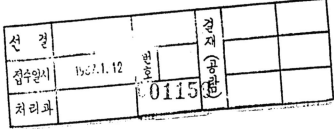

0002

다. 송용호、이태헌、김현순、김재관、정윤교、정선임、이동항 석방진정

     Mr.Hugh Sherry

     2 Hillcrest St

     Wahroonga, NSW 2076

라. 김병규、박용숙、임성희 및 김성은(86.11.26 구속)석방진정

     Ms.Julie Blake

     Flat 2, 110 Station St

     Thomastown, VIC 3074

마. 백기완 석방요구(86.7.19 명동성당 집회관련 12.7 구속)

     Ms.Clare Maguire

     201 Trafalgar St,

     Annandale NSW 2038

바. 북괴방송청취 및 좌경단체 활동참여 관련 구속자 10명(86.12.11자

Korea Times   보도)석방진정

     Miss E.Reeve

     13/62 Norfolk Rd

     Epping NSW 2121

2. 상기 "다""마""바"항 관련 당국의 해명자료 송부 바랍니다. 끝.

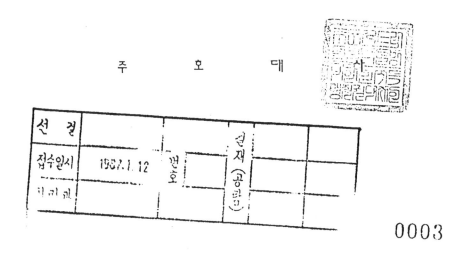

주 호 대

선 결					
접수일시	1987.1.12	번호	전재(공람)		
처리과					

0003

외 무 부 착 신 전 문

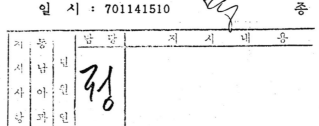

번 호 : AUW-0044   일 시 : 701141510   종 별 :

수 신 : 장관(국연,아동)

발 신 : 주 호주 대사

제 목 : 유엔인권위 대책

지 시 사 항	동 남 아 과	남 당	지 시 내 용
	린 인 과 인	정	

대: WAU-0791

1.대호건 1.14   GATES 북아시아 부국장 접촉시, 북한 움직임을 설명하고, 협조를
요청한바, 동 부국장은 현재까지 호주의 경우 북한측으로 부터 아무런 접촉시도가
없는 것으로 알고있으나, 만일 북한의 책동으로 아국 인권문제가 제기된다면, 이는
인권문제와는 별개 차원의 문제로서, 관계부서와 협의하여 협조하겠다고 말하고, 동
회의에는   ROBERTSON 주제네바 호주대사의 참석이 예상된다고 하였음을 우선 보고
함.

2.본건 주무국인 국제기구국과 재접촉 보고위계임.

(대사 임동원-차관)

예고:87.12.31.일반

국기국   차관실   1 차보   아주국   청와대   안 기   성문국

KOREAM MA30324 0

↓ 0
↑ WOIMUBU K24652
↓ AIAUST AA23206
14 JANUARY

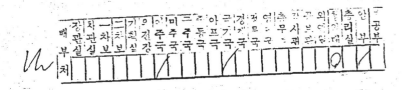

HIS EXCELLENCY PRESIDENT CHUN DOO- HWAN
SEOUL
REPUBLIC OF KOREA

URGE THAT PREVENTIVE CUSTODY ORDER AGAINST KANG JONG-KON
NOT BE RENEWED AND THAT HE BE IMMEDIATELY AND UNCONDITIONALLY
RELEASED

AMNESTY INTERNATIONAL AUSTRALIA
NSW BRANCH

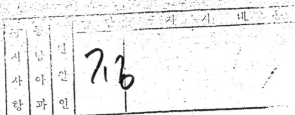

AIAUST AA232060
↑ WOIMUBU K24652

0005

↑ WOIMUBU K24651
↓ AIAUST AA23206

9 DEC., 1986
PRESIDENT CHUN DOO-HWAN
SEOUL
SOUTH KOREA

12-9 13 :08

RESPECTFULLY URGE DEATH SENTENCES IMPOSED ON YANG DONG-HWA AND
KIM SONG-MAN BE COMMUTED.
A. I. OPPOSES DEATH PENALTY UNCONDITIONALLY.

AMNESTY INTERNATIONAL AUSTRALIA
NSW BRANCH

MD

0006

외 무 부 착 신 전 문

일 시 : 70123 1500   종 별 :

번 호 : AUW-0082

수 신 : 장 관(국연, 아동)

발 신 : 주 호주 대사

제 목 : 유엔인권위 대책

대: WAU-0791

연: AUW-0044

1. 대호건 1.23 주재국 외무성 GERALD HARDING 인권담당관장을 추가 접촉한바, 동인은 상금 북괴측으로부터 아무런 접근 시도도 없었으며 의제에도 포함되어있지 않았다고 말하고, 호주는 ROBERTSON 주제네바 대사를 포함한 제네바 대표부지권 3명, 주유엔 호주대표부직원 1명및 외무성 직원 1명, 계 5명의 대표단이 참가예정이라고 밝힘.

2. 동건 북한 책동으로 아국인원문제가 제기된다면 이는 인권문제와는 별개차원의 문제임을 지적하고, 아국 주요 맹방의 하나인 호주가 적극협력해줄것을 요청한바, 동인은 유의하겠다는 반응을 보였음을 첨언함.

(대사 임동원-차관)

예고:87.12.31.일반

국기국   차관실   1 차보   아주국   청와대   안 기

한국 정세 및 인권문제에 대한 호주 반응, 1987 13

주 호 주 대 사 관

1987. 1. 22.

수신 장관

참조 아주국장

제목 인권진정

1. 아래와 같이 주재국인사로 부터 인권관련 진정이 있었음을 보고합니다.

　　가. 백기완 석방요구

Maureen Playdon

13 Tulip St

Chatswood 2067

Stephen Birch

60 A Pleasant Rd

Hawthorn East, Vic 3123

C.Bootsman

30 Campbell Grove

Dingley, Vic 3172

L.Max Baker

Talent search Pty.LTD

155 Drummond St

Carlton, Vic 3053

선 결			결재 (과장)		
접수일시	1987.1.26	번호			
처리		005204			

0008

나. 송용호, 이태헌, 김현순, 김재관, 정윤교, 정선임, 이동항 석방진정

관심표명 및 진상요구

```
Maureen Playdon
13 Tulip St
Chatswood    NSW2067


Janet Keller
28 Sailors Bay Rd
Northbridge NSW 2063


Amanda Currie
8 Tahlee Pl
Vermont South, Vic 3133
```

다. 건국대학 소요사태 관심 표명

```
Robyn Alders
ANU
P.O.BOX 334
Canberra City A.C.T.  2601
```

라. 김태홍, 신홍범, 김주온(기자 86.12. 구속)석방 요구

```
Paul and Louise Vinnane
4 Bransby Ave.
North Plympton, S.A. 5037


Clare Maguire
201 Trafalgar St
Annandale, NSW 2038
```

마. 김병규、박용숙、임성희、김성은 석방진정

```
Noel S. Havenhand
1 Hillingdon Cres.
Kiama, NSW 2533

Mr.John Frame
11 Brown Street
Newport Vic 3015

Glenda Jones
P.O.BOX 628
Lakes Entrance Vic 3909
```

바. 양동화、김성만 사형선고 감형요구

```
D.N.& R.Madill, Members of Amnesty International
2 Mungari St
Dingley Vic 3172

Mr.& Mrs. Doumos,Members of Amnesty International
7/75 Edinburgh St
Richmond, Vic 3121

Miss B.A.Besley, Member of Amnesty International
13 Third Ave.
Moana, 5169
```

사. 조정식、이민용、이동엽、박정식、천원하등 석방진정

```
L.Chamas
228 Forest Rd
Arncliffe, NSW 2205
```

0010

아. 홍기선.이효인 석방 진정

    M.S.Ward, SRN, JP

    391 Wickham Terrace

    Brisbane, QLD 4000

2. 상기 "라"항 관련 당국의 해면자료 송부 바랍니다. 끝.

주   호   대

0011

주 호 주 대 사 관

호주(정)2000-91   1987. 2. 20.

수신 장관

참조 아주국장

제목 인권진정

1. 아래와 같이 주재국 인사로부터 인권관련 진정이 있었음을 보고합니다.

　가. 재일교포 강종곤(KANG Jong-Kon   )에 대한 예방구속조치항의

　　　Irene Sills, Member of Amnesty International

　　　82 Denning St

　　　South Coogee 2034

　　　Meg Spicer,Member of Amnesty International

　　　185 Victoria St

　　　Brunswick 3056

　　　John Green

　　　39 Main Rd.

　　　Moonah 7009

　　　Geoff ¢ Heather Rundell

　　　24 Worthing Ave,

　　　East Burwood, Vic 3151

　　　성명미상
　　　5 Titree Grve

　　　Parkdale 3194 Vic

　나. 김태홍、신홍범、김주은 석방요구

　　　Barbara Stroud

　　　P.O.BOX 4

　　　South Wagga Wagga, NSW 2650

선 결			결재(공람)		
접수일시	1987. 2. 23	편호			
처리과	011358				

0012

Andrew Goldie
11 Brighton Parade
Blackwood, SA 5051

Mary Holyoake,Member of Amnesty International
16 Park Ave
Richmond, Vic 3121

Judith H. Reidal
P.O.BOX 42
North Hobart 7002

Judith G.Wallace
"GLENOGIL" Harkaway 3806

Mary Holyoake
16 Park Avenue
Richmond, Victoria 3121
Melbourne, Australia

Clare Maguire
201 Trafalgar St.
Annandale 2038

Robin Sevenoaks
Jamieson Farm
Berndale 2628 NSW

다. 송용호、이태헌、정선임.정윤교、이동항、김재관、김현순 석방진정   외8명

Amanda Currie
8 Tahlee Pl
Vermont South, Vic 3133

0013

Noel S. Havenhand
1 Hillingdon Cres.
Kiama, NSW 2533

라. 박종철 고문 치사사건

John P.Brown, Director of Commission for Mission
4th Fl. 123 Clarence St
Sydney NSW 2000

마. 신영복

Peter Bennett
62 Fitzroy St
Burwood, NSW 2134

바. 백기완 석방요구

Vic.Mitchell
413 Wellington Street
Clifton Hill, 3068 Vic

2. 상기 "가"항 관련 당국의 해명자료 송부 바랍니다. 끝.

주   호   대

0014

주 호 주 대 사 관

호주(정)2000-122   1987. 3. 6.

수신 장관

참조 아주국장

제목 인권진정

　　　1. 아래와 같은 주재국 인사로 부터 87..2.12 불온서적 출판혐의로

구속된 나평식 및 7명의 석방 진정이 있었음을 보고합니다.

　　　　　　　Mr & Mrs J. Bongiorno
　　　　　　　701 Dana Street
　　　　　　　BALLART VIC 3350

　　　　　　　Ms J.D.Smith
　　　　　　　1/11 Sturdee Street
　　　　　　　BROADVIEW SA 5803

　　　　　　　Mr.Philip Ruddock, MP
　　　　　　　Member for Dundas
　　　　　　　Suite 302
　　　　　　　Eastwood Centre
　　　　　　　160 Rowe Street
　　　　　　　Eastwood NSW.. 2122

　　　2. 동건 관련 당국의 해명자료 송부바랍니다.   끝.
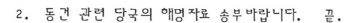

주　　　호　　　대

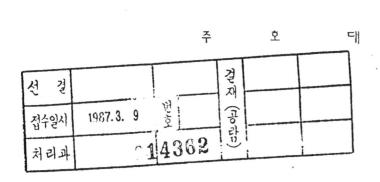

선결				결재	
접수일시	1987.3. 9	번호		(공람)	
처리과		14362			

0015

간보기

주 호 주 대 사 관

호주(정)2000-*175*   1987. 4. 2.

수신 장관

참조 아주국장

제목 인권관련 진정

1. 아래와 같이 주재국 인사로부터 인권관련 진정이 있었음을 보고합니다.

　가. 정성현(87.3.2구속) 석방진정

　　　Philip Ruddock
　　　Member of Australian Parliament(House of Rep.),
　　　Member for Dundas
　　　George Petersen
　　　Member of Parliament,N.S.W.(Legislative Assembly):
　　　MP for Illawarra

　　　John Bongiorno 외 27명
　　　701 Dana St
　　　Ballarat, Vic 3350

　　　Noel S.Havenhand
　　　1 Hillingdon Cres.
　　　Kiama, N.S.W. 2533

　　　Michael Jones
　　　P.O.BOX 759
　　　Belconnen A.C.T. 2616

　　　Dr.A.M.Healy
　　　PO BOX 1144
　　　Wollongong NSW 2500

선 결			결재(공람)		
접수일시	1987.4. 6	번호			
처리과	020696				

0016

나. 박우정(87.3.4 구속)정상모 석방요구

(Mrs.)Rae Goth,Member of Amnesty International
58 Lough Ave.
Guildford, N.S.W. 2161

Noel S.Havenhand
1 Hillingdon Cres
Kiama,N.S.W. 2533

Mr.H.Sherry
2 Hillcrest Street
Wahroonga NSW 2076

다. 백기완

B.R.Speed
Fairfield Hospital
Fairfield, Vic 3078

Dr.W.J.Quilty
115 Sobraon Street
Shepparton VIC 3630

David Birks
Moe South Road
Moe, Vic 3825
Malcom Douglas
Medical Practioner

라. 김상근 구속항의 및 김용권 자살진상 설명 요구

Ian Tanner
President of Uniting Church in Australia

마. 김용권 고문 항의

John P.Brown
Director of the Uniting Church in Australia
4th Fl.123 Clarence St
Sydney, NSW 2000

바. 나명식(87.2.12 구속) 석방진정

Judith G.Wallace
"Glenogil"
Harkaway, Vic 3806

0017

사. 최민화(대전교도소 수감중) 석방시기문의
    Ms.N.Searles
    P.O.BOX 342
    Midland WA 6056

2. 상기 "가""""나""""라""""사"항 관련 당국의 해명자료 송부합니다. 끝.

대   호   주

0018

WOIMUBU K24651
AIAUST AA23206

1 APRIL, 1987

HIS EXCELLENCY PRESIDENT CHUN DOO-HWAN,

SEOUL,

SOUTH KOREA.

WE URGE IMMEDIATE AND UNCONDITIONAL RELEASE OF SOH
JOON-SHIK AND KANG JONG- KON, PRISONERS OF CONSCIENCE,
DETAINED FOR NON-VIOLENT EXPRESSION OF BELIEFS.

AMNESTY INTERNATIONAL AUSTRALIA.

배부실	장관실	차관실	一차보	二차보	기획실	의전장	아주국	미주국	구주국	중동국	아동국	국가국	경제국	정문국	영사국	총무과	감사관	공보관	의연실	협력단	총리실	안기부	두공부
					/	/	/	/									a						

DD

김(정)

주 호 주 대 사 관

호주(정) 2000-204   1987.4.16.

수신   장관

참조   아주국장

제목   인권관련진정

        아래와 같이 주재국인사로부터 인권관련 진정이 있었음을
보고합니다.

1. 서준식 및 강종건 석방진정

    Ms A. Lenos, Member of Amnesty International
    14 Churchill Avenue
    CHADSTONE VIC 3148

    Mrs Beverley Lewis, Member of Amnesty International
    3 Stawell Street
    PRAHRAN VIC 3181

2. 정성현석방진정

    Ms Susan B. Hewett, Member of Amnesty International
    Amnesty International Australian Group 505
    Box 2196
    WHYALLA NORRIE SA 5608

    Mrs Margaret Hewitson, Member of Amnesty International
    Amnesty International Australian Group 505
    Box 2196
    WHYALLA NORRIE SA 5608

    Ms Ann M. Burgin
    274 Douglas Parade
    NEWPORT VIC 3015

    K.E. Taylor
    (No address given)

선 결			결재 (공람)		
접수일시	1987.4 20				
처리과	28975				

1

0020

3. 박우정 석방진정

Mr D.M. Chancellor
Box 34
BLACKWOOD   SA   5051

Mr Ian C. Clayton
28 Blackdown Street
ELIZABETH WEST   SA   5113

4. 백기완 석방진정

G.L. Gillam
99 Burke Road North
EAST IVANHOE   VIC   3079

주   호   대

2

0021

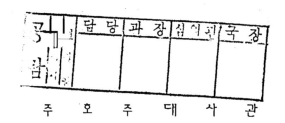

호주(정) 2000- 23ㅏ   1987. 5. 15.

수신 장관

참조 아주국장

제목 인권 관련 진정

선 결			결재 (공람)		
접수일시	1987.5 18	번호			
처리과	C29730				

1. 아래와 같이 주재국 인사로부터 인권 관련 진정이 있었음을 보고합니다.

  가. 서준식、강종건 석방 요구

    Mr. S. McIntyre, Member of Amnesty International
    33 Canadian Bay Rd.
    Mt. Eliza, VIC 3930

    Mrs. F. Nichols
    30 Cardinal Ave.
    Beecroft, NSW 2119

    Ms. M. LaScala
    9 Sherwood Rd.
    Ivanhoe, VIC 3079

    Mr. Robert Sulter
    1/58 Whitmuir Rd.
    Bentleigh, VIC 3204

    Mr. Ian Clayton, Member of Amnesty International
    28 Blackdown St.
    Elizabeth West, S.A. 5113

    Concerned Students
    Amnesty International, Melbourne University
    c/o Student Activities
    University of Melbourne
    Parkville, VIC 3052

  나. 한성문、배문종、하연수 석방 요구 및 옥중 대우 관심 표명

    Miss Christine Phillips
    c/- Alice Springs Hospital
    Alice Springs, N.T. 5075

    Concerned Students
    Amnesty International, Melbourne University Group
    c/o Student Activities
    University of Melbourne
    Parkville, VIC 3052

0022

```
Ms. Sarah Austin
41 Tennyson Street
Kew 3101 Victoria
Australia

Mr. Harry Collins, Member of Amnesty International
10 Bourke St.
Pymble, NSW 2073
```

다. 박우정 석방 요구

```
Ms. Joyce Trevitt
46 Morton Rd.
Burwood, VIC 3125
```

2. 상기 "나", "다"항 관련, 당국의 해명자료 송부 바랍니다.   끝.

주   호   주   대

0023

김(까리)

주 호 주 대 사 관

호주 (정) 20000-*288*   87. 6. 12.

수신   장관
참조   아주국장
제목   인권 관련 진정

1. 아래와 같이 주재국 인사로부터 인권 관련 진정이 있었음을 보고합니다.

                    - 아   래 -

   가. 김문수 고문 항의

       K.J. Clancy, Member of Amnesty International, Chavelier College
       Bowral, NSW 2576

       H & C.A. Lott, Member of Amnesty International
       Tasmania I.B. 134
       Currie, King Island 7256

       (Miss) M. Bulstrode
       53/695 Hawthorn Road
       East Brighton, Vic. 3187

1987. 6. 1 2
주호대사관

   나. 한성문、 배문종、 하연수 제적학생의 옥중 대우 관심 표명 및 석방요구

       Noel S. Havenhand
       1 Hillingdon Cres.
       Kiama, NSW 2533

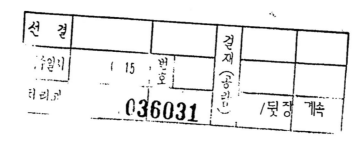

선 결			결재 (공란)		
년월일	15 번호				
처리과	036031			/뒷장 계속	

0024

다. 김성식、 윤성구、 이선희、 김설수、 유강근、 민최、 민병두 옥중고문
   항의 및 석방 요구
   Joyce R. Trevitt, Member of Amnesty International
   46 Morton Rd.
   Burwood, Vic. 3125

라. 이민용、 이동엽、 박시정、 김진호 옥중 대우 관심 표명
   Paul J. Meenters, Member of Amnesty International
   17 Kerrimuir St.
   Box Hill North, Vic. 3129

마. 박종철 사건 관심 표명
   Dr. S. Hofirek
   Secretary, Chrishan Democratic Association of Central
   Eastern European Australia,
   Flat 5, 159 Melrose St.
   North Melbourne
   Victoria 3051

바. 등현 (Dung Hyun   : 발행인) 석방 요구
   Mr. Niall Brennan
   "Kingajanik"
   RSD 202
   Gladysdale
   Victoria 3797

2. 상기 "가"、 "다"、 "라"、 "바" 항 관련、 당국의 해명자료 송부 바랍니다.
                                              끝.

        주   호   주   대

                                              0025

외 무 부   착신전문

원 본

번 호 : AUW-0786   일 시 : 706301820   종 별 :

수 신 : 장 관 (아동,정일)

발 신 : 주 호주 대사

제 목 : 국내정세에 대한 헤이든 장관 성명 (자료응신 166호)

헤이든 주지국 외무장관은 금 6.30 저녁, 노태우 민정당 대표의 발표와 관련 다음과
같이 환영성명을 발표하였음.

별첨 : 환영성명

(주호주대사 임동원-국장)

별첨 :

DEVELOPMENTS IN KOREA

THE MINISTER FOR FOREIGN AFFAIRS, MR BILL HAYDEN M.P., SAID TODAY THAT THE AUST
RALIAN GOVERNMENT WELCOMES THE IMPORTANT AND FAR-REACHING STEPS IN THE REPUBLIC
OF KOREA TOWARDS A PEACEFUL AND DEMOCRATIC ELECTORAL PROCESS AND THE REMOVAL OF
RESTRICTIONS ON FREEDOM OF SPEECH.

MR HAYDEN POINTED TO THE STATEMENT ON 29 JUNE BY CHAIRMAN OF THE RULING DEMOCRA
TIC JUSTICE PARTY, ROH TAE WOO (PRONOUNCED 'NO TAY OO'), WHICH CALLED FOR:

- CONSTITUTIONAL REFORM TO ALLOW DIRECT ELECTIONS FOR THE SUCCESSOR TO PRESIDEN
T CHUN DOO HWAN (WHO IS DUE TO RETIRE IN FEBRUARY 1988):

- AMNESTY FOR PROMINENT OPPOSITION LEADER KIM DAE JUNG: AND

- THE RELAXATION OF VARIOUS RESTRICTIONS ON DEMOCRATIC FREEDOM.

HE SAID THAT THESE PROPOSALS BY MR ROH APPEARED TO ENJOY WIDESPREAD SUPPORT IN
KOREA, FROM THE RULING AND OPPOSITION PARTIES, FROM RELIGIOUS GROUPS, BUSINESS O
RGANISATIONS, AND FROM SOUTH KOREANS IN ALL WALKS OF LIFE. ON THIS BASIS, THERE
NOW SEEMED TO BE BRIGHT PROSPECTS FOR THE FORMATION OF A NEW PULULARLY ELECTED G

차보   정문국   청와대   안 기   문공부

PAGE 1

OVERNMENT NEXT YEAR IN ACCORDANCE WITH THE DEMOCRATIC ASPIRATIONS OF THE SOUTH K

OREAN PEOPLE AS A WHOLE. IT WOULD BE A TRAGEDY FOR SOUTH KOREA, AND A MAJOR BLOW

TO ITS STANDING IN THE WORLD COMMUNITY, IF REFORM DID NOT PROCEED OR WAS OBSTRU

CTED BY INTERESTS INSIDE OR OUTSIDE THE COUNTRY.

MR HAYDEN SAID THAT THE AUSTRALIAN GOVERNMENT HAD IN RECENT YEARS MADE CONSISTE

NT REPRESENTATIONS TO THE ROK GOVERNMENT ON THE NEED FOR LIBERALISATION AND DEMO

CRATISATION OF ITS POLITICAL SYSTEM. THE AUSTRALIAN EMBASSY IN SEOUL, ON THE GOV

ERNMENT'S INSTRUCTIONS, HAD KEPT IN REGULAR CONTACT WITH LEADING OPPOSITION POLI

TICIANS, INCLUDING KIM DAE JUNG AND KIM YOUNG SAM. AS RECENTLY AS LAST MONTH, TH

E GOVERNMENT EXPRESSED STRONG RESERVATIONS TO THE ROK GOVERNMENT OVER MOVES BY T

HE LATTER TO BAN THE MAJOR OPPOSITIONRE PARTY.

MR HAYDEN ADDED THAT THE AUSTRALIAN EMBASSY IN SEOUL HAS BEEN INSTRUCTED TO REI

TERATE TO BOTH GOVERNMENT AND OPPOSITION POLITICIANS AUSTRALI'S STRONG DESIRE TH

AT THE GOVERNMENT AND OPPOSITION GROUPS WILL ENTER INTO A CONSTRUCTIVE POLITICAL

DIALOGUE, AND A PEACEFUL AND DEMOCRATIC ELECTORAL PROCESS CAN BE ACHIEVED BY SU

CH A DIALOGUE.

END

외 무 부 착신전보

번 호 : SNW-0260   일 시 : 706301130   종 별 :

수 신 : 장 관 (아동)

발 신 : 주 시드니 총영사

제 목 : 호주연방 야당의 아국사태 관련 신문 발표문

금일 당관에 입수된 NEIL BROWN 연방 야당 부당수겸 야당 외상의 아국사태 관련 언론발표문 (6.28.자 시드니발) 전문을 아래 타전하니 참고바람.

- 아 래 -

THE LIBERAL PARTY VIEWS WITH COPNCERN THE GROWING UNREST IN SOUTH KOREA. POLITICAL INSTABILITY IN SEOUL AND OTHER CITIES HAS THE POTENTIAL TO AFFECT ADVERSELY THE SECURITY NOT ONLYOF SOUTH KOREA BUT OF THE ASIAN REGION AS A WHOLE. DEMOCRACY IN SOUTH KOREA IS THE BEST DEFENCE AGAINST NORTH KOREA AND OTHER DICTATORSHIPS IN THE REGION.

IT IS THEREFORE TO BE HOPED THAT THE ONGOING PROBLEMS IN SOUTH KOREA CAN BE RESOLVED GY DIALOGUE BETWEEN THE GOVERNMENT AND OPPOSITI ON PARTIES THAT WILL LEAD TO A STRENGTHENING OF THE DEMOCRATIC PROCESSES. IN PARTICULAR, WE WOULD WELCOME THE REOPENING OF DIALOGUE ON REFORM OF THE CONSTITUTION AND DIRECT PRESIDENTIAL ELECTIONS. WITH THE APPROACH OF THE SEOUL OLYMPICS NEXT YEAR, WORLD ATTENTION WILL FOCUS INCREASINGLY ON POLITICAL DEVELOPMENTS IN SOUTH KOREA. AUSTRALIA AND OTHER DEMOCRACIES WILL WATCH THESEDEVELOPMENTS CLOSELY: IT IS IN OUR INTEREST AND THAT OF SOUTH KOREA TO ENCOURAGE AND FOSTER THE DEMOCRATIC PROCESS IN THAT COUNTRY. THE HAWKE GOVERNMENT'S COMPLETE SILENCE ON THE ISSUE SHOWS THAT, AS USUAL, IT IS OUT OF TOUCH WITH EVENTS IN ASIA, INDIFFERENT TO THE GROWING CRISIS AND HAS NO ANSWERS TOTHE SOUTH KOREAN PROBLEM

(총영사 진관섭-국장)

아주국   1 차보   청와대   안 기   정문국

PAGE 1   87.07.01 11:37
                                              외신 1과 통제관

0028

34 한국 인권문제 민주화 관련 기타 자료 2

외 무 부

착 선 전 보

번 호 : AUW-0802   일 시 : 70702 1130   종 별 :
수 신 : 장 관 (아동)
발 신 : 주 호주 대사
제 목 : 국내사태에 대한 주재국 여야 성명

연 : AUW-0786

1. BROWN 주재국 야당 외교문제 대변인은, 민정당 노대표 발표전일인 6.28. 시드니에 서 한국 국내사태에 관한 별첨과 같은 신문 발표문을 발표하였음.

2. 상기 발표중 마지막 부분에서, 동 대변인은 호크정부의 침묵을 비난하였는바, 연 호 헤이든 외상의 성명중 하반부는 오는 7.11 총선거를 의식, 동 야당의 공격에 대한 정부측의 대응으로 보여짐.

(대사 임동원-국장)

별첨 : 발표문

SOUTH KOREA

THE LIBERAL PARTY VIEWS WITH CONCERN THE GROWING

UNREST IN SOUTH KOREA

POLITICAL INSTABILITY IN SEOUL AND OTHER CITIES HAS THE POTENTIAL TO AFFECT ADV

ERSELY THE SECURITY NOT ONLY OF SOUTH KOREA BUT OF THE ASIAN REGION AS WHOLE.

DEMOCRACY IN SOUTH KOREA IS THE BEST DEFENCEAG AINST NORTH KOREA AND OTHER DICTA

TORSHIP IN THE REGION. IT IS THEREFORE TO BE HOPED THAT THE ONGOING PROBLEMS IN

SOUTH KOREA CAN BE RESOLVED BY DIALOGUE BETWEEN THE GOVERNMENT AND OPPOSITION PA

RTIES THAT WILL LEAD TO A STRENGTHENING OF THE DEMOCRATIC PROCESSES. IN PARTICUL

AR, WE WOULD WELCOME THE REOPENING OF DIALOGUE ON REFORM OF THE CONSTITUTION AND

DIRECT PRESIDENTIAL ELECTIONS.

WITH THE APPROACH OF THE SEOUL OLYMPICS NEXT YEAR, WORLD ATTENTION WILL FOCUS IN

아주국   1 차보   청와대   안 기   정문국   반공부

PAGE   1

87.07.02   13:35
외신 1과

0029

CREASINGLY ON POLITICAL DEVELOPMENTS IN WOUTH KOREA. AUSTRALIA AND OTHER DEMOCRA
CIES WILL WATCH THESE DEVELOPMENTS CLOSELY: IT IS IN OUR INTEREST AND THAT OF SO
UTH KOREA TO ENCOURAGE AND FOSTER THE DEMOCRATIC PROCESS IN THAT COUNTRY.
THE HAWKE GOVERNMENT'S COMPLETE SILENCE ON THE ISSUE SHOWS THAT, AS USUAL, IT I
S OUT OF TOUCH WITH EVENTSIN ASIA, INDIFFERENT TO THE GROWING CRISIS AND HAS NO
ANSWERS TO THE SOUTH KOREAN PROBLEM.
END

PAGE   2

정 리 보 존 문 서 목 록

기록물종류	일반공문서철	등록번호	2020010118	등록일자	2020-01-20
분류번호	701	국가코드	GE	보존기간	영구
명 칭	한국 인권문제 관련 독일 동향, 1989-91				
생 산 과	서구1과	생산년도	1989~1991	담당그룹	
내용목차	＊ 독일인 Juergen Meier 입국 불허 문제 ＊ 이해학, 홍근수 목사 석방요구 독일인 1,127명 서명 ＊ 독일지 DAAD 초청, 1991.10월 홍성담 작품 전시회 개최				

0001

주한 독일대사 면담자료

(인 권 문 제)

1989. 12.

서 구 1 과

0002

o 금일 귀대사를 이자리에 초치한것은 아국의 인권상황에 대한 이해를
  돕기위한 것으로 우리 인권문제에 대하여 더이상의 오해가 없기를
  바라는 차원에서인 것임.

o 1988년2월 제6공화국 출범이후 한국정부는 확고한 민주화 의지하에
  우리사회 전반에 걸친 민주화 추진노력을 기울여 왔으며, 이에따라
  인권문제에 있어서도 몇차례의 사면을 통해 소위 정치범이나 반체제
  인사를 전원 석방 조치하였으며 UN의 "국제인권규약" 가입을 추진
  하고 있는등 한국내에는 더이상의 인권문제가 존재하지 않음을
  대내외에 강조해 왔음.

o 그러나 인권분야에 대한 이러한 한국정부의 노력과 최근의 실상이
  일부 우방국정부에 정확하게 인식되지 못하고 있다는 사실에
  접할때마다 우리정부는 당혹감과 함께 깊은 유감의 뜻을 표하지
  않을수 없음.

o 특히, 금번 아국대통령의 귀국방문시 거론된 바 있는 문익환,
  홍성담, 김형규 문제는 정치범 구속과 같은 인권문제의 차원을
  벗어나는 것으로, 이들은 공히 친북 반체제 활동이나 간첩활동
  또는 정부의 사전 허가없이 방북하는등 우리나라의 실정법
  (국가보안법 및 형법)을 명백히 위반하는 활동을 한자들임.

o 현재 문익환, 홍성담에 대한 사법절차가 진행중에 있으며
  김형규는 적법절차에 따른 재판결과 복역중에 있음. 아국정부는
  이들에 대한 사법부의 결정을 존중한다는 것이 기본입장임.

0003

o 본인은 독일이 인권문제에 각별한 관심을 갖고 있으며, 아국의
   인권상황에도 민감한 반응을 보여온 점을 잘 알고 있읍니다.
   독일이 과거 나치 독일치하 유태인 인권문제로 인한 역사적
   교훈을 명심하고 있는 것이나 귀대사께서 아국내 Gestapo 라는
   명칭을 가진 cafe에 대하여 보여주신 반응등은 좋은 실례라고
   생각함.

o 같은 분단국으로서 귀국이 갖고 있는 동·서독 관계에 대한
   시각으로 남북한 관계를 바라보는 것은 한반도 분단상황의
   정확한 인식을 저해하는 근본원인이 될 것임.

o 따라서 이번 기회에 귀대사께 동·서독 관계와 남북한 관계간의
   근본적인 차이점 몇가지를 지적하고저 함.
   - 첫째, 동·서독은 동족간의 전쟁을 치르지 않았으나 남북한은
     동족상잔의 전쟁을 경험하여 아직도 상호간에 심각한 적대
     상태에 있음.
   - 둘째, 서독은 경제 군사면에서 월등히 앞서 있으므로,
     동독은 자신의 주도하의 통일을 실현 가능한 것으로 생각치
     못하고 있음. 반면, 남북한간에는 경제력은 남한이 앞서
     있어도, 군사력에 있어서는 북한이 월등한 우위에 있으므로
     북한은 아직도 무력을 통한 통일야욕을 버리지 않고 있음.
   - 셋째, 북한은 버마아웅산 터러사건, 대한항공기 폭파사건
     등에서 볼 수 있듯이 테러행위를 계속 자행하고 대남공작을
     계속 책동하고 있음.

o 향후 귀대사께서 이미 설명한 바와 같은 한국이 처해있는
   제반상황에 대한 인식을 새롭게 하시어 양국간 보다 긴밀한
   우호관계가 지속될 수 있도록 힘써주실 것을 당부하는 바임.

0004

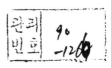

법 　 무 　 부

검삼202-/♪7　　　　　(503-7055)　　　　1990. 10. 27.

수신　외무부장관

참조　구주국장

제목　의견 통보

　　구일 202-2584(90.10.23)로 요청한 문익환, 홍성담, 김형규에

대한 당부의 조치사항 및 입장을 별첨과 같이 통보합니다.

　　첨부　: 의견서 1부.　끝.

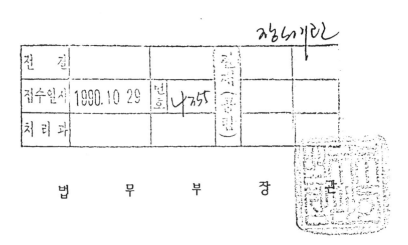

법　　무　　부　　장

0005

```
┌─────────────────────────┐
│     문  익  환          │
└─────────────────────────┘
```

1. 인적사항

    o 연 령 : 18. 6. 1. 생 (72세)

    o 직 업 : 전민련 고문

    o 주 거 : 서울 도봉구 수유2동 527-30

    o 본 적 : ████████████████

2. 처리상황

    o 구속일자 : 89. 4. 13.

    o 재판확정 : 90.6.8. 징역,자격정지 각 7년

3. 범죄사실

    o 재일 북괴공작원 정경모의 지령에 따라 89.3.25. 반국가단체가
      지배하는 북한지역으로 탈출

    o 89.3.25. 부터 동년 4.3.까지 북한에 체류하면서 반국가단체
      구성원과 회합하고, 한국을 비방하면서 북한의 활동을 찬양.고무하고
      그 주장에 동조

                                              0006

                        ㄱ-1

o. 89.4.2. 북한고위간부인 허담으로 부터 금품을 수수

o 89.4.3. 일본으로가 북한 고위간부인 허담의 지령에 따라 북한의
   활동에 동조하는 기자회견, 강연회등을 개최후 동년 4.13. 국내에
   잠입

4. 조치사항

o 동인은 지병으로 인하여 수형생활을 감내할 수 없다는 판단에 따라
   90.10.20. 형집행정지 결정을 하여 석방하였음.

홍　성　담

1. 인적사항

    ○ 연　　령 : 55. 8. 28. 생 (35세)
    ○ 직　　업 : 화가
    ○ 주　　거 : 광주 서구 화정동 640
    ○ 본　　적 : ███████████████

2. 처리상황

    ○ 구속일자 : 89. 8. 3.
    ○ 죄　　명 : 국가보안법위반
    ○ 1심선고 : 90. 1.30.　징역,자격정지 각 7년
    ○ 2심선고 : 90. 6. 1.　징역, 자격정지 각 7년
    ○ 3심선고 : 90. 9.25.　원심파기

3. 범죄사실

    ○ 88.4.4 ~ 6.28.간에 서독에서 북한의 지령을 받은 유럽민협 국제
      부장 성낙영과 회합하여 독일화 2,000마르크 및 미화 1,500달라
      를 수수하고, 국내운동권 상황이나 정세를 분석한 책들을 송부해 주기로
      약속

0008

7-3

o 88.7. 초순 - 11. 중순간에 "문화운동론"1,2권, "한국민족민주
   운동의 쟁점", "말"지 11월호, "흐름"지 11월호, "역사비평" 가을호,
   "미술운동1" 등을 서점에서 구입, 성낙영에게 발송

o 89.1.경 차일환등과 공모하여, 민족해방민중민주주의혁명이론에
   입각하여 학생과 민중들에게 투쟁의식을 고취, 각성시킬 목적으로
   갑오경장에서 조국통일운동까지 근현대사를 민족해방운동사라는 제목의
   대형 걸개그림 1폭으로 제작하여 각 대학에 순회전시하고, 슬라이
   드로 제작, 북한에 송부

o 89.2. 하순 조선혁명의 현 단계와 미술인의 임무등의 내용이 수록된
   이적표현물 "미술운동" 2호 제작

4. 관용요청에 대한 의견

o 동인은 아국의 실정법을 위반하여 현재 제2심에 계류중 (90.9.25.
   대법원에서 파기환송)에 있으므로 동 재판결과에 따라 처리되어야
   할 것임.

0009

ㄱ-4

```
┌─────────────────────┐
│   김    형    규      │
└─────────────────────┘
```

1. 인적사항

   o 연   령 : 50.10.25.생 (40세)

   o 직   업 : 전 서독 광부 (독일국적 취득자)

   o 주   거 : 서독 함부르크 60 에드빈 샤르프링 49

   o 본   적 : ████████████████

2. 처리상황

   o 구속일자 : 87. 10. 6.

   o 재판확정 : 89. 4. 3. 징역,자격정지 각 9년

   o 죄   명 : 국가보안법위반, 간첩

   o 형종료일 : 96. 10. 10.

   o 집행기간 : 3년 10일 (33.9%) 집행

   o 잔   형 : 5년 11월 20일 (66.1%)

   o 수용교도소 : 대전교도소

3. 범죄사실

   o 74.11.30. 도독하여 서독광부로 취업중 80.3.초 북괴와 긴밀한
      관계를 맺고 있던 "재독 조국통일 해외기독자회" 편집부장 김성수
      에게 포섭되어 82.4.17. 체코 북괴대사관을 방문, 공작교육을 받고,

                                                    0010

                           7-5

o 83.10.7. 체코 북괴공작아지트 및 모스크바 북괴대사관을 경유하여
  입북, 간첩밀봉교육을 받은 후 83.10.15. 서독으로 귀환하여 그때
  부터 북괴로 부터 지령을 받으면서 암약하던중

o 86.4 - 86.7.간 미국,케나다 등을 여행하며 교포들의 생활실태 및
  사상동향을 파악하여 북괴에 보고하고,

o 87.4 - 87.5.간 아르헨티나 등을 여행한 후 87.7.2. 체코 및
  소련을 경유, 재차 입북하여 남미여행보고서를 제출한 후 노동당에
  입당하고,

o 87.9.3. 국내에 잠입하여 9.20.까지 서울,안동,포항,청송 등지를
  전전하며 중요시설물 위치, 국내정세등을 파악 및 사진촬영하는 등
  간첩활동

4. 가석방에 대한 의견

   o 법률상 기결수는 형기의 1/3을 경과하고 행장이 양호하여 개전의
     정이 현저한 때 가석방을 할 수 있음 (형법 제72조)

   o 그러나 실제 당 부의 공안사범에 대한 가석방 기준은 행장이 양호한
     자로서 형기의 75%이상을 집행할 것을 원칙으로 하고 있음

0011

7-b

° 동인의 경우는 형기의 1/3(33.4%)은 집행하였으나 집행기간이 가석방 실무기준에 미달하고 죄과에 대한 반성의 정이 없는 행장 불량자임

° 따라서 현재로서는 당 부의 가석방기준에 비추어 가석방을 검토하기 어려우나 독일관계요로에서 자국민보호등을 이유로 각별한 관심을 표명하고 있는 점등에 비추어 동인이 죄과를 반성하고 개전의 정을 보이는 경우 국익상 필요하다면 강제퇴거를 전제로 가석방을 검토할 수도 있을 것임.

0012

7-7

이 준희 과장 귀하

그동안 본부의 분주한 업무에 수고많을줄 믿습니다.
이곳 주독대사관도 본부의 여러지시에 부응하기 위해 많은 노력을 하고
있습니다.

오늘 특파편에 대사님 지시로 급히 글을쓰는것은, 명년초 우리공관의
가장 주요한 현안인 바이체커 대통령 방한과 관련된 문제 때문입니다.
특히 최근 공전으로도 보도되고 있는 아국 인권문제에 관한 독일정부의
관심표명이 대사님 이하 정무팀에서 가장 신경을 쓰고있는 사안이라
생각됩니다.

이미 공전(WGE-1760. (임경측위우 함소보면))으로 보고했읍니다만 관계기관에 대한 설명을 위해
89년 방독행사시 독일측에서 아측에 명단을 전달한 3명(문 익환, 홍 성담,
김 형규)에 대한 설명자료가 시급 필요합니다.

이와관련, 12.20 소생이 외무부 Schoenfelder를 만났는바, 동인도 상기사안과
최근 백림 3자회담 참석자 구속건에 관해 보고하라는 대통령실의 지시를 받고
이에 관해 자료를 작성중에 있다고 말하였읍니다.

소생이 대통령실이 관심을 갖고 있는 인사를 구체적으로 확인하자 구체명단에
관하여는 상기3인 외에도 통일문제 관련 방북한 문 익환, 유 원호(문 익환을
동반 방북함), 임 수경에 관해서도 관심이 크다고 알려주었읍니다.

상기인들에 관한 자료는 당관에도 일부 와있긴 합니다만 시일이 경과된
자료들이며, 이곳에서 보완하기가 어려운 형편이니 최신자료를 지급 송부
바랍니다. 자료송부 간트래에 명인흥부니 근개박처운 각수처럼 예방니다.

동 대통령 방한전에 상기인들에 대한 아측의 관련조치가 나오면 당관으로서는
매우 편리하겠으니 본부에서도 당관의 입장을 관계부처에 적극 설명해 주시기
바랍니다.

새해에도 좋은일 많이 있기를 기원합니다.

1990.12.21.

0013

관리
번호 90 -1428

報 告 事 項

3

1990.12.17.
情報文化局
情報2課(51)

題 目 : 베를린 3者會談 參加者 拘束關聯

1. 政府는 조용술 牧師等 전민련 관계인사 3인이 11.19-20 남북한, 해외동포간 3者 會談에 參加하고 歸國(11.30)한 즉시 國家保安法 違反 혐의로 拘束한 바 있습니다. 이와관련 최근 獨逸 및 카나다 外務省의 關係官은 同 拘束에 人權次元의 關心을 表明하였는 바, 이에대해 아래와 같이 措置하였음을 報告드립니다.

2. 對獨逸 措置事項

　　가. 本部, 駐獨大使館에 下記 要旨의 說明指針 下達(12.3, 12.11)
　　　o 동건은 實定法 違反에 대한 법적제재에 不過할 뿐 人權事案이 아님.
　　　o 同人들의 犯法内容
　　　　- 政府의 參加不許 通報를 무시, 實定法을 고의로 違反하여 會談參加
　　　　 (南北交流協力에 관한 法 第 9 條, 國家保安法 第 8 條)
　　　　- 南韓政府를 일방적으로 非難하는 共同 聲明發表 (國家保安法 第 7 條)
　　　o 政府는 同 會談이 南北交流에 관한 政府의 基本方針에 背馳되므로 參加不許
　　　o 3者會談은 北韓의 對南 革命戰略의 一部

　　나. 駐獨大使館 上記指針에 따라 獨 外務省側에 說明
　　　o 全 參事官, 獨外務省 Schonfelder 韓國課長 面談 (12.4)
　　　o 安公使, 獨外務省 Zimmermann 東亞局長 代理 面談 (12.12)
　　　　- 獨逸側은 바이체커 大統領 訪韓前 同人들에 대한 적절한 措置 希望

　　다. 駐韓 獨逸大使館앞 理解 促求
　　　o 정보2과장, 주한 독일대사관 관계관 면담 (12.17)
　　　　- 會談開催 過程에서의 北側 策動事實等 詳細說明

3. 主要 公館에 指針下達
　　　o 21個 主要公館에 동건에 대한 弘報 指針 下達(12.15)
　　　　- 駐美, 英, 日 大使館 및 美洲地域 主要 總領事館 等 包含.

첨 부 : 공동성명서 요지. 끝.

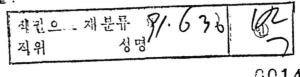

─── 베를린 3자회담 참가자 구속관련 ───
주한 독일 대사 면담 자료

1990. 12.

정 보 문 화 국

0015

목   차

I. 베를린 3자회담 참석자 구속관련 정부입장

  1. 구속관련 사실

  2. 독일정부의 관심 표명

  3. 정부입장

II. 영문 설명자료

첨 부 :

  1. 베를린 3자회담 개최경과

  2. 베를린 3자회담 참가대표 공동선언 요지

0016

베를린 3자회담 참석자 구속관련 정부입장

==

1. 구속관련 사실

가. 구속자 인적사항

  0 조용술(목사, 범민족대회 남한측 추진본부 공동 본부장)

  0 이재학(목사, 범민족대회 남한측 추진본부 집행위원장)

  0 조성우(범민족대회 남한측 사무처장)

나. 회담 개최 및 구속경위

  0 90.8.18. 판문점 범민족대회 참가자(남측대표는 불참), 3개월내 베를린
    에서 남·북·해외동포 3자회담 개최키로 합의

   - 상설 민간 통일기구 결성이 목적

  0 10.28. 상기 구속자들, 베를린회담 참가를 위한 북한주민 접촉 승인서
    제출

  0 11.13. 통일원 동 신청에 대한 불허 방침 통보

   - 동인들, 정부측 통보를 기다리지 않고 사전 베를린 향발

  0 11.18. 주베를린 공보관, 현지에서 동인들 접촉시 3자회담에 불참 촉구

   - 동인들, 사후 구속되더라도 참가를 강행하겠다고 언급

  0 11.19-20, 베를린 3자회담 개최

   - 참가대표

     . 북한 : 전금철(최고인민회의 대의원, "조평통" 부위원장)

     . 해외 : 황석영 외 미주대표 2명

     . 남한 : 상기구속자 3인

  0 11.30. 귀국즉시 국가보안법 위반 혐의로 구속

2. 독일정부의 인권차원 관심표명

가. 독일측 관심표명

  0 12.3. 독일외무부 한국과장, 아측대사관에 동건 관심표명, 설명요청

  0 12.12. 외무부 동아국 국장대리, 안공사 면담

   - 91.2. 하순 바이체커 대통령 방한전 동인들에 대한 적절한 조치희망

0017

나. 아측 조치사항

　　O 독일외무성측에 동건관련 정부입장 상세 설명(12.4,12.12)

　　O 정보2과장, 주한 독일대사관 관계관 면담(12.17)

　　　- 회의개최 과정에서의 북측책동 사실등 상세설명

　　O 주독대사앞 장관친전(12.21)

3. 동 구속관련 정부 입장

가. 기본입장

　　O 동인들의 구속은 당사자들의 실정법 위반에 대한 법적제재에 불과할 뿐,
　　　인권차원에서 거론할 사안이 아님

나. 구속자 법법사실

　　(1) 실정법을 고의로 위반하여 회담참가(남북교류협력에 관한법)

　　　- 동인들은 실정법에 따라 동 3자회담 참석을 위해 사전 정부허가 신청

　　　- 정부의 불허방침을 접수하고도 고의로 이를 무시, 회담 참가

　　(2) 남한정부를 일방적으로 비난하는 성명발표(국가보안법)

　　　- 남북고위급회담의 의제를 비롯한 남북한 현안에 대해 전적으로 북한의
　　　　주장만을 되풀이하고, 남한정부를 일방적으로 비난(Ⅱ '성명요지'참조)

다. 정부의 베를린 3자회담 참가불허 이유

　　O 남북교류에 관한 정부의 기본방침에 배치

　　　- 통일문제는 국민적 대표성을 가진 정부당국을 중심으로 논의해야 함

　　　- 민간차원의 교류도 국민적 공감대가 형성된 기반위에서 추진되어야 함

　　O 동 회담은 북한의 통일전선 전술상의 대남선동 책략의 일환

　　　- 북한은 당 고위급인사를 민간대표로 가장하여 파견

　　　- 전민련 계열의 "추진본부"만을 남한측 회담대표로서 일방적으로 제한

　　　- 회담 준비과정에서 친북성향의 해외교포인사들을 수시로 접촉, 참여유도

0018

Main points for the explanation

90.12.21.

A. Our government's basic position

The arrest of the three South Korean representatives to the
Berlin conference should be viewed in terms of an enforcement
of positive law againt violators.

Even though there are some people who intend to portray the
incident as a human right issue, we believe that it is
nothing more than an enforcement of the relevant laws and
regulations.

B. The reason of the arrest of the South delegates

(1) They violated knowingly the positive law

o The three South delegates initially filed their application
forms with the relevant government agency in order to gain
government permission for their participation in the Berlin
conference.

They did so in accordance with the Law on South-North Exchanges
and Cooperation, which regulates the procedure for South
Koreans to contact with North Koreans.

According to the law, any South Korean who wishes to have a
contact with a North Korean is required to file an application
for the contact with the Board of National Reunification.

(2) They announced a joint statement unilaterally reiterating North
Korea's scheme for reunification.

0019

o The participants of the Berlin conference were seen to be in a
   blatant favor of the North all through the conference. Their
   partial attitude was clearly demonstrated in the Statement
   in which their manner of delivering the current inter-Korean
   issues was utterly pro-North. In actuality, the statement is
   nothing but a fine reproduction of the North positiions in
   every aspect.

C. The reason of not permitting the South delegation to participate
    in the Berlin conference.

o Based on the following facts, the Berlin conference runs contrary
   to the government's basic policy on the South-North exchanges.

   - The North disguised Chun Kum-chul, a member of the Superme
      People's Assembly, as non-governmental delegate to the
      conference. This is an obvious attempt to put the conference
      under its influence.

   - Besides, the North Korean authorities have begun to inter-
      fere with the preparation of the conference since 1988,
      and "designated" as the South delegation the Pan-National
      Democratic Movement, the most famous dissident group in
      our society.

o Meanwhile, the government's policy on inter-Korean exchanges
   is based on the following principles

0020

- The unification problem should be dealt with according
  to the Korean people's opinion. Hence, the government
  authorities should take the responsibility of conducting
  the South-North dialogue.
- In case of civilian exchanges, it should also be
  maintained on the basis of the general agreement of
  the Korean people.
  And its content should be condusive to our government's
  efforts to improve the South-North relations.

o In light of the above principles, the Berlin conference cannot
  be an appropriate device for the promotion of inter-Korean
  exchanges.
  We believe that the North responded positively to the conference because the North can exploit the conference to undermine
  our government's dignity and to thrust our society into disorder.

0021

(첨 부)

1. 베를린 3자회담 개최경과
   o 89.1.   아국의 '전국민족민주운동연합'(전민련), 범민족대회
                남북공동 개최 및 이를 위한 판문점 예비실무회담(89.3.1)제의
   o 89.2.   정부, 범민족대회 추진 중지 촉구
   o 89.7.   북한의 '조국평화통일위원회'(조평통), 범민족대회 90.8.15.
                개최제의
   o 90.3.   전민련, 8.15 범민족대회 개최결의
   o 90.6.   제1차 예비실무회담(베를린)개최
                - 전민련은 정부의 불허 방침으로 불참
   o 90.7.26-27. 제2차 예비실무회담(서울)
                - 우리정부가 북한측 참가를 허용하였으나, 북한대표 불참
   o 90.8.6-7. 제3차 예비실무회담(평양)
                - 정부는 전민련의 대표성을 이유로 북한방문신청 불허
   o 90.8.15.   북한, 해외동포대표들 참가하에 판문점 북측지역에서 범민족
                대회 개최(남측대표 불참)
   o 90.8.19.   동참가자들은 상설민간 통일기구로서 "조국통일 범민족 연합"을
                3개월내에 구성키로 결의
   o 90.11.19-20.베를린 3자회담에서 범민련 결성

2. 베를린 3자회담 참가 대표 공동선언문(요지)
   o "조국통일 범민족 연합" 결성 선포
     - 7.4 남북공동 성명의 3대원칙과 범민족대회에서의 결의를 기본강령으로
       통일운동의 대중화와 단결을 위해 활동
   o 남한당국도 분열과 대결의 자세를 청산하고 범민련의 대열에 참가할 것을
     촉구
   o 향후 활동 방향
     - 반전.반핵운동 전개를 통하여 한반도 주둔 외국군 및 핵무기 철수 실현
     - 국가보안법등 제반 악법의 철폐를 위해 투쟁
     - 물리적 장벽의 제거를 통한 남북간 자유왕래와 전면개방 실현
     - 유엔분리가입 반대운동 전개
     - 불가침선언 채택 촉구

0022

**Botschaft
der Bundesrepublik Deutschland
Embassy
of the Federal Republic of Germany**

RK 531 SE Kim

VN No. 1/91

<u>Verbal Note</u>

The Embassy of the Federal Republic of Germany presents its compliments to the Ministry of Foreign Affairs of the Republic of Korea and with reference to its Verbal Note No. 73/90 has the honour to ask again for the Ministry's kind assistance in the following matter:

The German citizen Mr. Adrian Kim actually serving a a nine-year-term in the correctional center of Taejon has informed this Embassy that his health condition is deteriorating and that he is, therefore, suffering from severe pains. He argues that, however, the prison authorities concerned seem to be reluctant to grant him the necessary medical care. Mr. Kim asked, therefore, again to be transferred to another correctional center as soon as possible.

In this connection it would be appreciated if the Ministry could inform this Embassy whether an early release from custody is possible due to the deteriorating health condition of Mr. Kim. In the meantime this Embassy would be grateful if the necessary steps could be taken in order to make sure that the indispensable medical assistance is provided.

The Embassy of the Federal Republic of Germany avails itself of this opportunity to renew to the Ministry of Foreign Affairs of the Republic of Korea the assurances of its highest consideration.

Seoul, January 4, 1991

To the
Ministry
of Foreign Affairs
of the Republic of Korea
<u>Seoul</u>

0023

주 ＥＣ 대 표 부

이씨정 202-2   1991. 1. 10.

수신 : 외무부 장관

참조 : 구주국장

제목 : 구주의회 의장서한

      대 : WEC-0005

      연 : ECW-0845

      연호, 간첩죄로 수감중인 Adrian KIM에 관한 구주의회 의장 서한에
대하여 당관은 91.1.9. 대호 내용에 의거, 별첨과 같이 본직명의 회신서한을
동 의장에게 송부하였음을 보고합니다.

      첨부 : 상기 서한 사본 1부.   끝.

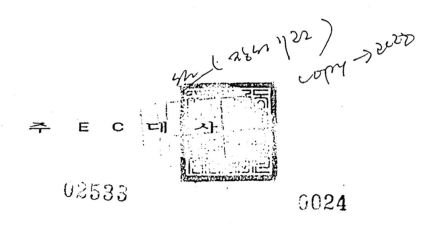

주 ＥＣ 대 사

02533   0024

MISSION
OF THE
REPUBLIC OF KOREA
TO THE EUROPEAN COMMUNITIES
AVENUE DE TERVUREN 249 - BOX 2
1150 BRUSSELS

January 9, 1991

Your Excellency:

I would first like to express my great appreciation for the warm hospitality which you showed me when I visited your office in Strasbourg last November. At that time, I was deeply impressed by your clear-cut and firm position with regard to the relations between the European Parliament and North Korea.

I am also pleased to acknowledge the receipt of your letter dated December 11, 1990, concerning the case of Adrian KIM. As soon as I received your letter, I transmitted it to my government for due consideration.

Mr. Kim had been working as a miner in West Germany since 1974. During that period, he was recruited by North Korean agents and visited North Korea several times for secret espionage training. Afterwards, on North Korean instruction, he went to South Korea in 1987, and while engaging in espionage activities for North Korea, was arrested by Korean authorities.

As Mr. Kim has violated Korean law, and since the law should be carried out with equal justice to all, there are certain barriers which keep the Korean government from granting special amnesty to him.

Nevertheless, I hope that this case will be taken into favorable consideration in the near future by Korean authorities, in light of your humanitarian request.

May I wish you, Your Excellency, a Happy New Year and every success in your high endeavors throughout the year.

Yours faithfully,

Tong-Man KWUN
Ambassador

H.E. Mr. Enrique BARON CRESPO
President of the European Parliament
Rue Belliard 79-113
1040 Bruxelles

0025

獨逸 大統領 訪韓과 獨逸僑胞 김형규 問題

-서기관 작성-

1. 事件概要

o 김형규, 1974년 독일 광부로 취업후, 북한공작원에게 포섭되어
83.10-87.7간 3회에 걸쳐 방북, 간첩 밀봉 교육 받음.

o 87.9.2. 북한의 지령에 따라 국내잠입, 간첩활동중 동년 10월 구속

o 89.4.3 징역 9년의 확정판결을 받고 현재 대전교도소에서 복역중
(3년 3개월)

2. 獨逸側 要請

o 독일측, 동인이 독일 시민권자임을 감안 동인에 대한 특별 사면
고려 요청

- 88.2. 겐셔 외무장관, 주독대사에 특별사면 고려 요청

- 88.7. 한.독 외무장관 회담시 선처 요청

- 89.10. 브란트 전독일수상, 국무총리와의 오찬시 선처 요청

- 89.11. 노대통령 방독시, 바이쩨커 대통령 및 겐셔 외무장관
관심 표명

o 그간 아측은 사면이나 석방은 현행법상(최소한 형기의 1/3이상
복역, 행형성적 양호) 어렵다는 입장 견지

3. 關聯問題 및 對策

(관련문제)

o 폰 바이쩨커 대통령 방한시 김형규 문제를 비롯한 시국관련
구속자 문제 거론 예상

- 89.11. 노대통령 방독시에도 폰 바이쩨커 대통령, 상기 문제 거론

* 독일측 관심표명 구속자: 김형규, 문익환(석방), 홍성담, 유원호,
임수경 및 백림 3자회담 참가자(조용술 목사 등 3명)

0026

(대 책)

o 1.22 외무부 제1차관보 주재로 열린 관계부처 대책회의에서 아래와
  같이 결정
  - 폰 바이제커 대통령 방한에 즈음, 동 대통령을 위시한 독일 정부
    요로의 김형규에 대한 지속적인 관심표명 및 한.독간 우호관계를
    고려, 동인을 강제 퇴거를 전제로 가석방
  - 폰 바이제커 대통령과 개인적 친분관계가 있는 강원룡 목사를
    독일에 파견, 아국 입장을 설명하고 방한시 아국 인권문제 거론
    자제 요청토록 함.

(기조치 사항)

o 법무부의 김형규 가석방 방침 통보에 따라, 독일 정부측에 동 방침
  통보 및 대통령 방한시 아국 인권문제 거론 자제 요청토록 주독
  대사에 지시(2.1)

o 공보처와 협의, 강원룡 목사 2.19-21간 독일 파견 결정
  - 폰 바이제커 대통령 면담 일시확정 : 2.20(수) 18:00시

첨부 : 김형규 인적사항 1부. 끝.

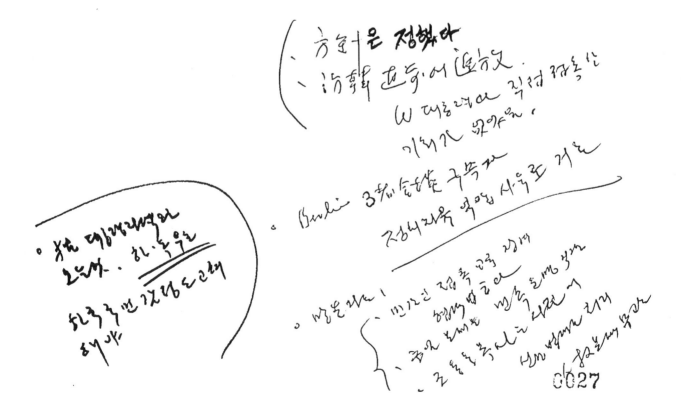

0027

인 적 사 항

○ 성   명: 김형규(金炯圭)

    * 독일명: Adrian Kim

○ 생년월일: 1950년생(41세)

○ 본   적: ███████████████████

○ 주   소: 서독 함부르크 60 에드윈 샤르프링 49

    * 플라스틱 제조회사 연마공

○ 학   력: 삼척공전 광산과 졸업(69)

○ 경   력:

    74.12   광부로 도독

    86.12   서독 시민권 취득

    87.9.3   입국, 9.25 피검

    89.4.3   간첩행위 혐의로 징역 9년형 확정

    현재   대전교도소 복역중(3년4월 복역, 잔형 5년8월)

0028

법   무   부

인권 202- 7   503-7045   1991.1.14

수선 외무부장관

참조 구주국장

제목 아국 인권상황 관련자료 송부

　　　구주의회 아국 인권 결의문과 관련, 귀부에서 요청한 인권상황에
대한 설명자료를 별첨과 같이 송부합니다.

첨부 : 1. 개인별 관련자료 1부.
　　　　 2. "법과 질서 그리고 인권" 영문책자 1권

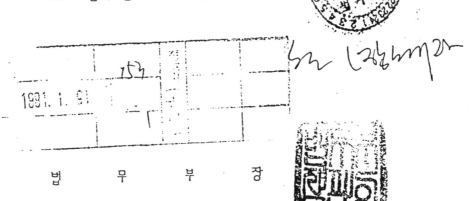

법   무   부   장

직권으로 재분류(91· 6·30)

직위   성명

0029

임   수   경

1. 인적사항

   . '68. 11. 6생 (21세)

   . 학생 (한국외국어대 용인분교 불어과 4년)

2. 범죄사실

   . '89.5.18 북한을 이롭게 할 목적으로 구성된 이적단체인
     전대협 평양축전 준비위원회 구성원으로 가입함

   . 전대협 대표자격으로 평양에서 개최되는 제13차 세계청년
     학생축전에 참가할 목적으로 '89.6.30 북한지역으로 탈출함

   . '89.7.12 및 8.12 반국가단체 구성원으로부터 북한화
     30원과 금목걸이를 교부받고 금품을 수수함

   . '89.6.30부터 동년 8.15까지 북한에 체류하면서 대학가
     실태 및 학생운동권의 활동상황을 북한의 조선학생위원장에게
     보고하여 반국가단체에 군사상 이익을 제공하고 대한민국을
     비방하면서 북한의 활동을 찬양.고무하고, 반국가단체 구성원과
     회합함

   . '89.8.15 판문점 군사분계선을 넘어 국내에 잠입함

0030

3. 처리상황

　　. '89. 8.20　구속 (안기부)

　　. '89.10. 7　구속기소 (서울지검)

　　. '90. 2. 5　제1심 선고 (징역10년, 자격정지10년)

　　. '90. 6.11　항소심 선고 (징역5년, 자격정지5년)

　　. '90. 9.25　상고기각, 확정

0031

문 규 현

1. 인적사항

   • 본 적 : 전북 익산
   • 주 기 : 미국 뉴욕주
   • 생년월일 : '49. 10. 1
   • 직 업 : 신부

2. 범죄사실 (국가보안법 위반)

   • '89.6.1 북한 외교의원회 위원장이 보낸 항공료 1,600불을
     수령하고, 동년 6.5 북경을 통해 평양에 들어가서 6.20까지
     체류하는 동안 남한에 주둔하는 미군과 핵무기가 통일을 저해하는
     요소라는 등 대한민국을 비방하고 북한을 찬양

   • '89.7.26 당시 전대협 대표자격으로 평양에서 개최되는 제13차
     세계청년학생축전에 참가키 위하여 밀입북하여 북한에 체류중이던
     임수경을 대동 기환할 목적으로 북경을 거처 평양에 도착하여 수회에
     걸쳐 조국분단의 원인은 미제국주의자들이 남한을 점령하고 있으며,
     그 하수인인 남한정권이 통일을 원치 않고 있기 때문이라는 등
     북한의 선전활동에 동조하는 내용의 연설을 하고, 8.15 임수경과
     함께 군사분계선을 넘어와 국내에 잠입

3. 처리상황

   • '89. 8.15   구속 (서울시경)
   • '89. 9.29   구속기소 (서울지검)
   • '90. 2. 5   1심선고 징역, 자격정지 각8년 (서울지법)
   • '90. 6.11   2심선고 징역, 자격정지 각5년 (서울고법)
   • '90. 9.25   상고기각, 확정

0032

임수경, 문규현 사건에 대하여
====================================

1. 북한의 평화통일 선전에 대하여

   ○ 1945년 일제식민통치에서 해방되면서 대한민국은 소련과
     미국이 각각 진주함으로써 분열되었고 이제까지 40여년간
     동서 이데올로기의 대립과 갈등이라는 냉전구조속에서
     남북간의 첨예한 이념적,군사적,정치적 대결상태를
     유지하여 왔음

   ○ 북한의 제1목표는 한반도 전역을 공산화하는데 있으며
     그 의도는 1950년 6.25전쟁, 미국 푸에블로호 납치사건,
     청와대 습격사건, 판문점 도끼만행사건, 미얀마 아웅산
     폭파사건, 칼기 폭파사건, 휴전선 각 지역에서의
     남침용 땅굴 발견사건, 각종 무장간첩사건 등에서 보는
     바와 같이 의심의 여지가 없음

   ○ 북한은 이와같은 직접적인 도발외에, 한편으로는 우리
     사회의 불만세력과 좌익세력을 이용하여 내부혼란을
     조성하여 왔으며, 그러면서도 대내외적으로는 평화통일
     선전을 하면서 오히려 미군의 주둔 등을 이유로 남한은
     미제국주의의 신식민지이며 우리 정부를 반통일세력이라고
     선동하여 왔음

0033

○ 대한민국 정부는 이러한 직접적인 도발과 선전·선동
전술을 감내하여 왔으며, 1988년 제6공화국의 출범
이후 사회 각 분야에서의 광범한 민주화 추진과 함께
'7.7 특별선언'을 통해 북한을 민족공동체의 일원으로
포용, 동반자관계를 지향하겠다는 입장을 표명하고,
남북한간의 교류·협력과 공산권 국가와의 관계개선을
적극 추구해 나갈 것을 천명하였으며, 이에 따라
그동안 동구 각 국과의 수교, 그리고 최근의 한·소
정상회담 등이 이루어졌음

○ 그러나 북한은 이러한 대한민국의 전향적 대북정책을
거부하고 여전히 지난 40여년간 유지해 온 인민민주주의
혁명전략을 포기하지 않고 대남적대정책을 지속하면서
그 일환으로 임수경 등을 밀입북시켜 이들을 소위
그들의 평화통일 선전전술에 이용하였음

2. 우리 사회의 좌익세력에 대하여

○ 우리 사회의 좌익세력은

. 남한은 일본의 식민지에서 벗어나면서 미군의
강점으로 미국의 식민지로 재편되었고

0034

- 미제는 군사파쇼정권을 내세워 남한의 급속한
  자본주의화를 추진했으며 이 과정에서 노동자,
  농민의 생활조건과 처지는 더욱 비참해지고
  부익부, 빈익빈 현상이 심화되었으며

- 미.일 외세와 이에 의존하고 있는 군사독재와
  독점재벌은 분단을 통해 막대한 이익을 얻고 있기에
  분단의 고착화를 바라고 있다고 역사와 현실을
  인식하고

- 이러한 모순을 해결하기 위해서는 친미세력,
  매판자본가, 소수 정치군인을 배제한 노동자, 농민,
  학생 등 모든 민주세력이 일치 단결하여 미.일
  외세와 군부독재를 타도 (반미자주, 반파쇼민주)
  하고 민족자주국가를 수립해야 한다고 생각하고 있음

o 위와같이 현실을 인식하고 있고, 우리 정부의 통일노력은
  민주세력의 요구에 마지못해 움직이는 가정된 행위라고
  생각하고 있기 때문에, 임수경을 밀입북시킨 전국대학생
  대표자 협의회 (전대협) 등에서는 자신들의 행위가
  진정한 통일열망에 의한 것이라고 주장하고 있음

0035

3. 국가보안법의 위반에 대하여

○ 미국에서도 전쟁중에 있는 적국이나 분쟁중에 있는 외국에
   대하여 정부의 허가없이 교섭하거나 교류하는 경우에는
   처벌을 하고 있으며(Logan법), 그 이유는 그와같은
   경우에 교섭의 주체는 정부가 되어야 하며, 개인들의
   자의적인 교섭이나 교류는 오히려 혼란을 초래하여 적국에
   유리하고, 아국에 불리한 상황이 초래될 수 있기 때문일
   것임

○ 원래 하나의 국가였고, 같은 민족이므로 통일은 우리의
   열망이고 과제이기는 하지만, 우리 헌법은 자유민주적
   기본질서에 입각한 통일정책을 수립, 시행할 것을 선언하고
   있고, 그 책무를 대통령에게 부과하고 있음

○ 그것은 아직도 적대국인 상황에서 통일정책의 수행은
   헌법과 국민적 합의에 기초하여 정부의 주도하에 단계적으로
   이루어져야 하며 개개인이 정부를 배제한 채 자의적으로
   북한과 접촉하여 이루어질 문제가 아니기 때문임

○ 임수경, 문규현은 위와 같은 헌법과 국가보안법의 규정을
   무시하고, 정부를 배제한 채 여전히 대치관계에 있는
   북한에 밀입북하여 통일논의를 빙자, 대한민국의 통일정책을
   비난하여 결과적으로 북한의 대남분열공작책동에 동조함으로써
   정부의 정통성과 대표성을 부정하는 행위를 하였기 때문에
   부득이 사법처리하지 않을 수 없었음

0036

o   이것은 자기 나라와 분쟁중인 적대국가에 몰려 들어가
    분쟁을 평화적으로 종식시키려고 교섭을 모색하고 있는
    자기 나라가 분쟁 종식에는 관심이 없다고 비난함으로써
    적대국가에 동조하는 행위와 다름없음이 이해되어야
    할 것임

o   임수경, 문규현의 이러한 행위는 국민들에게 크나큰
    충격과 분노를 안겨 주었으며, 당연히 실정법을 위반
    하였으므로 법과 판결에 따라 처리되어야 함

0037

홍 성 담

1. 인적사항

    · 본 적 : ████████████

    · 주 거 : 광주 서구 화정동 640 주공(아) 20동 405호

    · 직 업 : 화가

    · 연 령 : '55. 8. 28생

2. 범죄사실 (국가보안법 위반)

    · '88.4.3 서경원의 알선을 받아 서독으로 출국하여 동년 6.28
      귀국시까지 북괴공작원 성낙영 등과 수차 회합하고 동인들로부터
      3,000불과 4,200마르크를 수수

    · 동년 7월 초순경 성낙영에게 "한국민족민주운동의 쟁점" 등
      국내상황에 대한 서적들을 수집, 제공하여 국가기밀 누설

    · 동년 10월 중순경 조선대학교 축제 초청강연시 "우리의 적은
      미국이다"는 취지의 연설을 하여 이적 동조

    · '89.4경 민중혁명의식을 고취하는 내용의 대형 걸개그림
      "민족해방운동사"를 제작한 후 순회 전시하고, 동 그림을
      슬라이드로 제작하여 북한에 보내어 평양축전장소에 전시

3. 처리상황

    · '89.9.20 구속기소
    · '90.1.30 제1심에서 징역7년, 자격정지7년, 일부무죄
    · '90.6.1 2심에서 징역7년, 자격정지7년, 일부무죄
    · '90.9.25 대법원 파기환송

0038

홍성담 사건에 대하여
========================

1. 홍성담의 국가보안법 위반내용

　○　AI측에 의하면 동인의 범죄사실이 단순히 자신의 그림을
　　　슬라이드 사진으로 제작하여 북한에 보내고, 서독에 있는
　　　한국인에게 책을 보냈다는 것으로 되어 있음

　○　그러나 동인의 범죄사실에 대한 AI측의 위와 같은 견해는
　　　기소된 범죄사실의 내용과 동인에게 적용된 법률의 조문 등
　　　가장 기본적인 사실을 아무런 근거도 없이 무시하고 당사자나
　　　그 주변에서 동인의 범죄사실을 은폐, 미화하기 위해 행하는
　　　주장을 그대로 반복한 것임

　○　동인의 범죄사실을 이해하기 위해서는 먼저 북한의 대남적화
　　　혁명전략과 통일전선전술을 이해하여야 함

　　　-　1945년 일제식민통치에서 해방되면서 대한민국은 소련과
　　　　　미국이 각각 진주함으로써 분열되었고, 이제까지 40여년간
　　　　　동서 이데올로기의 대립과 갈등이라는 냉전구조속에서
　　　　　남북간의 첨예한 이념적, 군사적, 정치적 대결상태를
　　　　　유지하여 왔음

0039

- 특히 피고인이 직접 담당한 "광주항쟁부분"에 대하여는
  민중을 억압 착취하는 군부독제와 미제 등 외세의 한국침탈에
  대항하여 싸운 민중의 항쟁으로 광주사태를 승화시켜 형상화
  하기로 합의하여, 5월 광주민중항쟁이 반미·반파쇼 민주화
  투쟁의 시각에서 일어난 것이라는 내용으로 그림을 제작함으로써
  북한의 선전·선동에 동조하였던 것임

o 또한 홍성담이 책을 보낸 서독거주 성낙영은, 북한이 한국의 해외
  여행자,유학생, 취업자 등을 포섭, 입북시켜 사상교양후 간첩으로
  침투시키거나 친북 동조세력 확산을 위해 일본, 유럽, 미주지역에서
  활용하고 있는 전위조직의 일원으로서, 홍성담에게 서독에서는
  한국책을 구하기가 어려우니 책을 부쳐주되 국내운동권 상황이나
  정세를 분석한 책들이 필요하다고 요청하였고, 이에 따라 동인은
  수회에 걸쳐 국내정세, 운동권이론, 주한미군의 강간·살인 등
  범죄사례, 노동문제, 농민운동, 도시빈민운동, 학생운동 등의
  동향, 6.25 전쟁에 관한 새로운 이론, 미술운동의 나아갈 방향
  및 미술운동의 흐름 등에 관한 자료가 수록된 책자를 송부하였음

o 이들 자료는 북한이 한국내의 좌익세력과 불만세력의 동향을
  파악하여 선동전술을 계획하고 조종하는데 필요로 하는 것들로서
  1심 판결에서도 동 자료들의 국가기밀성을 인정하였음

0040

- 북한의 제1목표는 한반도 전역을 공산화하는데 있으며, 그 의도는 1950년 6.25전쟁, 미국 푸에블로호 납치사건, 청와대 습격사건, 판문점 도끼만행사건, 미얀마 아웅산 폭파사건, 칼기 폭파사건, 휴전선 각 지역에서의 남침용 땅굴발견사건, 각종 무장간첩사건 등에서 보는 바와 같이 의심의 여지가 없음

- 북한은 이와 같은 직접적인 도발외에, 한편으로는 우리사회의 불만세력과 좌익세력을 이용하여 내부혼란을 조성하기 위해 선동선전전술을 계속 자행하여 왔음

- 즉, 남한은 일본의 식민지에서 빗어나면서 미군의 강점으로 미국의 식민지로 재편되었고, 미제는 군사파쇼정권을 내세워 남한의 급속한 자본주의화를 추진했으며, 이 과정에서 노동자, 농민의 생활조건과 처지는 너무 비참해지고 부익부, 빈익빈 현상이 심화되었으며, 미.일 외세와 이에 의존하고 있는 군사독재와 독점재벌은 분단을 통해 막대한 이익을 얻고 있기에 분단의 고착화를 바라고 있다고 선전하고, 이러한 모순을 해결하기 위해서는 친미세력. 매판자본가. 소수 정치군인을 배제한 노동자, 농민, 학생 등 모든 민주세력이 일치단결하여 미.일 외세와 군부독재를 타도(반미자주. 반파쇼민주)하고 민족자주국가를 수립해야 한다고 선동하여 왔음

0041

o 홍성담도 위와 같은 북한의 선전·선동과 같이 "한국사회는

신식민지적 국가로서 미제국주의에 의해 지배받고 있으며,

이러한 외세와 결탁한 매판독재세력에 의해서 민중이 억압받고

수탈당하고 있고, 자본주의 체제의 모순으로 빈부의 격차가

심화되어 노동자, 농민 즉 민중들은 생활고에 시달리고 있다.

이러한 사회구조의 모순은 노동자, 농민, 도시빈민 등 소외계층

민중의 연대투쟁을 통해서만이 해결될 수 있으며, 사회변혁도

가능하다"고 인식하였으며, "미술활동도 현실에 참여하는

민중미술운동을 통해서 모순된 사회현실을 민중에게 알리고

의식화시켜 사회구조적 모순을 타파해야 한다"고 믿고,

"노동자, 농민의 고달픈 삶" 등 판화전시회를 개최하고,

반미투쟁 선동을 내용으로 하는 "해방의 횃불" 등을 출품

하였으며, "막스레닌주의 미학의 기초" 등을 학습하는 등

소위 민중미술을 통한 투쟁방법을 모색하여 왔음

o 동인이 주동하여 15폭의 대형 걸개그림으로 그려 이를 슬라이드로

제작, 북한에 보낸 "민족해방운동사"라는 제목의 그림은

    - 소위 NLPDR (민족해방민중민주주의혁명) 이론에 입각하여

      남한학생과 민중들에게 투쟁의식을 고취, 각성시키자는 것이

      제작목적이었으며

0042

o 그밖에도 동인은 동인이 대표로 있는 민족민중미술운동 전국연합

   건설준비위원회(미미연 건준위) 명의로 기관지인 '미술운동

   제2호'를 제작, 발간하였던 바, 동 기관지의 내용은

   - 미술가 대중조직에 있어서 지도중심은 마르크스-레닌주의적

     미술사상과 올바른 정치사상적 입장을 체현하고 이를 관철하여

     신망을 받을 수 있는 사람이어야 한다

   - 선진 미술가조직은 국민대중의 예술표현요구를 조직화하여

     각 계급 계층운동을 지원 보조하고, 민중이 문예창작의 주인으로

     나서는 데 보조해야 한다

   - 미술운동의 사회의 변혁을 앞당기고 변혁운동 자체에 높고

     힘있는 기여를 하게 하는 것이다 등 마르크스-레닌주의에

     입각하여 계급투쟁을 선동하는 내용으로 역시 북한의 주장과

     활동에 동조하는 기관지를 제작하였던 것임

o 위에서 설명한 바와 같이 홍성담의 범죄사실은 단순히 그림을

   그렸다거나 책을 해외에 보냈다는 것이 아니며, 그와 같은

   사실만으로는 현행법상 범법행위가 결코 될 수도 없음

0043

2. 양심수라는 주장에 대하여

○ 국가가 개인의 정치적인 신념에 대한 자유를 보장해 주어야
   한다는 점에 대해서는 이론이 없음

○ 그러나 어떤 개인이 공산주의 사상이나 좌익, 좌경사상을
   자신의 신념으로 갖고 있는 것과 이를 실현하기 위해 계급
   혁명을 선동하여 자유민주주의 체제의 전복을 기도, 조장하는
   것과는 다른 차원의 문제라고 생각함

○ 홍성담의 경우, 자신의 사상을 단순히 내면의 신념으로만 갖고
   있었던 것이 아니며 항상 그 사상을 실현하기 위해 실천방법을
   모색하여 왔으며, 그 실천방법이 실정법에 저촉되게 된 것임

○ 그리고 AI에서는 홍성담의 경우, 폭력을 사용하거나 옹호한
   경우가 아니라고 하나, 헌법과 법률에 따라 선거에 의하여
   선출된 대통령과 정부를 매판독재세력이라고 주장하면서
   타도해야 한다고 할 때 과연 어떤 방법으로 타도해야 한다는
   것인지 묻지 않을 수 없음

0044

o 우리 사회의 좌익혁명세력의 경우, 헌법과 법률에 정한 절차에
   따라 정부를 교체하고, 빈부격차 등 사회문제를 해결하자는
   것이 아니며, 헌법과 법률을 비롯하여 모든 정치,사회,경제
   체제가 매판독재세력의 장기집권과 민중에 대한 착취, 탄압을
   보장해 주는 구조로 되어 있기 때문에 현 체제하에서 합법적이고
   평화적인 방법으로는 변혁이 있을 수 없고, 결국 노동자, 농민,
   학생 등 민중의 연대에 의한 폭력혁명만이 변혁을 가능하게
   한다고 주장하고 있음

o 따라서 홍성담의 경우, 정치적 신념만으로 구금되었거나 폭력을
   옹호한 경우가 아니라는 주장은 전혀 사건에 대한 깊이있는
   이해에 입각한 주장이 아님

3. 변호인의 조력을 받을 권리

   o 대한민국의 헌법과 형사소송법은 변호인의 조력을 받을 권리를
      보장하고 있으며 수사기관도 이를 준수하고 있음

   o 홍성담 사건에 있어, 1심 법원은 국가안전기획부에서 동인을
      조사할 때 변호인의 접견신청이 거부당하였으며, 법원의 접견허용
      결정에 따라 접견이 이루어진 '89.8.24. 이전에 작성된

0045

증거에 대해서 증거능력을 부인하였으나, 8.25부터 9.18까지 사이에 작성된 증거는 변호인의 접견 교통권이 보장된 상태에서 이루어진 것이므로 증거능력을 인정하였으며, 증거능력이 인정된 증거의 범위내에서 유죄가 선고되었음

o 이 사건의 판결은 수사기관에서 커다란 교훈을 주었으며, 수사 기관들은 더욱 변호인의 접견 교통권을 보장하는데 주의를 기울이게 되었음

4. 가혹행위 주장에 대하여

o 홍성담은 수사기관의 조사를 받는 동안 잠을 못 자고 구타를 당했다고 주장하고 있으나, 검찰 송치당일 그는 건강상태를 묻는 검사의 질문에 대하여 신체에 별다른 이상이 없으며, 그동안 가혹행위를 당한 사실도 없을 뿐만 아니라 건강하다고 명백히 대답하였음. 그리고 그는 검사실에서 조사받는 도중 법조출입 기자들이 들어와 그들과 환담까지 나누었다고 함

o 홍씨는 자신 이외에는 알 수 없는 내용을 검찰에서 자연스럽게 진술하였고, 조서의 세세한 부분까지 자필로 수정하거나 자신에게 유리한 내용의 문구를 조서 말미에 보태기까지 하였음.

0046

이는 곧 홍씨가 수사기관에서 강압에 의해 진술했던 것이 아님을

반증하는 것이라 아니할 수 없음.

법원에서도 홍씨의 고문주장은 받아들여지지 않았음

o 다만, 홍씨의 가족들이 서울지방검찰청에 고소장을 제출하여

수사가 진행중에 있으므로 곧 그 결과가 나오게 될 것임

0047

┌─────────────────────┐
│   조　용　술   │
└─────────────────────┘

o 인적사항

　주　소 : 군산시 나운동 유원아파트 3동 1305
　생년월일 : 1920. 12. 1. 생
　직　업 : 목사

o 범죄사실요지 (국가보안법위반)

－ 전민련 산하 조국통일위원회 소속 범민족대회 추진본부 공동위원장
　　조용술, 동 집행위원장 이해학, 동 사무처장 조성우등 3명은 89.
　　10. 3. 및 11. 9. 이른바 범민족 통일온동체 결성을 추진한다는
　　명분하에 베를린에서 열기로 한 남.북.해외동포 3차회담에 참석
　　하기 위해 관광을 빙자 각각 은밀히 출국

－ 89.11.19.부터 20.사이 베를린시청 회의실에서 북측대표인
　　조통위 부위원장 전금철 등을 만나 소외 조국통일 범민족연합을 결성,
　　그 집행기관으로 공동사무국등을 설치키로 합의한 후 우리 정부를
　　반통일세력으로 매도하고 한반도주둔 외국군 및 핵무기칠수, 유엔
　　동시가입반대, 국가보안법철폐등 내용의 공동선인문과 유엔 사무총장
　　에게 보내는 편지를 발표하여 반국가단체인 북한의 구성원과 회합,
　　통신하면서 그들의 주장, 활동에 동조한 것임

o 처리상황

　서울지방검찰청에서 수사중
　90년 11월30일 구속 (치안본부)

0048

```
┌─────────────────────────────┐
│                             │
│      유    원    호          │
│                             │
└─────────────────────────────┘
```

1. 인적사항

   o 본 적 : ████████████████████

   o 주 거 : 서울 은평구 응암4동 261-4

   o 생년월일 : 30. 7. 3

   o 직 업 : (주) 중원엔지니어링 대표

2. 범죄요지

   o '89.3.25 재일 북한공작원 정경모의 지령에 의해 문익환과
      함께 평양으로 탈출하였다가 동년 4.13 귀국하여 잠입

   o 2회에 걸쳐 국가기밀을 수집하여 위 정경모에게 보고하고
      한민통 (한국민주회복통일추진국민회의) 구성원 곽동의로부터
      정치자금 명목으로 일화 200만엥 수수

3. 처리상황

   o '89. 4.14   구속 (안기부)

   o '89. 5.31   기소 (서울지검)

   o '89.10. 5   1심선고, 징.자 10년 (서울지검)

   o '90. 2.10   2심선고, 징.자 7년, 일부 무죄

0049

＊　무죄이유 :　특수잠업중 지령수수에 대한 증거가 없어

　　이점에 대해 이유에서 일부 무죄설시하고, 반국가단체의

　　지령에 의해 범행한 것이 아니라고 범행을 부인하고

　　이에 대한 증거가 없어 이점에 대해 이유에서 일부

　　무죄설시

ㅇ　'90. 6. 8　상고기각, 확정 (대법원)

0050

```
┌─────────────────────┐
│   김   진   업        │
└─────────────────────┘
```

o 인적사항

　　주　　소 ： 오스트레일리아국 뉴사우스웨일즈주 시드니시 켄시파크
　　　　　　　　스트리트 80

　　생년월일 ： 64. 1. 12.생

　　직　　업 ： 치과의사

o 범죄사실요지 (국가보안법위반)

　　89.5. 약혼너 김승일(호주국적)로부터 전대협대표 평축참가를 지원할
　　것을 지시받고, 동년 6월 전대협 정책위원장 정은철등과 접촉하여 임수경의
　　밀입북경로등에 대하여 조인하고, 정은철에게 임수경과 유럽민협측과의
　　연락 및 접촉방법등을 상의한 후 그 사항을 호주에 거주하는 김승일로
　　하여금 유럽민협의 어수갑에게 연락토록 하여 임수경의 밀입북행위에
　　대하여 편의제공

o 처리상황

　　-　89. 9. 4　　　구속 (안기부)

　　　　89.10.21　　구속기소 (서울지검)

　　　　90. 2.20　　 1심선고　징.자2년 (서울지법)

　　　　90. 6.15　　 2심선고　징.자1년6월 (서울고법)

　　　　90. 9.14　　 상고기각 (대법원)

　　　　90. 9.14　　 확정

0051

공   란

공 란

공 란

공   란

공   란

공   란

공　　　　란

공   란

공   란

공　　　　란

공 란

공   란

공   란

공　　　란

공 란

공   란

공   란

공   란

공 란

공　　　란

공 란

공   란

공   란

공   란

공 란

공   란

공　　　　란

공   란

공　　　란

공   란

공 란

공   란

공 란

공   란

공 란

공 란

洪性淡피고인
간첩혐의 無罪
大法환송 高法선고

서울고법 형사2부(재판장
朴駿緖부장판사)는 31일 대
법원 파기환송된 국가보안법위반
형결개그룹 실라인등을 편
낮혹전에 보낸 혐의등으로 구

속기소된 洪性淡피고인(35.
민족미술인총연합 공동대표)
에대한 국가보안법위반 파기
환송사건 선고공판에서 대법
원의 선고대로 洪피고인에게
적용된 간첩죄부분등 주요공
소사실에 대해 무죄를 선고
했다.

재판부는 그러나 洪피고인
에게 적용된 국가보안법상의
이적표현물 제작반포등 혐의
에대해서는 원심대로 유죄를
인정, 징역3년 자격정지3년
을 선고했다.

공 란

공　　　란

공   란

MINISTRY OF FOREIGN AFFAIRS
REPUBLIC OF KOREA

14. Maerz 1991

An
Herrn Andreas Guendel
Fachbereich Informatik-Lehrstuhl V
Uebersetzerbau und Programmiersysteme
Universitaet Dortmund
Postfach 50 05 00
4600 Dortmund 50
Bundesrepublik Deutschland

Betr.: Kang, Che-Hyong

Sehr geehrter Herr Guendel,

Fuer Ihr Schreiben an Herrn Vizeminister Yoo, Chong-Ha vom
25. 11. 1990 danke ich Ihnen. Sie berichteten in Ihrem Schreiben
ueber den Fall Herrn Kang, Che-Hyong.

Nach der Information vom zustaendigen Ministerium wurde Herr Kang
als Redakteur einer Hochschulzeitung mit der Beschuldigung der
widerrechtlichen Veroeffentlichung und Verteilung der Zeitung
am 26. 5. 1990 verhaftet, die einen Artikel zur Umwerfung des
kapitalistischen Systems durch die Volksrevolution enthielt.
Der Inhalt dieses Artikels verletzt das Recht Koreas und ist
eine offene Herausforderung der Demokratie unseres Landes.

Herr Kang wurde am 12. 9. 1990 zu einer Haftstrafe von einem
Jahr mit Bewaehrung von zwei Jahren verurteilt und wurde selbstver-
staendlich am selben Tag aus der Haft freigelassen.

Ich hoffe, dass ich hiermit Ihre Frage beantwort habe und danke
Ihnen fuer Ihr Interesse an Korea.

Mit freundlichen Gruessen

Kwon, Youngmin
Leiter der Abteilung Europa

0092

1991년 3월 14일

친애하는 권델씨,

  귀하가 1990.11.25일자로 유종하 차관에게 보낸 강제형씨 사건에 관한
서신 잘 받아 보았습니다.

  본인이 이 사건에 관해 해당 부처로부터 받은 보고에 의하면, 강제형씨는
1990. 5. 26 한성대 교지 편집위원장으로서 이적 표현물 제작 및 반포
협의로 구속되었습니다.

  동 교지에는 현 한국의 자본주의 제도를 민중의 혁명으로 변혁시켜야
한다는 글이 게재되었던 바, 이는 한국의 법에 저촉되며 또한 민주주의
제도에 대한 정면 도전인 것입니다.

  강씨는 1990.9.12. 재판에서 징역 1년 집행유예 2년의 형을 선고 받고
동일자로 석방되었습니다.

  본인은 귀하의 질문이 이것으로서 대답되었기를 바라며, 귀하의 한국에
관한 관심에 감사드립니다.

권영민
구주국장

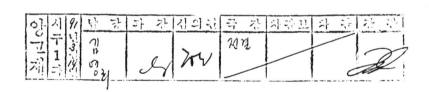

분류기호 문서번호	국연 2031- 124	( )	협조문용지	결 재	담당	과장	국장
시행일자	1991. 4. 6.						
수 신	미주국장, 구주국장	발 신		국제기구조약국장 (서명)			
제 목	아국 인권문제						

1. 제 6공화국 출범이래 정부가 인권신장을 위하여 적극 노력

하고 있고 특히 아국이 90.7.10. 국제인권규약에 가입함에 따라 국제

사회에서의 아국 인권현황에 대한 인식과 관심이 한층 제고되고

있습니다.

2. 당국은 유엔내 인권관련회의 대책수립과 이행, 국제인권

규약 가입에 따른 의무이행에 관련된 인권업무 및 A.I. 관련업무를

담당하고 있으나 간혹 재외공관으로부터 상기 유엔차원의 인권논의

와는 무관한 주재국 정부, 의회 또는 민간단체, 인사들로 부터의

질의.청원 관련 문건을 당국에 송부하여 오는 경우가 있습니다.

3. 상기 각국정부 또는 단체등이 제기하는 아국 인권관련 문건

등은 접수즉시 귀국으로 이첩할 예정이며 사안에 따라 법무부로부터

당국이 기접수한 설명자료가 있는 경우는 첨송할 예정임을 알려드립니다.

끝. 0094

1505 - 8 일 (1)
85. 9. 9 승인 "내가아끼 좋아 하짠 늘여나는 나라살림"

190㎜×268㎜ (인쇄용지 2 급 60g / ㎡)

長 官 報 告 事 項

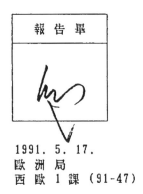

報 告 畢

1991. 5. 17.
歐 洲 局
西 歐 1 課 (91-47)

題 目 : 獨逸人 Juergen Meier 入國 不許 問題

獨逸 綠色黨 全國 代表委員 中 1人인 Juergen Meier 가 1991.5.16
我國 入國이 拒否된 바, 關聯事項 아래 報告 드립니다.

ㅇ 동인은 광주항쟁 11주년 기념행사에 참석차 91.5.16. 10:40 김포공항에
   도착 하였으나 법무부 당국으로부터 입국이 거부됨.

ㅇ 5.17(금) 주한 독일 대사관은 동인의 입국 거부에 대한 법적근거를 문의해옴.

ㅇ 이와 관련한 법무부의 입장은 하기와 같음.
   - 양국간 사증면제협정 제 6항<특정 외국인(undesirable person)에 대한
     입국허가 유보권리>을 근거로하여 입국을 불허함.
   - 동인은 88년 8월 한국을 방문하여 여러가지 불법 정치집회에 참석한
     이유로 사증 발급 규제 대상자로 분류

※ 동인은 현재 동경에 체류중임.   끝.

0095

長 官 報 告 事 項

報 告 畢

1991. 5. 17.
歐 洲 局
西 歐 1 課 (91-47)

題 目 : 獨逸人 Juergen Meier 入國 不許 問題

獨逸 綠色政黨 全國 代表委員 中 1人인 Juergen Meier 가 1991.5.16
我國 入國이 拒否된 바, 關聯事項 아래 報告 드립니다.

---

o 동인은 광주항쟁 11주년 기념행사에 참석차 91.5.16. 10:40 김포공항에
  도착 하였으나 법무부 당국으로부터 입국이 거부됨.

o 5.17(금) 주한 독일 대사관은 동인의 (한국) 입국 거부에 대한 법적근거를
  문의해옴.

o 법무부 입국 심사과에 문의 하카 요지로 답변

  - 양국간 사증면제협정 제 6항<특정 외국인(undesirable person)에 대한
    입국허가 유보권리>을 근거로하여 입국을 불허함.

  - 동인은 88년 8월 한국을 방문하여 여러가지 불법 정치집회에 참석한
    이유로 사증 발급 규제 대상자로 분류

※ 동인은 현재 동경에 체류중임. 끝.

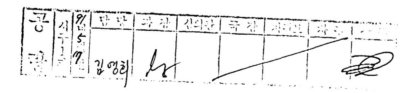

독일인 Juergen Meier(녹색정당 전국 대표중 1인) 입국 거절문제

ㅇ 동인은 91.5.16, 10:40 김포공항에서 입국을 거절당함.

ㅇ 5.17 독일 대사관은 동인의 입국거절 법적 근거를 문의해 옴.(전화로)

ㅇ 법무부 입국심사과의 이에대한 대답은 아래와 같음.
  - 동인은 88년 8월 한국을 방문하여 여러가지 불법 정치집회에 참석한 바 있음.
  - 위의 근거로 하여 동인은 사증발급 규제 대상자로 규정됨.
  - 대한민국 정부와 독일연방 공화국간의 사증면제협정 제 6항을 근거로 하여
    입국을 불허함.

* 첨부: 사증면제 협정 1부. 끝.

0097

AGREEMENT ON THE WAIVER OF
VISA REQUIREMENTS BETWEEN THE GOVERNMENT OF THE REPUBLIC OF KOREA AND THE GOVERNMENT OF THE FEDERAL REPUBLIC OF GERMANY

Effected by Exchange of Notes
at Seoul November 17, 1972
Entered into force January 24,
1974

The Ambassador of the Federal Republic of Germany
the Minister of Foreing Affairs

Seoul, November 17, 1972

Excellency,

I have the honour to propose on behalf of the Government of the Federal Republic of Germany that, with a veiw to facilitating travel between the Federal Republic of Germany and Republic of Korea, the following Arrangement be concluded on the basis of the respective national legislation of both countries:

1. Germans who possess a valid German passport and do not intend to engage in gainful activities may enter the Republic of Korea without a visa, stay there for a period not exceeding sixty days and leave the terrotiry without the necessity of obtaining an exit permit.

An extension of stay for another thirty days will be granted to Germans by the Korean authorities concerned without delay upon receipt of an application for extension and residence report.

2. Germans who intend to stay for a period exceeding sixty days in the Republic of Korea or to engage in gainful activities there may enter the Republic of KOrea and stay there if they posses a valid German passport and visa issued by the appropriate diplomatic mission or consular post of the Republic of Korea.

3. Nationals of the Republic of Korea who possess a valid passport

of the Republic of Korea and do not intend to engage in gainful activities may enter the Federal Republic of Germany without a residence permit (visa, and stay there not longer than three months and leave the territory without the necessity of obtaining an exit permit).

4. Nationals of the Republic of Korea who intend to remain longer than three months in the Federal Republic of Germany or to engage in gainful activities there may enter the Federal Republic of Germany and stay there if they possess a valid passport of the Republic of Korea and a residence permit in the form of a visa issued by the appropriate diplomatic mission or consular post of the Federal Republic of Germany.

5. The waiver of the visa requirements shall not exempt Germans and nationals of the Republic of Korea from the obligation to observe the laws and regulations of the Republic of Korea and of the Federal Repbulic of Germany relating to the entry, sojourn (temporary or permanent), as well as the employment or professional activity of aliens.

6. The appropriate authorities of both countries reserve the right to refuse permission to enter or stay in their respective territory to any persons who are considered undesirable or who, on other grounds, have to be refused permission according to general regulations for foreigners.

7. The Government of the Republic of Korea shall readmit to the Republic of Korea at any time and without special permission nationals of the Republic of Korea whom the authorities of the Federal Republic of Germany intend to remove from the Federal Republic of Germany and shall issue them, if necessary, the papers they require for their return to the Republic of Korea.

8. The Government of the Federal Republic of Germany shall readmit to the Federal Republic of Germany at any time and without special permission Germans whom the authorities of the Republic of Korea intend to remove from the Republic of Korea, and shall issue them, if necessary, the papers they require for their return to the Federal Republic of Germany.

9. The Government of either Contracting State may suspend the foregoing provisons temporarily either in whole or in part for reasons of public safety or order. Such suspension shall be notified immedia-tely to the Government of the other Contracting State through the diplomatic channel. The same procedure shall be adopted when the suspension is lifted.

10. The present Arrangement shall also apply to Land Berlin provided that the Government of the Federal Republic of Germany does not make a contrary declaration to The Government of the Republic of Korea within three months of the entry into force of this Arrangement.

11. The present Arrangement shall enter into force when both Governments have informed each other that the national prerequisites thereto have been fulfilled. It may be denounced at any time subject to two months' notice.

Such denunciation shall be notified to the Government of the other Contracting State through the diplomatic channel.

If the Government of the Republic of Korea agrees to the proposals contained in paragraphs 1 to 11 above, the present Note and Your Excellency's Note in reply thereto shall constitute an Arrangement between our two Governments.

Accept, Excellency, the renewed assurances of my highest consideration.

Wilfried Sarrazin
Ambassador

His Excellency
Kim Yong Shik
Minister of Foreign Afffairs

0099

독일녹색당 대표 입국 불허

'광주'행사 참석 무산

광주항쟁 11주년 기념행사에 참석하려던 유럽녹색당연합 위르겐 마이어(28) 독일대표가 16일 정부의 입국금지조치로 입국하지 못한 채 김포공항에서 만하로 일본으로 떠났다.

마이어는 이날 오전 10시20분 5·18기념식참가진위인회(위원장 이광우) 초청으로 독일 녹색당연합유럽녹색연합의 한국 대표로 대한항공편으로 도착했으나 공항당국이 입국을 불허해 오후 1시40분 일본행공 952편기로 도쿄로 떠났다.

마이어는 서독 녹색당 중앙위원으로 있다. 지난 88년 8월 서울에서 개최된 제1세계·진대협 등이 주최한 '한반도 평화와 통일'을 위한 세계대회에 서독 대표로 참가한 적이 있어 '입국 사증발급 규제 자가 된 것으로 알려졌다.

한편 마이어는 이번 입국이 불허되자 "기구상에서 한국은 어떤 이유로도 추방할 수 있는 유일한 나라"라며 "한국정부의 조치에 강력히 항의한다"고 밝혔다.

한국과 독일 사이에는 지난 74년 1인 사증면제협정이 체결돼 독일인의 입국에는 사증이 필요 없어 입국이 가능하다.

"돌아오시면 안됩니다"
광주항쟁 11주년 기념식에 참석하기 위해 16일 오전 김포공항에 도착한 유럽 녹색당연합 독일 대표 위르겐 마이어가 입국무 관계자로부터 입국불허통보를 받고 있다. 〈이상기 기자〉

5·18행사 참석예정
獨人인사 정부서不許

전남도 녹지과 대표단을 인솔했고 현 유럽 녹색당 동일대변인 위르겐 마이어씨 (33) 가 16일 상오 10시 20분 한화원에서 전기료납부하라며 정부당국 의 불허방침으로 일본으로 돌아갔다.

마이어씨는 이날 5·18 광주 민중항쟁기념사업추진 위 초청으로 입북, 26일까지 머물면서 광주민주화항쟁 11 주년기념식및 각종행사에 참석할 예정이었다.

한국일보 91. 5. 17

0101

외 무 부

종 별 : 지급

번 호 : GEW-1083

수 신 : 장관(영사, 구일)

발 신 : 주독 대사

제 목 : 독일인 입국거부

일 시 : 91 0517 1730

5.17. 외무부 SCHEEL 동아국장은 안공사에게, 독일인 JUERGEN MAIER 가 최근 김포공항에서 입국을 거부당하고 현재 동경에서 대기중인바, 입국할수 있도록협조요청해온바, 입국거부 경위등 관련사항 회시바람.

(대사-국장)

예고:91.12.31. 까지

검도필(1)91.6.30

예고문에 의거 재수구(1991. 12. 31.)
지위 성명 기

영교국   구주국

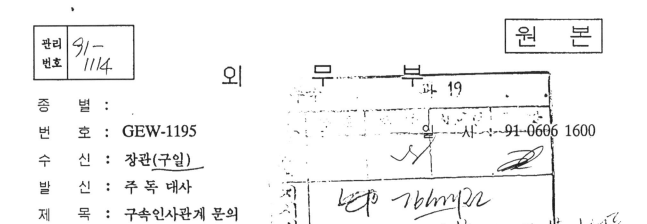

| 관리
번호 | 91-
1114 |

원　본

외　　무　　부

종　별 :

번　호 : GEW-1195

수　신 : 장관(구일)

발　신 : 주독 대사

제　목 : 구속인사관계 문의

일　시 : 91 0606 1600

6.6. 안공사는 대통령실 VON DER PLANITZ 대외정책및 의전담당 국장과 오찬을 가진바, 동국장은 바이체커 대통령의 방한시 KLEINER 대사를 통하여 아측에 전달한바 있는 홍성담등 구속인사 관계 진전사항을 문의하였는바, 회보바람.

(대사-국장)

예고:91.12.31.일반

검토필(1991.6.30)	
예고문에의거 재분류(1991.12.31.)	
직위　　　　　　성명	

구주국　　　차관　　　1차보　　　2차보

PAGE 1

91.06.07　　00:04

외신 2과　통제관 CF

0103

〈참고자료〉

독일측 거론 예상 구속자 및 아국 정부 입장

가. 김형규 문제

(사건개요)

o 1974년이후 서독 광부로 취업중 83.10-87.7간 3회에 걸쳐 방북,
  간첩 밀봉교육 받음.
o 87.9. 북한의 지령에 따라 국내잠입, 간첩 활동중 동년 10월 구속
o 89.4.3 징역 9년의 확정판결을 받고 현재 대전교도소에서 복역중

(독일측 요청)

o 동인이 독일 시민권자임을 감안, 동인에 대한 특별사면 고려 요청
   - 88.2. 겐셔 외무장관, 주독대사에 트결사면 고려요청
   - 88.7. 한.독 외무장관 회담시 선처 요청
   - 89.10. 브란트 전독일수상, 국무총리와의 오찬시 선처 요청
   - 89.11. 노대통령 방독시, 바이쩨커 대통령 및 겐셔 외무장관
            관심표명

(아측 입장)

o 그간 아측은 사면이나 석방은 현행법상(최소한 형기의 1/3이상
  복역, 행장성적 양호 등) 어렵다는 입장을 견지해 왔으나
o 폰 바이쩨커 대통령을 위시한 독일정부 요로의 동 문제에 대한
  지속적인 관심표명 및 한.독간 우호관계를 고려,
o 가석방은 실제 관행상 형기의 3/4이상 복역한 자에 한해 시행해
  왔음에도 불구, 형기의 1/3 이상을 복역한 동인에 대하여 국외추방을
  전제로 가석방 조치

0104

나. 법민족 3자회담 참가자 문제

(사건개요)

ㅇ 90.10.28 조용술, 이재학, 조성우 3인, 베를린 개최 법민족 3자회담
  참가를 위한 북한주민 접촉 승인서 통일원에 제출

ㅇ 90.11.19-20 상기 3인, 정부측 불허방침 통보에도 불구 3자회담
  참가 강행

ㅇ 90.11.3 귀국 즉시 국가보안법 위반 혐의로 구속, 현재 재판 계류중

(독일측 관심표명)

 ㅇ 90.12. 독일 외무부 동아국장대리, 독일 인권단체들이 독일 대통령
   방한과 관련 동 문제를 제기할 가능성에 비추어 방한 실현전 아국정부의
   적절한 조치 희망

(아측 입장)

ㅇ 동인들의 구속은 실정법 위반에 따른 사법적 조치이며 인권차원에서
  거론할 문제가 아님.

ㅇ 독립된 사법부에 의해 재판 계류중인 사안이므로 행정부가 이에
  관여할 수 없음.

* 정부의 법민족 3자회담 참가 불허이유
  - 통일문제는 국민적 합의를 바탕으로 국민대표 기관인 정부나
    국회의 주도하에 신중히 추진되어야 함.
  - 동 회담은 북한이 당고위급 인사를 민간대표로 가장하여 파견하고
    전민련 계열만을 남한측 회담대표로 제한하는 등 북한의 통일전선
    전술상의 대남선동 책략의 일환임.

0105

다. 여타 시국관련 구속자 문제

(기타 독일측 거론 예상 구속자)

　　ㅇ 임수경 :　89.8.20　국가보안법 위반으로 구속, 징역.자격정지

　　　　　　　　　　　　　　각 5년형 확정

　　ㅇ 문익환 :　89.4.13　국가보안법 위반으로 구속, 징역.자격정지

　　　　　　　　　　　　　　각 7년형 확정

　　　　　　　90.10.20　지병에 따른 형 집행정지 결정으로 가석방

　　ㅇ 유원호 :　89.4.14　국가보안법 위반으로 구속, 징역.자격정지

　　　　　　　　　　　　　　각 7년 확정

　　ㅇ 홍성담 :　89.8.3　국가보안법 위반으로 구속, 2심에서

　　　　　　　　　　　　　징역.자격정지 각 7년 선고,

　　　　　　　90.9.25　대법원에서 원심파기 환송

　　　　　　　91.1.31　고법에서 징역.자격정지 각 3년 확정

(정부 입장)

　　ㅇ 문익환 :　법원의 형집행 정지 결정으로 기 가석방

　　ㅇ 임수경, 유원호, 홍성담 : 이들에 대한 사법부의 결정을 존중한다는 입장이며

　　　　　　　특별사면이나 가석방은 고려하지 않고 있음.

0106

관리 번호	9 1 - 7279			

분류기호 문서번호	구일 202- 750	기 안 용 지	시 행 상 특별취급	
보존기간	영구.준영구 10. 5. 3. 1		장 관	
수 신 처 보존기간				
시행일자	1991. 7. 10.			

보조 기관	국 장	전결	협조기관			문 서 통 제
	심의관					접수 1991. 7.10
	과 장					
기안책임자		김 영 희				발 송 인

경 유		발신명의	
수 신	주독대사		
참 조			

제 목	임수경 등 구속자 관련 자료 송부

대 : GEW - 1195

대호, 독일측에서 관심을 표명하고 있는 구속자들에 관한

법무부 제공자료를 별첨 송부하오니 동 자료를 참조, ~~von der Planitz~~

~~국장~~에게 적의 설명 하시기 바랍니다.

예고문에의거재분류(1991. 12.31.)
직위   성명 김○○

첨 부 : 상기자료.   끝.

예 고 : 91.12.31. 일반

0107

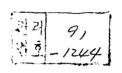

법   무   부

검삼 202-28   (503-7055)   1991. 7. 1.

수신 외무부장관

참조 구주국장

제목 임수경등 관련자료 회신

1. 구일 202 - 647 ('91.6.10)호 및   -1195(91.6.10)
호와 관련입니다.

2. 귀부에서 요청한 자료를 별첨과 같이 송부합니다.

3. 조용술, 이해학, 조성우에 대한 당부의 입장은 검삼0160-87호
('91.4.22. 대외비) "보안법위반 구속자"로 송부한 베를린 3자회담 참
가자 구속관련 대응자료를 참고하시기 바랍니다.

첨부 : 설명자료 4부. 끝.

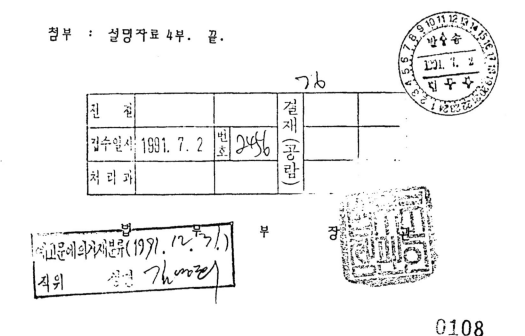

전 결			결재(공람)		
접수일시	1991. 7. 2	번호	2456		
처 리 과					

법   무   부   장

예고문에의거재분류(1991. 12. 31)
직위   실명 김OO

0108

예고문 [일반문서 : 91. 12. 31]

임수경 (여, 22세, 외대 용인분교 불어과 4년)

o 범죄사실 요지

  - 89.5.18. 이적단체인 전대협산하 "평양축전준비위원회"에 정책
    기획실장으로 가입

  - 제13차 세계청년학생축전에 참가할 목적으로 89.6.30. 일본,
    동독을 거쳐 평양에 도착, 지령을 받고 북한지역으로 탈출

  - 89.6.30.-8.14. 북한에 머물면서 반국가단체구성원과 회합,
    찬양고무 및 북한의 조선학생위원장에게 학생운동권 활동상황등을
    보고하는등 자진하여 군사상이익 공여

  - 89.7.12. 및 8.12. 반국가단체구성원으로부터 북한화 3,000원과
    금목걸이 시가 15만원상당 금품수수

  - 89.8.15. 판문점을 통해 입국 지령을 받고 북한지역으로부터 잠입

o 적용법조

  - 국가보안법 제5조제1항, 제4조제1항제1호, 형법제99조,국가보안법
    제5조제2항,제6조제2항,제7조제1항,제3항,제8조제1항,제14조

o 처리상황

  - 89.10. 7   구속기소
  - 90. 2. 5   서울형사지법, 징.자 각10년
  - 90. 6.11   서울고법, 징.자 각5년
  - 90. 9.25   대법원, 상고기각 확정

0109

○ 당부입장

- 통일이 우리의 시급한 과제이기도 하나, 우리 헌법은 자유민주적
  기본질서에 입각한 통일정책을 수립, 시행할 것을 선언하고 있고,
  그 책무를 대통령에게 부과하고 있음

- 통일논의는 자유롭게 개방되어 있다고 하더라도 자유민주적기본질서에
  입각한 통일의 범위를 벗어날 수 없으며, 그 정책의 수립후 시행은
  대통령과 정부의 주도하에 질서있게 순차적으로 추진되어야 함

- 북한의 적화혁명 통일이나, 소위 민중혁명에 의한 민중정권 수립후의
  연공·연북 통일을 지지하거나, 정부의 통일정책과 대북정책을 무시한
  채 자의적으로 밀입북하여 그들과 개별적으로 통일논의를 전개하거나
  우리의 체제를 비방하고 북한의 활동을 찬양하는 등의 행위는 정부와
  국민사이를 이간시켜 국론을 분열시키고 궁극적으로 한반도 전역에서
  공산혁명의 달성을 기도하는 북한의 대남분열공작책동에 휘말려
  드는 것 이외에 아무것도 아님

- 임수경 자신은 통일을 촉진시키기 위하여 밀입북했다고 주장하나
  일반 국민이 그의 독단적이고 무분별한 행동을 결코 지지하지도
  않을 뿐만 아니라, 그의 행동은 남·북한과의 점진적인 교류협력을
  증진시켜 상호 신뢰의 기반을 조성하고 북한의 개방을 유도함으로써
  자유민주적기본질서에 입각한 평화통일을 달성하려는 우리 정부와
  국민의 통일열망에 찬물을 끼얹는 행위로서 오히려 평화통일에
  장애가 되는 것이라 아니할 수 없음

0110

- 참고로 미국에서도 전쟁중에 있는 적국이나 분쟁중에 있는 외국에 대하여 정부의 허가없이 교섭하거나 교류하는 경우에는 처벌을 하고 있음. (Logan 법), 그 이유는 그와같은 경우에 교섭의 주체는 정부가 되어야 하며 개인들의 자의적인 교섭이나 교류는 오히려 혼란을 초래하여 적국에 유리하고 아국에 불리한 상황이 초래될 수 있기 때문임

홍 성 담 (남 35세 화가)

1. 범죄사실 요지

   o 88.1.경 서경원으로부터 독일행권유를 받고, 4.3. 출국 독일에
     도착하여 북한공작원 성낙영의 집에 기거하면서 국내운동권동향
     및 정세를 파악보고하라는 지령과 함께 독일화 2,000마르크,
     미화 1,500달러를 수수하고 6.28. 입국하여 반국가단체의
     지령을 받은자와 회합 및 지령수수 잠입

   o 88.6.하순경 광주에서 성낙영에게 안부전화하여 통신연락

   o 88.7.경 성낙영의 전화지시에 따라 "문화운동론"책자를 구입
     우송하여 통신연락 및 간첩

   o 88.9경 "한국민족민주운동의 쟁점" 책자를 구입, 성낙영에게
     우송하여 간첩

   o 88.10경 조선대 운동장에서 "5월 민중항쟁과 민족민중미술운동"
     제하의 강연을 하여 찬양고무

   o 88.11.초순경 광주에서 성낙영이 보낸 재독교포로부터 한화
     금 50만원과 성낙영의 편지를 전달받아 통신연락 및 금품수수

0112

o 88.11. 중순경 말지 11월호, 흐름지11월호, 역사비평 가을호,
  미술운동 제1호등 책자 4권을 구입, 성낙영에게 우송하여 간첩

o 88.11. 하순경 전남대에서 "남북한 미술의 발전비교" 제목
  으로 북한미술의 전통성과 우월성을 강연하여 찬양고무

o 88.11경 차일환, 정하수등과 공모하여 갑오경장에서 조국통일
  운동까지를 형상화한 "민족해방운동사"제목의 대형걸개그림
  15폭을 제작키로 합의하고 89.2.하순경 "광주항쟁부분"을
  형상화하여 이적표현물제작

o 89.2.경 계급투쟁을 선동하는 내용의 미술운동제2호 책자 700부
  를 제작·배포하여 이적표현물 제작·반포

o 89.2경 성낙영에게 전화하여 통신연락

o 89.4.14경 서울대에서 "민족해방운동사" 제목의 대형걸개그림
  11폭을 설치 전시하는등 그시경부터 6.30경까지 각대학등을
  순회전시하여 이적표현물 반포

o 89.6.15.경 "민족해방운동사" 제목의 걸개그림 슬라이드필림을
  미국을 통해 북한에 송부, 평양축전 미술전람회에 전시케하여
  이적동조

0113

2. 적용법조

  ○ 국가보안법 제4조제1항 제2호, 제5조제2항, 제6조제2항,제7조
    제1항 제5항, 제8조제1항, 제14조,형법 제98조제1항
    제37조, 제38조

3. 처리상황

  ○ 89.9.20   구속기소

  ○ 90.1.30   서울형사지법 징.자 각7년 일부무죄
    - 88.6경 북한공작원 김평원등과 3회 회합 (주문 무죄)
      · 피고인이 범죄사실을 부인하고 사법경찰관작성증거는 부동의
        하며 검사작성의 1회 피의자신문조서는 구속이후 20여일
        동안 가족 및 변호인과의 접견이 거부된 상태에서 작성된
        것이므로 형사소송법상의 적법절차가 무시된 채 위법한
        방법으로 수집된 증거로서 증거능력없고 그외달리 증거없음

    - 89.9경 성낙영에게 "비류벽제와 일본의 국가기원" "탈춤의
      역사와 원리"라는 서적송부하여 간첩 (이유무죄)
      · 순수한 학술서적에 불과하여 국가기밀이라 볼수 없음

  ○ 90.6.1 서울고법 징.자 각7년 일부무죄
    - 88.11.하순경 전남대에서 "남북한 미술의 발전비교"제목으로
      북한미술의 전통성과 우월성을 강연하여 찬양고무 (주문무죄)
      · 남북한 미술의 단점도 비교강연한 것이므로 대한민국의
        존립안전을 위태롭게 하거나 자유민주적기본질서에 실질적
        위해를 줄 위험성이 있다고 볼수 없음

0114

o 90. 9. 25. 대법원 파기환송

- 증거없이 범죄구성의 주관적 요건사실을 인정, 판결에 영향을 미침

o 91. 1. 31. 서울고법 징.자 각3년, 일부무죄

- 회합,잠입,통신연락 금품수수 간첩은 무죄

  · 성낙영이 북한의 지령을 받은자라는 것외에 피고인에게 그와같은 지령을 받은 자라는 데에 대한 인식이 있었음을 인정할 증거없음

o 91. 5. 24. 대법원 상고기각 확정

유원호 (남 60세, 중원엔지니어링 대표)

○ 범죄사실요지

- 88. 3.14 동경에서 반국가단체인 한국민주회복통일추진국민회의
 (한민통) 사무총장 곽동의와 만나 일화 200만엔 수수하여 회합
 및 금품수수

- 88. 9. 7 일본에서 북한지령받은 정경모로부터 문익환의 밀입북
 관련 지령을 받고 입국하여 잠입

- 88.12 - 89. 1 정경모와 회합, 통신, 지령수수잠입

- 89. 2. 6 동경에서 정경모에게 전민련조직체계도, 구성원등을
 보고하여 회합 및 목적수행간첩

- 89.2 - 89.3 정경모와 회합 통신, 지령수수 잠입,탈출

- 89. 3.25 문익환, 정경모와 함께 북경을 거쳐 평양에 도착,
 지령수수탈출

- 89.3.25 - 4.3 북한에 머물면서 김일성등과 회합

- 89. 4. 2 허담으로부터 산삼1상자, 자개병풍 1개등 선물을
 받아 금품수수

- 89. 4.13 북경, 일본을 거쳐 입국하여 지령수수잠입

0116

o 적용법조

  - 국가보안법 제4조제1항제2호, 형법제98조제1항, 국가보안법
    제5조제2항, 제6조제2항, 제8조제1항, 제14조

o 처리상황

  - 89. 5.14   구속기소

  - 89.10. 5   서울형사지법, 징·자 각10년(지령수행목적 간첩을
                 자진지원 국가기밀누설로 인정)

  - 90. 2.10   서울고법, 징·자 각7년 (간첩을 자진지원 국가기밀
                 누설로 인정하고, 4.13. 입국행위에 대해 지령
                 수수 인정할 증거없어 단순잠입으로 인정)

  - 90. 6. 8   대법원, 상고기각 확정

o 당부의 입장

  - 임수경에 대한 당부입장과 같음

0117

결 번

넘버링 오류

전민련산하 조국통일위원회 소속 범민족대회추진본부(범추본) 관련사건

o 인적사항

   - 조용술 (남 70세, 군산복음교회 목사, 범추본 공동본부장)
   - 이해학 (남 46세, 성남주민교회 목사, 범추본 집행위원장)
   - 조성우 (남 41세, 평화연구소장, 범추본 사무처장)

o 범죄사실요지

   - 소위 조국통일범민족연합(범민연)을 결성하려는 목적으로 90.11.19 -
     11.20. 베를린시청에서 범추본 남북해외 3자회담을 개최하여 북측
     대표인 조평통 부위원장 전금철등과 만나 범민연의 조직구성, 공동사무국
     설치, 사업내용을 결정하는등 반국가단체 구성원과 회합

   - 90.11.20. 베를린시청에서 미군철수, 유엔동시가입반대, 국가보안법
     철폐등을 내용으로 하는 '베를린 3자실무회담 공동선언문"과 '유엔
     사무총장에게 보내는 편지'를 발표하는등 이적동조

o 수사처리상황

   - 90.11.30   치안본부 각 구속
   - 91. 1.16   서울지검 각 구속기소
   - 91. 5.13   서울형사지법 조용술 징1년6월, 자2년,집유2년
                              이해학 징1년6월, 자2년
                              조성우 징1년6월, 자2년
   - 91. 5.20   검사.피고인 각 항소

0119

```
┌─────────────────────────────────────────────┐
│   베를린 3차회담 참가자 구속관련  대응자료   │
└─────────────────────────────────────────────┘
```

o 통일전 동서독의 안보상황과는 다른 우리나라 안보상황의 특성상 불가피한

   조치임

   - 동서독간에는 1972년 기본조약의 체결을 전후하여 상호 교류를 위한

      각종 협정이 체결되었으며 수차례의 동서독 정상회담이 개최되는등

      오랜 기간동안 통일의 여건을 다져온 데 비하여, 북한은 일찌기

      전쟁을 도발한 이래 현재까지 각종 무력도발을 감행하는등 극도의

      군사적 위협을 가하고 있으며, 최근 화해와 개방이라는 세계사의

      흐름마저 거부한 채 폐쇄정책과 대남적화혁명 기본전략을 고수하고

      있어 현재까지 남북한간에는 아직 단 한건의 협정도 체결하지

      못하고 있음

   - 동서독 주민들간의 접촉과 왕래가 동서독 정부간의 수차례에 걸친

      협상의 결과임을 감안하면 우리나라와 같이 남북이 첨예하게

      대치하고 있는 특수한 안보상황하에서 남북간의 대화와 접촉은

                                                            0120

역시 국민적 합의를 바탕으로 국민대표기관인 정부나 국회의 주도하에

신중히 추진되어야 할 것이고 무분별하고 자의적인 대북접촉은 북한

북한의 대남적화전략전술에 이용될 가능성이 있을 뿐만 아니라 국내적

으로도 통일문제에 관한 혼란과 반목등 국론분열을 초래하여 국익을

손상할 우려가 있으므로 이에 대하여는 사법조치가 불가피한 실정임

o 명백한 실정법위반 행위임

   - 대한민국은 대한민국의 특수한 안보상황에 대한 국민들의 인식과

      국민적 합의를 기초로 하여 국가의 안전과 자유민주체제를 수호하기

      위한 법률적 장치를 마련하고 있음. 따라서, 이러한 법률을 위반

      하는 행위에 대하여는 국가의 안전과 체제수호차원에서 단호히

      대처할 수밖에 없으며 이는 또한 법치주의의 기본원리상 당연한 것임

   - 우선 남북교류협력에관한법률 제9조는 남한의 주민이 북한의 주민과

      접촉하고자 할 때는 정부의 승인을 받도록 되어 있음에도 베를린회담

      참가자들은 정부의 승인을 받지 않고 참가함으로써 실정법을 무시

      하였음

0121

- 나아가, 이번 배틀린회담은 민간단체로 가장하고 있는 북한의 조국
  평화통일위원회 (약칭 조평통)의 실질적 주도하에 남한내의 반체제
  세력과의 연합전선을 구축, 남한사회에 반국가세력을 부식함으로써
  적화통일을 앞당긴다는 그들의 소위 통일전선전술의 일환으로 개최된
  것으로서, 회담 합의내용 역시 국가보안법 폐지, 주한미군철수,
  남북한 유엔동시가입 반대등을 표방하고 있어 북한의 주의주장과 일치
  하고 있음

- 이는 결국 우리 사회의 갈등과 혼란, 통일문제에 관한 국론분열을
  야기하는등 북한의 대남전략입지를 강화시키고 우리의 국가안보를
  위태롭게 함으로써 국내 실정법인 국가보안법에 저촉되는 것이므로
  동 법률에 따라 처리할 수밖에 없음. 이건 이외에도 전민련관계자
  들의 정부를 배제한 자의적인 대북접촉에 대하여는 이미 법원의
  유죄판결이 수회 선고되어 확정된 바 있음

- 이렇듯 자국의 안전과 체제수호를 위한 입법례는 각국의 안보상황에
  따라 정도의 차이는 있지만 대부분의 나라들이 갖고 있으며 특히

0122

통일이전의 서독형법에는 남북한과 같은 현실적인 안보위해요인이

없음에도 자유민주체제를 수호하기 위한 각종 규정들을 두고 있었을

뿐만 아니라 통일된 현재까지 그러한 조항들의 기본적인 내용은

그대로 유지하고 있으며 통일독일당국은 동서분단당시의 서독의 국가

기밀을 탐지하는등 서독의 안보를 위협한 동독의 비밀경찰요원들을

체포하고 있는 것으로 알고 있음

o 국가의 권위와 전체 국민의 의사를 무시한 행위임

  - 전민련 관계자들의 베를린회담 참가는 통일을 앞당기는데 전혀

     도움이 되지 않을 뿐만 아니라 우리 사회의 혼란을 조성하기 위한

     북의 대남전략전술에 말려들게 되어 국익에 위해한다는 이유로

     정부는 동인들의 대회참가신청을 불허하면서 강행시에는 사법처리가

     불가피함을 경고하였음에도 이를 무시하고 참가하였음

  - 이들은 또한 범국민적 대표임을 자처하고 있지만 국민적 대표성을

     인정할 수 없고 베를린회담 추진역시 국민적 합의에 기초한 것이

0123

아니어서 대다수 국민의 뜻에도 어긋나므로 이들의 경거망동에

대하여는 대부분의 국민들도 분개하고 있음

- 우리나라 뿐만 아니라 미국에서도 정부의 허가없이 분쟁 또는 대립

관계에 있는 외국의 정부요원들을 함부로 만나는등 접촉하는 것을

법으로 금지하고 있음 (The Logan Act)

0124

X 참고자료

○ 조국평화통일위원회 (약칭 조평통)

- 연혁 및 성격

    . 61.5.13. "4.19"직후 "가자 북으로, 오라 남으로" 등
       우리 학생, 재야등의 통일운동 격화시기에 남한의 각계각층
       인사들의 민주주의 역량을 단합, 적화통일을 실현하기 위하여
       북한내 제정당, 사회단체, 각계인사를 망라하여 급조한
       노동당의 외곽단체임

- 기능 및 임무

    . 남한의 각계각층인사 및 해외동포들을 상대로 통일실현 투쟁
       고취

    . 노동당의 통일·남북대화정책 대변

    . 한국내 주요사건 또는 새로운 정책 발표시마다 소위 "조평통
       서기국 보도" 등을 발표, 이를 비난

0125

- 조직

  - 위원장(1명, 허담), 부위원장(12명)등 간부 대부분이 당정치국원, 당비서, 최고인민회의 대의원등을 겸하고 있는 당정고위간부임

  - 특히 부위원장중 4명 (윤기복, 전금철, 임춘길, 조명일)과 서기국장(안병수)은 남북대화관련 서울왕래 인물임

  - 이번 베를린회담 북한측 참가자 전금철은 조평통의 부위원장으로서, 남북국회회담 준비접촉 북측대표 단장이기도 함

○ 로간법 (The Logon Act).

  - 미국법전 제18편 제953조

    - '미국시민으로서 정부의 허가없이 미국과 분쟁 또는 대립관계에 있는 외국정부나 관리 또는 그 대리인의 조치 또는 행동에 영향을 미치거나 미국의 국가정책을 저지시키기 위하여 외국정부나 관리 또는 그 대리인과 직접·간접으로 통신 또는 접촉을 개시

0126

여기나 거주한 기간 그가 어디에 있든 기간에 3년이하의 징역
또는 5,000불이하의 벌금에 처한다.'

- 입법배경

    · 미국독립전쟁직후 필라델피아에 살고 있는 로간(Logan)
    이라는 목사가 미국과 전쟁직전 상태에 있는 프랑스를 방문
    하여 프랑스혁명 정부와 개인적으로 강화조약에 관한 협상을
    벌이고 귀국

    · 당시 미국국민들은 그를 두고 나라를 팔아먹은 자라고 비난
    하였고 이러한 배경하에 미국국민과 외국정부간의 사적접촉.
    교류를 금지하기 위한 로간법(The Logan Act)을 제정함.

0127

한국 기독교 교회 협의회

○ 설립 목적

　　교회 에큐메니칼 정신 구현

　　통일된 신앙적 결단을 통해 정의와 평화 구현

○ 소재지

　　종로구 연지동 136　기독교회관 705호

○ 연　혁

　　46.10.　조선 기독교 연합회 창립

　　70. 2.　한국 기독교 교회협의회로 개칭

○ 가입교단

　　기독교 장로회

　　예수교 장로회(통합)

　　기독교 감리회

　　기독교 복음교회

　　성공회

　　구세군

0128

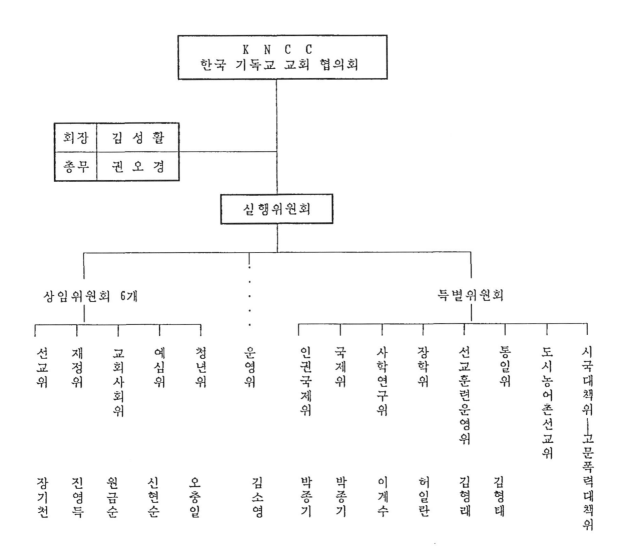

```
                    ┌─────────────────────┐
                    │      K N C C        │
                    │  한국 기독교 교회 협의회  │
                    └─────────────────────┘
                              │
        ┌───────────┐         │
        │ 회장 │ 김 성 활 │      │
        │ 총무 │ 권 오 경 │──────┤
        └───────────┘         │
                      ┌──────────────┐
                      │  실 행 위 원 회  │
                      └──────────────┘
                              │
        ┌─────────────────────┴─────────────────────┐
   상임위원회 6개          · · · · ·              특별위원회
   ┌──┬──┬──┬──┬──┐       │        ┌──┬──┬──┬──┬──┬──┬──┬──┐
   선  재  교  예  청       운        인  국  사  장  선  통  도  시
   교  정  회  심  년       영        권  제  학  학  교  일  시  국
   위  위  사  위  위       위        국  위  연  위  훈  위  농  대
          회                        제     구     련     어  책
          위                        위     위     운     촌  위
                                            수     영     선  ─
                                                   위     교  고
                                                          위  문
                                                              폭
                                                              력
                                                              대
                                                              책
                                                              위

   장  진  원  신  오       김        박  박  이  허  김  김
   기  영  금  현  충       소        종  종  계  일  형  형
   천  득  순  순  일       영        기  기  수  란  래  태
```

O 주요 동향

80. 1. 이후   매주 목요예배
              사회문제 비판, 구속자 석방, 언론자유보장 등

86. 3.   시국 대책위 (위원장 김지길 목사) 구성
              시국선언 발표, 직선제 개헌 저지운동 전개

86. 4.   CBS 기능 정상화 100만인 서명
              KBS TV 시청료 납부 거부 운동

86. 8.   한·북미 교회 협의회 주관 " 통일문제와 교회의 역할 " 제하
              세미나
              - 무분별 통일 주창

87. 1.   박종철 사건 관련 고문수사 정권 매도 획책

87. 2.   카츄사 김용전 자살관련 고문폭력대책위 명의 성명서 발표

※ 6 共 이후 침체기

- 언론 활동증대
- 정부 민주화
- 윤석양건 발표(90.10)

0130

ㅇ 김성활　███████████

　　구세군 전장 서기관장(수석 참모)

　　경북

　　███████████

　　서울 서대문 천연 117

　　49. 4～50. 3　　중앙 신학교 졸

　　58. 9～59. 6　　구세군 사관학교 졸

　　79. 1～79. 3　　대구 구세군 국제사관대 수료

　　85. 8～89.10　　대구 구세군 사관대 수료

　　62.11～76. 2　　구세군 서대문 영문교회　　사관

　　71. 6～73.10　　서대문 신애관　　　　　　관장

　　76. 2～81. 6　　구세군 사관학교　　　　　교관

　　81. 6～82. 6　　구세군 경북지방　　　　　경북지방장관

　　82. 6～86. 6　　구세군 사관학교　　　　　학교장

　　86. 6　　　　　구세군　　　　　　　　　부회장

　　88. 2～90. 2　　KNCC　　　　　　　　　부회장

　　90. 2　　　　　KNCC　　　　　　　　　회장

　　90. 6　　　　　CBS 자율성 수호위　　　위원장

0131

ㅇ 권오경 ███████████

목사 , KNCC 총무

███████████████

서울 강남 방배 900-41

48. 3∼54. 3   울산국교

54. 4∼58. 3   홍산중

62. 3∼65. 2   한영고등학교 졸

69. 1∼71. 5   서울 새밭교회 전도사

83.11∼86. 4   NCC 인권위 사무국장

85. 9∼89. 4   아시아 교회협의회(홍콩)
              도시산업선교회 간사

89. 2.   KNCC 총무

0132

o KNCC 와 서독과의 관계

- 통일문제 관련
  격년제 한-서독 교회협의회
  서독측으로 부터 매년 외원자금 KNCC 접수
  (90 후 90만원) 지원
- 70년대, 한국 인권문제 서독(EZE)을 통한 해외 여론화 창구 역할
- 한국통일문제 지원 요청
- 인권문제(1400명 주장)등 거론 예상

Weizsaecker Richard 20. 4. 15 생
  독일정치가, 슈투트가르트 출생
  복음주의 신도대회 의장
  기독교 민주동맹(CDU) 당원
  84 서독 대통령
  * 철학자 칼 프리드리히 폰 바이쩨커의 동생

· 90. 3 JPIC 세계대회 (WCC 주최, 정의평화 창조 질서의 보존)
  서울대회 형참석

報告畢

1991. Ⅴ. 16.
國際機構條約局
國際聯合課 (47)

長官報告事項

題 目 : 政治犯 및 良心囚의 概念定義

김내기22
~copy 서구22

國際赦免委(A.I.)의 7.18. 年例報告書 發表, 我國政府의 "市民的.
政治的 權利에 관한 國際人權規約" 加入에 따른 7월말 人權報告書
提出, 그리고 우리의 유엔加入은 我國의 人權狀況에 대한 國內外의
關心을 고조시킬 可能性이 있는 바, 현재까지 政府의 對應時 混用해
왔던 「政治犯」 및 「良心囚」의 概念을 명확히 구분할 必要性이
있다고 사료되어 아래 報告드립니다.

1. 國際赦免委(A.I.)의 概念定義

○ 政治犯(political prisoner)은 良心囚보다 훨씬 包括的 槪念

- 불법정당 참가등 純粹한 政治的 성격의 法違反은 물론, 犯法
行爲에 政治的 要素 내지는 動機가 조금이라도 있으면 政治犯으로
分類. 즉, 폭력.방화등 명백한 一般刑事犯도 政治犯으로 分類
될수 있음.

0134

- 이같이 넓은 槪念을 사용하는 理由는 이들이 政治的 理由때문에 苛酷行爲를 받거나 또는 正常的인 司法節次에서 除外될까봐 우려하는 것임.

- 따라서 A.I.는 政治犯에 대해서 다른 범법자들과 같은 迅速하고 公正한 裁判이 이루어질 것을 要望하는 것이며, 釋放을 요구하는 것은 아님.

○ 良心囚(prisoner of conscience)는 정치범과는 뚜렷하게 구별되는 개념인 바, "그들의 政治·宗敎·여타 믿음 또는 人種, 姓別, 言語 때문에" 拘束된 者들을 지칭함.

- 暴力을 사용 또는 옹호한 경우와 같이 一般刑事犯 要素를 내포한 경우는 除外

- A.I.는 良心囚에 대해서는 釋放을 要求함.

2. 人權問題關聯 政府對應時 留意事項

○ 政治犯과 良心囚를 區別하여 對應 必要

- 상기 定義에 비추어 政治犯은 人權先進國에도 얼마든지 있을 수 있음을 弘報

- 政治犯에 대해서는 公正한 司法節次를 거치고 있다는 것만 강조하면 됨.

- ✓. "우리나라에 정치범은 없다"라고 强辯하는 것은 오히려 逆效果 招來

○ 良心囚가 있다는 주장에 대해서는 그들의 犯法行爲를 구체적으로 밝히면서 그들이 良心囚가 아님을 주장

- 단, 實定法 違反이라고만 하는 것은 說得力 微弱. A.I.등에서는 國家保安法등 實定法 자체를 問題視 하는 경우가 있음.

0135

- 이는 우리의 安保 및 社會狀況 전반에 대한 認識의 부족에서 비롯되는 것이므로 人權團體들의 理解深化를 위한 弘報努力은 필요하지만, 소위 良心囚 개개인의 문제와 관련 지나치게 敏感하게 對應할 필요는 없다고 봄.

- 단, A.I.가 特定人을 나름대로 良心囚라고 결론짓기 전에 對處하는 것이 效果的

※ 최근 아측은 政治犯이란 용어가 誤解의 소지가 크다고 A.I.측에 수차례 지적했는 바, 우리나라에 대하여 政治犯이란 用語 사용을 自制하고 있는 듯함.(91 연례보고서에서는 예년과 달리 "political prisoner"라는 단어 불사용)

3. 其 他

o 상기와 관련 우선 法務部, 靑瓦臺등 關係部處 실무자들과 意見交換할 예정이며, 필요시 여타 關係部處 및 관련 在外公館에 배포 참고토록 할 예정임.

- 끝 -

0136

구속 국회의원 현황

범죄사실	해당의원	소속당		현 재 상 태
방 복	서경원	구 평민		형 집행중 (의원직 박탈)
뇌물외유	박진구 이재근 이돈만	민 신 신	자 민 민	집행유예로 석방 (5. 18) " "
수서사건	이태섭 오영운 김동주 김태식 이원배	민 민 민 신 신	자 자 자 민 민	재판 계류중 " " " "

0137

법 무 부

인권 2031-**11076**　　　　503-7045　　　　　　1991. 7. 30
수신　외무부장관
참조　구주국장
제목　이해학,홍근수 목사 석방요구 독일인 1,127명 서명에 대한
　　　설명자료 송부

　　　1. 한국기독교교회협의회 인권위원회의 이해학, 홍근수 목사
석방요구를 위한 독일인 1,127명의 서명자료 송부와 관련입니다.

　　　2. 위 서명자료는 1991.6.25-29간 개최된 독일 "교회의 날"
행사때 재독한인교회협의회 정의평화위원회 주선으로 독일교회의
목사,교수,변호사,의사 등으로부터 받은 것이라고 하며, 독일교회
에서는 위 서명자 명단을 독일교회 (Evangel ische Kirche in
Deutschland)의 공식문서로 채택, 모든 외교적 방법을 동원하여
위 두 사람에 대한 석방운동을 전개할 것이라고 합니다.

　　　3. 따라서 이에 대한 당부의 입장을 별첨과 같이 송부하오니
주독일대사관으로 하여금 적의 설명될 수 있도록 조치하여 주시기
바랍니다.

첨부 :　1. 한국기독교교회협의회 인권위원회 발신문서 사본 및
　　　　　 서명자 명단(일부) 사본 1부.

　　　　2. 설명자료 1부.　　끝.

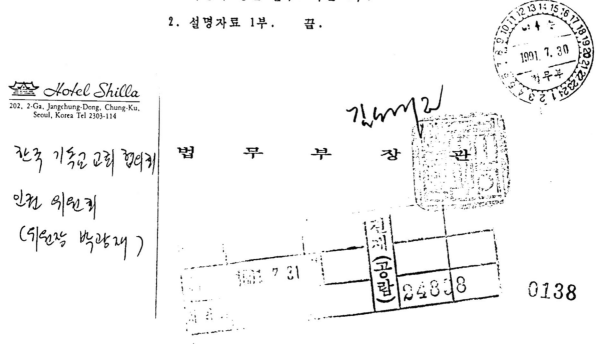

법　무　부　장　관

1991. 7. 30
법무부

전결
(공람) 24838

0138

이 해 학

1. 인적사항

- ○ 생년월일 : 1945. 3. 5 생
- ○ 직   업 : 성남주민교회 목사

2. 사건처리상황

- ○ '90.11.30   구속(치안본부)
- ○ '91.1.16   구속기소(서울지검)
- ○ '91.5.13   서울형사지방법원, 징역1년 6월 자격정지 2년
- ○ '91.5.20   검사, 피고인 각 항소 (2심 재판 계속중)
- ○ 현재 서울구치소 수감중

3. 범죄사실요지 (국가보안법위반)

- ○ 동인은 소위 전민련 산하 조국통일위원회 소속 범민족대회 추진본부(약칭:범추본) 집행위원장으로서 위 범추본 공동본부장 조용술(70세, 군산복음교회 목사), 동 사무처장 조성우(41세) 등과 함께 '89.10.3 및 11.9 이른바 범민족통일운동체 결성을 추진한다는 명분하에 베를린에서 열기로 한 남.북.해외동포 3자회담에 참석하기 위해 관광을 빙자, 각각 은밀히 출국

0139

o '89.11.19부터 20사이 베를린시청 회의실에서 북측대표인 조국
   평화통일위원회 부위원장 전금철 등을 만나 소위 "조국통일
   범민족연합(약칭:범민연)"을 결성하고 범민연의 조직구성, 공동
   사무국 설치, 사업내용 등을 결정하는 한편 우리 정부를 반통일
   세력으로 매도하고 한반도 주둔 외국군 및 핵무기철수, 유엔동시
   가입반대, 국가보안법철폐 등을 내용으로 하는 '베를린 3자 실무
   회담 공동선언문'과 '유엔사무총장에게 보내는 편지'를 발표하여
   반국가단체인 북한의 구성원과 회합, 통신하면서 그들의 주장활동
   에 동조한 것임

4. 수용동정 및 건강상태

최근 수용생활은 특이사항 없고 건강상태는 대체로 양호한 편임
(1991.6.24-6.27간 장인사망으로 일시 구속집행정지, 출소한 사실
  있음)

5. 정부입장

o 통일전 동서독의 안보상황과는 다른 우리나라 안보상황의 특성상
   불가피한 조치임

   . 동서독간에는 1972년 기본조약의 체결을 전후하여 상호교류를
     위한 각종 협정이 체결되었으며 수차례의 동서독 정상회담이
     개최되는 등 오랜 기간동안 통일의 여건을 다져온 데 비하여,
     북한은 일찌기 전쟁을 도발한 이래 현재까지 각종 무력도발을

0140

감행하는 등 극도의 군사적 위협을 가하고 있으며, 최근
화해와 개방이라는 세계사의 흐름마저 거부한 채 폐쇄정책과
대남적화혁명 기본전략을 고수하고 있어 현재까지 남북한간
에는 아직 단 한건의 협정도 체결하지 못하고 있음

. 동서독 주민들간의 접촉과 왕래가 동서독 정부간의 수차례에
걸친 협상의 결과임을 감안하면 우리나라와 같이 남북이 첨예
하게 대치하고 있는 특수한 안보상황하에서 남북간의 대화와
접촉은 역시 국민적 합의를 바탕으로 국민대표기관인 정부나
국회의 주도하에 신중히 추진되어야 할 것이고 무분별하고
자의적인 대북접촉은 결국 북한의 대남적화전략전술에 이용될
가능성이 있을 뿐만 아니라 국내적으로도 통일문제에 관한
혼란과 반목등 국론분열을 초래하여 국익을 손상할 우려가
있으므로 이에 대하여는 사법조치가 불가피한 실정임

O 명백한 실정법위반 행위임

. 대한민국은 대한민국의 특수한 안보상황에 대한 국민들의
인식과 국민적 합의를 기초로 하여 국가의 안전과 자유민주
체제를 수호하기 위한 법률적 장치를 마련하고 있음
따라서, 이러한 법률을 위반하는 행위에 대하여는 국가의
안전과 체제수호 차원에서 단호히 대처할 수밖에 없으며
이는 또한 법치주의의 기본원리상 당연한 것임

0141

· 우선 남북교류협력에관한법률 제9조는 남한의 주민이 북한의
 주민과 접촉하고자 할 때는 정부의 승인을 받도록 되어 있음
 에도 소위 "베틀린3자회담" 참가자들은 정부의 승인을 받지
 않고 참가함으로써 실정법을 무시하였음

· 나아가, 이번 베틀린3자회담은 민간단체로 가장하고 있는
 북한의 조국평화통일위원회(약칭:조평통)의 실질적 주도하에
 남한내의 반체제 세력과의 연합전선을 구축, 남한사회에
 반국가세력을 부식함으로써 적화통일을 앞당긴다는 그들의
 소위 통일전선전술의 일환으로 개최된 것으로서, 회담 합의
 내용 역시 국가보안법 폐지, 주한미군철수, 남북한 유엔동시
 가입 반대등을 표방하고 있어 북한의 주의주장과 일치하고
 있음

· 이는 결국 우리 사회의 갈등과 혼란, 통일문제에 관한 국론
 분열을 야기하는 등 북한의 대남전략입지를 강화시키고 우리의
 국가안보를 위태롭게 함으로써 국내 실정법인 국가보안법에
 저촉되는 것이므로 동 법률 및 재판결과에 따라 처리할 수밖에
 없음. 이건 이외에도 소위 전민련관계자들의 정부를 배제한
 자의적인 대북접촉에 대하여는 이미 법원의 유죄판결이 수회
 선고되어 확정된 바 있음

0142

. 이렇듯 자국의 안전과 체제수호를 위한 입법례는 각국의 안보
상황에 따라 정도의 차이는 있지만 대부분의 나라들이 갖고
있으며 특히 통일이전의 서독형법에는 남북한과 같은 현실적인
안보위해요인이 없음에도 자유민주체제를 수호하기 위한 각종
규정들을 두고 있었을 뿐만 아니라 통일된 현재까지 그러한
조항들의 기본적인 내용은 그대로 유지하고 있으며 통일독일
당국은 동서분단 당시의 서독의 국가기밀을 탐지하는등 서독의
안보를 위협한 동독의 비밀경찰요원들을 체포하고 있는 것으로
알고 있음

ㅇ 국가의 권위와 전체 국민의 의사를 무시한 행위임

. 전민련 관계자들의 베를린3자회담 참가는 통일을 앞당기는데
전혀 도움이 되지 않을 뿐만 아니라 우리 사회의 혼란을 조성
하기 위한 북의 대남전략전술에 말려들게 되어 국익에 위해
하다는 이유로 정부는 동인들의 대회참가신청을 불허하면서
강행시에는 사법처리가 불가피함을 경고하였음에도 이를 무시
하고 참가하였음

. 이들은 또한 범국민적 대표임을 자처하고 있지만 국민적
대표성을 인정할 수 없고 베를린3자회담 추진 역시 국민적
합의에 기초한 것이 아니어서 대다수 국민의 뜻에도 어긋나
므로 국가의 권위와 전체국민의 의사를 무시한 이들의 경거
망동에 대하여는 대부분의 국민들도 분개하고 있음

0143

· 우리나라 뿐만 아니라 미국에서도 정부의 허가없이 분쟁 또는
대립관계에 있는 외국의 정부요원들을 함부로 만나는 등 접촉
하는 것을 법으로 금지하고 있음 (The Logan Act)

0144

* 참고자료

ㅇ 조국평화통일위원회 (약칭:조평통)

- 연혁 및 성격
  . '61.5.13 "4.19"직후 "가자 북으로, 오라 남으로"등
    우리 학생, 재야 등의 통일운동 격화시기에 적화통일을
    실현하기 위하여 북한내 제정당, 사회단체, 각계인사를
    망라하여 급조한 북한 노동당의 외곽단체임

- 기능 및 임무
  . 남한의 각계각층 인사 및 해외동포들을 상대로 통일
    투쟁 고취
  . 노동당의 통일·남북대화정책 대변
  . 한국내 주요사건 또는 새로운 정책 발표시마다 소위
    "조평통 서기국 보도" 등을 발표, 이를 비난

- 조 직
  . 위원장(1명), 부위원장(12명)등 간부 대부분이 당정
    치국원, 당비서, 최고인민회의 대의원 등을 겸하고
    있는 당정고위 간부임
  . 특히 부위원장중 4명 (윤기복,전금철,임춘길,조명일)
    과 서기국장(안병수)은 남북대화관련 서울왕래 인물임
  . 이번 베를린회담 북한측 참가자 전금철은 조평통의
    부위원장으로서, 남북국회회담 준비접촉 북측대표 단장
    이기도 함

0145

○ 로간법 (The Logan Act)

- 미국법전 제18편 제953조

  . '미국 시민으로서 정부의 허가없이 미국과 분쟁
    또는 대립관계에 있는 외국정부나 관리 또는 그
    대리인의 조치 또는 행동에 영향을 미치거나 미국의
    국가정책을 저지시키기 위하여 외국정부나 관리
    또는 그 대리인과 직접.간접으로 통신 또는 접촉을
    개시하거나 계속한 자는 그가 어디에 있든지간에
    3년이하의 징역 또는 5,000불이하의 벌금에 처한다.'

- 입법배경

  . 미국 독립전쟁직후 필라델피아에 살고 있는 로간
    (Logan)이라는 목사가 미국과 전쟁직전 상태에 있는
    프랑스를 방문하여 프랑스혁명 정부와 개인적으로
    강화조약에 관한 협상을 벌이고 귀국
  . 당시 미국국민들은 그를 두고 나라를 팔아먹은 자라고
    비난하였고 이러한 배경하에 미국국민과 외국정부간의
    사적접촉.교류를 금지하기 위한 로간법(The Logan Act)
    을 제정함

○ 이해학과 함께 구속기소 되었던 조용술은 징역 1년6월
   자격정지2년 집행유예2년을, 조성우는 징역 1년6월 자격
   정지2년을 각 선고받아 이해학과 함께 항소하여 2심 재판
   계속중에 있음 (조용술은 1991.5.13 석방)

0146

홍 근 수

1. 인적사항

o 생년월일 : 1937. 8.15 생
o 직   업 : 향린교회 목사

2. 사건처리상황

o '91.2.20 구소 (안기부)
o '91.4.4 구속기소 (서울지검)
o 현재 서울형사지방법원에 재판계속중(1심), 서울구치소 수감중

3. 범죄사실요지 (국가보안법위반)

o '88.9.3 KBS 심야토론에 초청연사로 참석시, '88.9.22 한겨레
   신문 인터뷰시, '88.9.23 기독교회관에서 NCC목요예배시,
   '90.12.11 성남주민교회 설교시 북한의 고려민주연방제 통일
   방안 및 주체사상을 찬양하는 등 북한의 주의주장에 동조

o '89.3.1 범민족대회 예비회담을 구실로 소위 북한 조국평화통일
   위원회(약칭:조평통)예비회의 대표 윤기복 등과 회합하기 위해
   판문점으로 가는 등 반국가단체 구성원과 회합 예비

0147

o '89.10 북한의 주체사상을 찬양하는 "남북통일과 기독교" 책자 제작, 반포

o '90.8 북한의 주체사상, 사회주의를 찬양하고 남한의 예속성을 주장하는 "지금은 통일할 때" 책자 제작, 판매

o '90.7 숭실대 이삼열교수를 통해 북한 봉수교회목사 김운봉의 서신을 접수하여 통신연락

o '90.9 향린교회 부근 곰화랑에서 노동문학사 기자 장민성을 통해 국가보안법위반으로 수배중인 박기평에게 금 30만원 지원 하여 편의제공

o '91.1 위와 같은 내용의 향린교회 발행 유인물 "향린" 제5권 제1호 제작, 반포

o '91.1.23 이적단체 조국통일범민족연합(약칭:범민련) 남측본부 준비위원회 구성

4. 수용동정 및 건강상태

수용생활은 비교적 양호하고, 건강상태도 대체로 좋은 편임

0148

5. 정부입장

○ 대한민국은 대한민국의 특수한 안보상황에 대한 국민들의 인식과
국민적 합의를 기초로 하여 국가의 안전과 자유민주체제를 수호
하기 위한 법률적 장치를 마련하고 있음. 따라서, 이러한 법률을
위반하는 행위에 대하여는 국가의 안전과 자유민주체제 수호차원
에서 단호히 대처할 수밖에 없으며 이는 또한 법치주의의 기본
원리상 당연한 것임

○ 위와 같은 자국의 안전과 체제수호를 위한 입법례는 각국의 안보
상황에 따라 정도 차이는 있지만 대부분의 나라들이 갖고 있음

○ 우리 헌법은 전문과 제4조에서 "자유민주적 기본질서에 입각한
평화적 통일정책"을 수립하여 추진할 것을 천명하고 제66조에서
그 구체적인 책무를 국가원수이며 행정부의 수반인 대통령에게
부과함으로써 통일정책의 수립과 추진의 주체는 대통령과 대통령을
수반으로 하는 정부라고 하는 점을 명백히 하고 있음

○ 그러나 홍근수는 위와 같은 법질서를 무시하고 자의적으로 대북
접촉을 시도하였는가 하면 우리 정부를 외세에 예속된 식민지로
격하 비방하고 고려연방제통일방안 및 소위 주체사상 등을 지지
찬양하였으며, 국가보안법 폐지, 주한미군철수, 유엔동시가입반대
등 북한의 대남적화선전선동전략에 동조하는 단체를 구성하기도
하였음

0149

o 이는 결국 우리사회의 사상적 갈등과 혼란, 통일문제에 관한
  국론분열을 야기하는 등 북한의 대남적화전략입지를 강화시키고
  자유민주적 기본질서에 입각한 우리 정부의 평화적 통일정책
  및 우리의 국가안보를 위태롭게 함으로써 국내실정법인 국가보안
  법에 저촉되는 것이므로 정부로서는 동 법률 및 재판결과에 따라
  처리할 수밖에 없으며 위와 같은 실정법위반자에 대한 처벌에
  있어서 예외가 있을 수 없음

한국기독교교회협의회 인 권 위 원 회

(110-470) 서울시 종로구 연지동 136-46 기독교회관 708호
전화 : 764-0203, 744-3717, FAX : 744-6189

인권위 제91-15호   1991. 7. 4.
수신 : 이종남 법무부장관
제목 : 이해학.홍근수목사 석방요구 독일인 1,127명 서명에 관하여

　　법질서수호를 통한 국가발전을 위해 노심초사하시는 귀부처의 노고를 치하드립니다.
본회는 지난 7월 2일 재독한인교회협의회 정의평화위원회(위원장:전병탁)로부터 "홍근
수.이해학목사석방"을 요구하는 독일인 1,127명의 서명자명단을 전달받았습니다. 이
서명은 91년 6월 25-29일까지 개최된 "교회의 날"(독일의 국가적인 행사)행사때 재독
한인교회협의회 정의평화위원회가 주선하여 독일교회의 목사,교수,변호사,의사등으로
부터 받은 것입니다.　독일에서는 서명받기가 쉽지 않아 500명만 서명되면 독일교회의
정식사업으로 채택되고 있습니다. 또한 이번 서명숫자는 80년 광주민주화운동 당시 한
국의 민주화를 요구하는 독일인 5000명 서명 이후 최대규모입니다.　독일교회에서는
이서명자명단을 독일교회(Evangelische Kirche in Deutschland)의 공식문서로 채택하
였고 모든 외교적 방법을 동원하여 홍근수.이해학목사의 석방운동을 전개할 것임을 밝
혔습니다.　아울러 서명자명단은 법률사무소의 공증을 받은 것으로 공식적인 문서입니
다.
　　존경하는 장관님! 본회는 장관님께 홍근수.이해학목사의 석방을 간절히 바라는 세
계인들의 열망을 살피시고 두목사님의 석방을 신중히 고려하여 주실 것을 부탁 드리는
바입니다.

　　첨 부 : 1.서명자명단
　　　　　 2.공증서

　　　　　　　　　　　　　　　　　　　　　　한국기독교교회협
　　　　　　　　　　　　　　　　　　　　　　인 권 위 원
　　　　　　　　　　　　　　　　　　　　　　위 원 장　박

0151

Urkunde

des Notars

Wilhelm Dammeier

in Wiesbaden

0152

Nummer 169 der Urkundenrolle für 1991

Verhandelt

zu Wiesbaden am 21. Juni 1991

Vor mir, dem unterzeichneten Notar

Wilhelm Dammeier

mit dem Amtssitz in Wiesbaden

erschien heute:

Herr Dong Lack Jun, geboren am 18.04.1938, deutscher Staatsangehöriger, wohnhaft 6501 Essenheim, Zum Klopp 9.

Der Erschienene war koreanischer Staatsbürger und hat die deutsche Staatsbürgerschaft erhalten. Er wies sich aus durch Vorlage eines gültigen Personalausweises Nr. 2263129865.

Die Unterhaltung des Notars mit dem Erschienenen ergab, daß er der deutschen Sprache hinreichend mächtig ist und auf die Zuziehung eines Dolmetschers verzichtet werden konnte.

Der Erschienene bat um Beurkundung nachstehender
TATSACHEN:

Der Erschienene erklärte vorab:
Ich habe die Absicht, nach Seoul zu reisen, um dem Korean National Concil of Churches (KNCC) eine Petition zu überreichen, die das Ziel hat, die sofortige Freilassung der zwei in Südkorea inhaftierten Pfarrer Hong Gun Su, 54 Jahre alt, und Lee Hae Hak, 48 Jahre alt, zu erreichen. Zu diesem Zwecke werde ich dem Korean National Concil of Churches eine Liste übergeben, die die Namen, die Anschriften und die Unterschriften von eintausendeinhundertundsiebenundzwanzig Personen in der Bundesrepublik enthält, die sich für die Freilassung der vorgenannten Pfarrer einsetzen und den entsprechenden Aufruf des Komitees für Gerechtigkeit und friedliche Wiedervereinigung Koreas im koreanischevangelischen Gemeindekonvent in der Bundesrepublik Deutschland unterstützen. Der Erschienene legte mir hieraufhin eine Unterschriftsliste vor, die aus 79 Blättern bestand. Alle Blätter hatten den gleichlautenden Text. Eines dieser 79 Blätter ist beispielhaft in der Anlage beigefügt. Insgesamt tragen die 79 Blätter, wovon sich der Notar Gewißheit verschaffte, eintausendeinhundertundsiebenundzwanzig Namen nebst Anschrift und Unterschriften.

Nach Durchsicht und Überprüfung der Liste wurden die Dokumente dem Erschienenen wieder ausgehändigt.

Der Erschienene bat um Beurkundung dieser Tatsache, weil er befürchtete, daß ihm bei einer Einreisekontrolle die Dokumente behördlicherseits abgenommen werden würden und er dem KNCC für diesen Fall eine Ausfertigung dieser Notariatsurkunde zum Beweis vorlegen werde.

Das Protokoll wurde dem Erschienenen vorgelesen, von ihm genehmigt und eigenhändig wie folgt unterschrieben:

0153

Wir fordern die sofortige Freilassung der zwei inhaftierten Pfarrer!

Pfr. HONG Gun Su, 54J.alt.

Pfr.zu der Hyangrin-Gemeinde in Seoul.
Studierte Theologie an HANKUK-Theologischen-Hochschule,promovierte an der Lutherischen Theologischen Seminar in den USA.
Vorsitzender der theologischen Arbeitsgemeinschaft fuer Wiedervereinigung Koreas von Suedkorea-Sektion.

Pfr.LEE Hae Hak,48J.alt.

Pfr.zu Seungnam-Zumin-Gemeinde in In Chun.
Studierte Theologie an HANKUK-Theologischen-Hochschule.Seit 1974 er 15 Jahre Freiheitsstrafe verurteilt.Wegen Verstosses sonndergesetzes.
1975 kam er frei.1976 wurde er erneut wegen demselben Verstosses zur 3 Jahre Gefaegnisstrafe verurteilt.1978 wurde vorzeittig freigelassen.
1990 ist er Vorsitzender fuer die Sektion Suedkorea von PAN-KOREA-ALLIANZ fuer Wiedervereinigung.

Wir fordern die sofortige Freilassung der zwei Pfarrer und anderer politischen Gefangenen, die wegen ihrer Tätigkeit für die Demokratisierung und Wiedervereinigung Koreas inhaftiert sind.

Name, Vorname	Anschrift	Unterschrift
Pihlmann, Kristine	Waldeckring Str. 12 Braunweiss	R.P.Ph.
Drahaim, St.	Starweg 53, Ligollausto	S.Dr.
Karl Paulitz	Kreis 1	
S. Reuther	Chiegerlante 7, 87 Würzburg	
Erich Reuther	" "	Eg Rcc
Westerholt, Günter	Hans-Kruse-Str. 5 /5000 Soju	
Moritz, Kirsten	Karl-Löwe Str. 3 /4800 Berfeld	K. Moritz
von Günberg, Helge	Lina-Heinhigsb. 15/5090 Leverkus	
Bosbach, Henning	Wohnung 23 5250 verleisen	
Blank, Stephan	Böninger Str. 90 /4100 Duisburg	
GRUSSERT, NORMAN	Vod-Lenne-Str. 127// 4.1 Duisburg	
? Ilona	Cho-Hahn-Str. 8 /4.1 Duisburg 14	
Mühlmeier, Gerd	Düruch 53, 5300 Rom. 2	E.Mühlmeier
Lichtmann, Heike	Duckelman.str. 33 Aonhein 6	
Albrecht, Günter	Platanaush 7 8016 Dresden	

V.i.S.d.P.: D. L. Jun, Zum Klopp 9, 6501 Issenheim

0154

Vorstehende Ausfertigung stimmt mit der Urschrift überein. Sie wird hiermit
Herr Dong Lack Jun, Zum Klopp 8, 6501 Essenheim, erteilt.

Wiesbaden, den 21.06.91

Notar

분류기호 문서번호	구일.202- **27938**	기안용지		시 행 상 특별취급	
보존기간	영구.준영구 10. 5. 3. 1		장 관		
수 신 처 보존기간					
시행일자	1991. 8. 2.				
보조 기관	국 장	전 결	협조기관	국제기구조약국장	문 서 통 제 1991. 8. 03
	심의관				
	과 장				
기안책임자		김 영 희			발 송 인
경 유			발신명의		1991. 8. 03
수 신	주독대사				
참 조					
제 목	이해학, 홍근수 목사 석방요구 독일인 1,127명 서명				

    1. 한국기독교교회협의회 인권위원회(위원장 박광재)는 이해학,

홍근수 목사 석방요구를 위한 독일인 1,127명의 서명자료를 법무부에

제출하였다 합니다.

    2. 동 서명자료는 1991.6.25-29간 개최된 독일 "교회의 날"

행사때 재독 한인교회 협의회 정의 평화 위원회 주선으로 독일 교회의

목사, 교수, 변호사, 의사등으로부터 받은 것이라고 하며, 독일 교회

에서는 위 서명자 명단을 독일교회(Evangelische Kirche in Deutschland)

의 공식문서로 채택, 모든 외교적 방법을 동원하여 위 두 사람에 대한

계속....

0156

석방 운동을 전개할 것이라고 합니다.

    3. 귀관은 별첨(2) 설명자료를 참고, 독일교회(Evangelische

Kirche in Deutschland)측에 적의 설명 반응 보고바랍니다.

첨부: 1. 한국기독교교회협의회 인권위원회 발신문서 사본 및 서명자

      명단(일부) 사본 1부.

    2. 설명자료 1부. 끝.

**Botschaft
der Bundesrepublik Deutschland
Embassy
of the Federal Republic of Germany**

Pol 504.00 Choi

VN No. 148/91

Verbal Note

The Embassy of the Federal Republic of Germany presents its compliments to the Ministry of Foreign Affairs of the Republic of Korea and has the honour to transmit a letter of the President of the Trade Union Public Services, Transport and Traffic, Mrs. Monika Wulf-Mathies, to H. E. Prime Minister CHUNG Won Sik.

The union has asked the Federal Foreign Office to forward this letter to the addressee and this Embassy would be grateful if the letter could be forwarded to H. E. the Prime Minister by the Ministry.

The Embassy of the Federal Republic of Germany avails itself of this opportunity to renew to the Ministry of Foreign Affairs of the Republic of Korea the assurances of its highest consideration.

Seoul, July 23, 1991

Ministry of Foreign Affairs
of the Republic of Korea

S e o u l

0158

Gewerkschaft
Öffentliche Dienste,
Transport
und Verkehr

ÖTV-Hauptvorstand, Theodor-Heuss-Straße 2, 7000 Stuttgart 1

Prof. CHUNG Won Sik
Prime Minister
No. 77 Sechongro, Chongro-gu

Seoul 110-760
Republic of Korea

Hauptvorstand
Vorsitzende

Theodor-Heuss-Straße 2
7000 Stuttgart 1

Ihre Zeichen	Ihre Nachricht	Unser Zeichen	Fernsprech-Durchwahl	Tag
		HV-1-HJP/ma 242	(0711) 2097 21 10	24 June 1991

Dear Sir,

We were informed by the Public Services International that the Government of the Republic of Korea issued a warrant for the arrest of Mr. J.H. Choi, President of the Federation of Clerical and Financial Workers.

As we were told, you did so because Mr. Choi openly announced during the campaign for the municipal election that the workers should not elect those parties which are opposing union rights in your Republic.

On behalf of my union and its 2 million members, I urge you to draw back the warrant against Mr. Choi.

Union rights are also human rights!

Yours sincerely,

Monika Wulf-Mathies
President

Wir bitten, Zuschriften ausschließlich an die zuständige ÖTV-Verwaltung und nicht an Einzelpersonen zu richten.

Telefon (07 11) 2 09 71
Fernschreiber: 07 23 302
Telefax (07 11) 7 09 75 18
Postscheckkonto: Stuttgart 6 55 - 705 (BLZ 600 100 70)

Telegramm-Adresse oetveu Stuttgart
Bank für Gemeinwirtschaft AG, Stuttgart,
Konto 10 72 00 11 (BLZ 600 101 11)
Gimkasse Stgt., Konto 2 000 967 (BLZ 600 501 01)

0159

Doppel

**Botschaft
der Bundesrepublik Deutschland
Embassy
of the Federal Republic of Germany**

Pol 504.00 Choi

VN No. 148/91

<u>V e r b a l   N o t e</u>

The Embassy of the Federal Republic of Germany presents its compliments to the Ministry of Foreign Affairs of the Republic of Korea and has the honour to transmit a letter of the President of the Trade Union Public Services, Transport and Traffic, Mrs. Monika Wulf-Mathies, to H. E. Prime Minister CHUNG Won Sik.

The union has asked the Federal Foreign Office to forward this letter to the addressee and this Embassy would be grateful if the letter could be forwarded to H. E. the Prime Minister by the Ministry.

The Embassy of the Federal Republic of Germany avails itself of this opportunity to renew to the Ministry of Foreign Affairs of the Republic of Korea the assurances of its highest consideration.

Seoul, July 23, 1991

L.S.

Ministry of Foreign Affairs
of the Republic of Korea

<u>S e o u l</u>

0160

Pablo Richartz - Perez
Friedenstr. 68
4100 Duisburg 1
W. - Germany

Duisburg, den 12.12.1990

La paz , le paix , peace , Frieden

ABC der Erfolge: Arbeit --- Gerechte Arbeitsverträge
Bildung --- Schulpflicht für alle
Chor --- Gemeinsam beten, singen, reden
Dach über --- den Kopf für alle
Einheit --- Völkergemeinschaft
Freiheit --- Rechtsstaat

Völker müssen einen Frieden herstellen; ohne Krieg im Nahen Osten, der
die Einigkeit und die Gesellschaftsfähigkeit der Menschheit spaltet.
Daher bitten wir Kinder die Regierenden, sich um den Frieden noch mehr
zu bemühen.
  Was können wir sonst unseren eigenen Kindern sagen:
Wir wollten keinen Krieg, aber die Waffen haben gesprochen!
  Viele Kinder wachsen heute drei -und viersprachig auf, doch nach einem
Krieg ist keiner bereit miteinander zu sprechen. Wir werden nicht mehr
gehört, aber uns wird eingehämmert << Geht weiter, bleibt in euer Land,
wir wollen euch nicht, ihr seid nicht willkommen.>>
  Wir sehen und hören:
Was heute zählt sind Zahlen, Daten und Fakten. Gezählt wird nur der Erfolg, politisch und wirtschaftlich. Die Misserfolge werden als Folge-
kosten mehrfach bezahlt, dass will man heute nicht erkennen.
  Man sagt:
<< Der Irak hat viele Milliarden Schulden >> - also kann er auch keinen
verlorenen Krieg bezahlen. Die Frage braucht eine Antwort - wenn auch
die Mehrzahl der Welt gegen den Irak ist, bleibt die Frage: << Warum
hat ein Staatsoberhaupt so viele Anhänger? Somit hat er nicht nur Geg-
ner, auch Verbündete, deren Zahl eine Grössenordnung darstellt.
  Selbst wenn die Hälfte oder weniger seiner Anhänger den Krieg überleben,
deren Kultur und vieles mehr geschändet bleibt, wächst der Hass in
Generationen hinein.
  Somit werden die << lebendigen >> Sprachen, die wir heute erlernen zu
<< toten >> Sprachen, weil die Bereitschaft miteinander zu Sprechen,
verweigert wird.
  Bitte sagen Sie nicht gleich: << Kinder, wir haben jetzt viele wichtige
Dinge zu erledigen, stört uns nicht, wir haben keine Zeit.>> Kinder er-
warten Antworten auf Fragen.
  Ganz gewiss könnten wir, gleichaltrige Kinder aus verschiedenen Nationen
Friedensgespräche miteinander und sogar mit der irakischen Regierung in
Frankreich oder Spanien führen, da diese Länder gute Beziehungen zu den
Arabern haben.
  Die Vorteile der noch minderjährigen Jugendlichen (wie z.B. ich, der
14 Jahre bin) ist es, dass wir in friedlicher Absicht kommen und sind
nicht mit Waffen bestückt: So können wir den Herausforderer nicht be-
drohen.
  Meinen Sie solche Gespräche wären total nutzlos? Ja, wenn die Erwachse-
nen dazwischen reden, um ihre Interessen durchzusetzen. Lassen Sie uns
auch mitbestimmen. Wir Kinder verschiedener Länder, Kulturen und Reli-
gionsgemeinschaften können uns auf dem Schulhof oder auf dem Spielplatz
sehr gut verstehen.
  Uns Kinder schenkt man Fahrräder, doch keine Radwege. Wir, Kinder,
können der Welt Frieden schenken, auch wenn wir nicht die Welt reich
machen können.

0161

Wie sieht es heute in der Welt aus? Könnten Rüstungsausgaben nicht zur Schaffung von Wohlstand für alle verwendet werden?

Milliarden werden für Kriege finanziert, aber die Alten sollen noch länger arbeiten und die Jugend liegt auf der Strasse. Die Zahl der Arbeitslosen steigt sowie die Armut und Obdachlosigkeit.

Die Regierungen verschliessen die Augen. Parteien und Gewerkschaften zählen ihr Kapital und die Abgeordneten erhöhen einstimmig ihre Diäten. So kann man es aus Presse und Fernsehen entnehmen.

Die ganze Menschheit ist für den Frieden. Deswegen werde ich mich steht's für ihn einsetzen und bitte um Ihre Unterstützung.

Möge Gott uns Kinder beschützen, dass es meiner Generation gelingt eine heile Welt zu schaffen; damit später unsere Nachkommen das Erbe gerne antreten.

Wir wollen alle zu Gott gemeinsam beten, << JEDER IN SEINER SPRACHE, NACH SEINER GLAUBENSÜBERZEUGUNG >>.

Folgende Länder und deren Staatsoberhäupter erhalten diese Botschaft:

AFGHANISTAN ÄGYPTEN ALBANIEN ALGERIEN ANDORRA ANGOLA
ANTIGUA UND BARBUDA ARGENTINIEN ÄTHIOPIEN AUSTRALIEN BAHAMAS
BAHRAIN BANGLADESCH BARBADOS BELAU BELGIEN BELIZE BENIN
BHUTAN BOLIVIEN BOTSWANA BRASILIEN BRUNEI BULGARIEN
BURKINA FASO BURUNDI CHILE CHINA, TAIWAN CHINA, VOLKSREPUBLIK
COSTA RICA COTE D'LVOIRE DÄNEMARK DEUTSCHLAND DOMINICA
DOMINIKANISCHE REPUBLIK DSCHIBUTI ECUADOR EL SALVADOR FIDSCHI
FINNLAND FRANKREICH GABUN GAMBIA GHANA GRENADA GRIECHENLAND
GROSSBRITANNIEN UND NORDIRLAND GUATEMALA GUINEA GUINEA, ÄQUATORIAL
GUINEA-BISSAU GUYANA HAITI HONDURAS INDIEN INDONESIEN IRAK
IRAN IRLAND ISLAND ISRAEL ITALIEN JAMAIKA JAPAN JEMEN
JORDANIEN JUGOSLAWIEN KAMERUN KAMPUTSCHEA KANADA KAP VERDE
KATAR KENIA KIRIBATI KOLUMBIEN KOMOREN KONGO KOREA-NORD
KOREA-SÜD KUBA KUWAIT LAOS LESOTHO LIBANON LIBERIA LIBYEN
LIECHTENSTEIN LUXEMBURG MADAGASKA MALAWI MALAYSIA MALEDIVEN
MALI MALTA MAROKKO MARSHALL-INSELN MAURETANIEN MAURITIUS
MEXIKO MIKRONESIEN MANACO MONGOLEI MOSAMBIK MYANMA NAMIBIA
NAURU NEPAL NEUSEELAND NICARAGUA NIEDERLANDE NIGER NIGERIA
NORWEGEN OMAN OESTERREICH PAKISTAN PANAMA PAPUA-NEUGUINEA
PARAGUAY PERU PHILIPPINEN POLEN PORTUGAL RUMÄNIEN RWANDA
SAHARA SAINT CHRISTOPHER UND NEVIS SAINT LUCIA SAINT VINCENT/GRE-
NADINEN SALOMONEN SAMBIA SAMOA-WEST SAN MARINO SAO TOME UND
PRINCIPE SAUDI-ARABIEN SCHWEDEN SCHWEIZ SENEGAL SEYCHELLEN
SIERRA LEONE SINGAPUR SOMALIA SOWJETUNION SPANIEN SRI LANKA
SÜDAFRIKA SUDAN SURINAM SWASILAND SYRIEN TANSANIA THAILAND
TOGO TONGA TRINIDAD UND TOBAGO TSCHAD TSCHECHOSLOWAKEI
TUNESIEN TÜRKEI TUVALU UGANDA UNGARN URUGUAY VANUATU
VATIKANSTADT VENEZUELA VEREINIGTE ARABISCHE EMIRATE VEREINIGTE
STAATEN VON AMERIKA VIETNAM ZAIRE ZENTRALAFRIKANISCHE REPUBLIK
ZIMBABWE ZYPERN

Dieses Schreiben dürfen Sie an alle Gewerkschaften, Parteien und Arbeit-
geberverbände weitergeben, da diese zum Wohle aller beitragen können.

        Mit ergebenem Gruss
        Ihr Friedensbote

0162

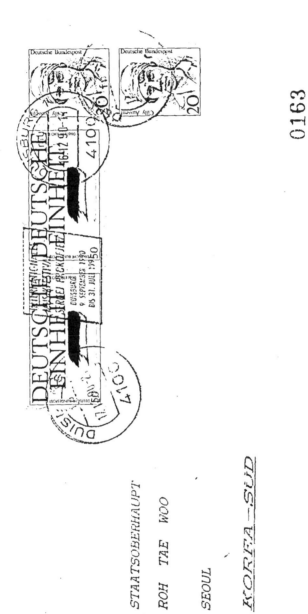

STAATSOBERHAUPT

ROH TAE WOO

SEOUL

KORFA—SÜD

0163

0164

Pablo Richartz - Perez
Friedenstr.68
4100 Duisburg 1
W. - Germany

Gunter Anreither
4040 Finkenberg 24

Österreich / Europa

An Seine Exzellenz
Präsident ROH Tae-woo

The Blue House
1 Sejong-no
Chongno-gu
Seoul
Republik Korea

Eure Exzellenz !

Viele Menschen in Österreich sorgen sich um die Menschenrechtssituation
in Ihrem Land. Ich habe während des vergangenen Jahres viele Informationen
über Nicht-Einhaltung von Menschenrechten in der Republik Korea erhalten.
Ich habe auch gehört, daß Sie und viele andere koreanische Politiker zahlreiche Briefe von besorgten Menschen auf der ganzen Welt erhalten haben.
Aber bisher haben diese Leute weder von Ihnen noch den anderen Politikern
auch nur eine einzige Antwort erhalten.
Sie können sich sicherlich vorstellen, wie enttäuscht ich über Ihren Mangel
an Interesse an Menschenrechten bin, da es für mich nur sehr schwer vor-
stellbar ist, daß Ihnen die Menschenrechtssituation in Ihrem Land nicht
wichtig erscheint.
Auch wenn Sie diesbezüglich anderer Meinung sind, so ist es bloß eine
Frage der Höflichkeit, auf Briefe von Menschen zu antworten, welche an
der Entwicklung größerer Sicherheit in Bezug auf Menschenrechte der Be-
wohner der Republik Korea interessiert sind.
Deshalb ersuche ich Sie, diese Briefe zu beantworten und alles in Ihrer
Macht stehende zu tun, um die Menschenrechte für jedermann in Ihrem Land
zu garantieren.
Hochachtungsvoll

0165

FÜRST
VOGELWEIDERSTR. 4
4600 WELS

Österreich / Europa

An Seine Exzellenz
Präsident ROH Tae-woo

The Blue House
1 Sejong-no
Chongno-gu
Seoul
Republik Korea

Eure Exzellenz !

Viele Menschen in Österreich sorgen sich um die Menschenrechtssituation
in Ihrem Land. Ich habe während des vergangenen Jahres viele Informationen
über Nicht-Einhaltung von Menschenrechten in der Republik Korea erhalten.
Ich habe auch gehört, daß Sie und viele andere koreanische Politiker zahlreiche Briefe von besorgten Menschen auf der ganzen Welt erhalten haben.
Aber bisher haben diese Leute weder von Ihnen noch den anderen Politikern
auch nur eine einzige Antwort erhalten.
Sie können sich sicherlich vorstellen, wie enttäuscht ich über Ihren Mangel
an Interesse an Menschenrechten bin, da es für mich nur sehr schwer vor-
stellbar ist, daß Ihnen die Menschenrechtssituation in Ihrem Land nicht
wichtig erscheint.
Auch wenn Sie diesbezüglich anderer Meinung sind, so ist es bloß eine
Frage der Höflichkeit, auf Briefe von Menschen zu antworten, welche an
der Entwicklung größerer Sicherheit in Bezug auf Menschenrechte der Be-
wohner der Republik Korea interessiert sind.
Deshalb ersuche ich Sie, diese Briefe zu beantworten und alles in Ihrer
Macht stehende zu tun, um die Menschenrechte für jedermann in Ihrem Land
zu garantieren.
Hochachtungsvoll

0166

HERBRIK GERHARD
Ballweg 3
4060 LEONDING.
Österreich / Europa

An Seine Exzellenz
Präsident ROH Tae-woo

The Blue House
1 Sejong-no
Chongno-gu
Seoul
Republik Korea

Eure Exzellenz !

Viele Menschen in Österreich sorgen sich um die Menschenrechtssituation
in Ihrem Land. Ich habe während des vergangenen Jahres viele Informationen
über Nicht-Einhaltung von Menschenrechten in der Republik Korea erhalten.
Ich habe auch gehört, daß Sie und viele andere koreanische Politiker zahlreiche Briefe von besorgten Menschen auf der ganzen Welt erhalten haben.
Aber bisher haben diese Leute weder von Ihnen noch den anderen Politikern
auch nur eine einzige Antwort erhalten.
Sie können sich sicherlich vorstellen, wie enttäuscht ich über Ihren Mangel
an Interesse an Menschenrechten bin, da es für mich nur sehr schwer vor-
stellbar ist, daß Ihnen die Menschenrechtssituation in Ihrem Land nicht
wichtig erscheint.
Auch wenn Sie diesbezüglich anderer Meinung sind, so ist es bloß eine
Frage der Höflichkeit, auf Briefe von Menschen zu antworten, welche an
der Entwicklung größerer Sicherheit in Bezug auf Menschenrechte der Be-
wohner der Republik Korea interessiert sind.
Deshalb ersuche ich Sie, diese Briefe zu beantworten und alles in Ihrer
Macht stehende zu tun, um die Menschenrechte für jedermann in Ihrem Land
zu garantieren.
Hochachtungsvoll

0167

Else B. Herbst Ww. BRD-West 6730 Neustadt/Weinstrasse
Grainstr. 15

Dem 26.4.1991

Sehr geehrter Herr Staatspräsident
Roh Tae Woo von Süd-Korea

Ich erlaube mir an Sie zu schreiben. Im Fernsehen
verfolge ich die Politik von Süd- und Nord-Korea, was allem
Anschein nach nicht immer leicht ist.

Wäre es nicht wünschenswert, wenn Süd- und Nord-
Kerea wieder ein Staat werden könnte, so wie es hier nach
4 Jahrzehnten in Deutschland geworden ist.

Natürlich ist das ein Kampf, denn jeder Politiker
sieht das immer nur von seiner Seite. Aber ein Sprcihwort
heisst: "wo ein Wille ist, ist auch ein Weg." - Sie werden
es mit der DLP-Mehrheit nicht immer leicht haben.
Wenn man sich ein Ziel setzt und mit Bedacht darauf zusteuert,
wird dieses Ziel auch erreicht werden, das wünsche ich
Ihnen von ganzem Herzen.

Darf ich bei dieser Gelegenheit eine Bitte und zu-
gleich Wunsch aussprechen.
Sie würden mir eine besonders grosse Freude bereiten,
wenn Sie mir ein Foto mit Wiedmung schenken wollten. Für Ihre
Liebenswürdigkeit sage ich Ihnen schon heute meinen allerherz-
lichsten Dank.

Mit freundlcichen Grüssen

Frau M. Herbst

0168

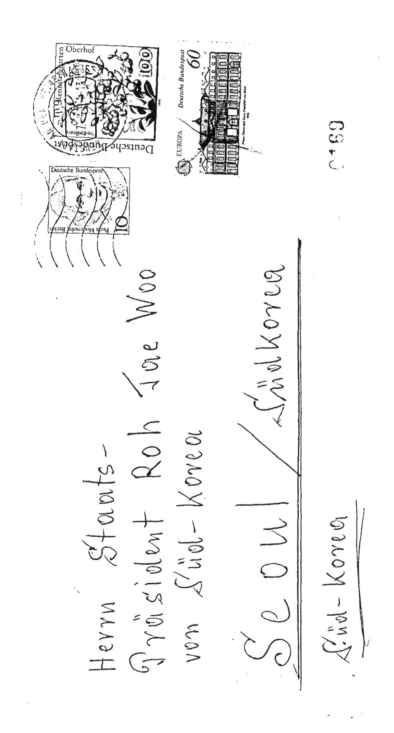

Herrn Staats-
Präsident Roh Tae Woo
von Süd-Korea

Seoul / Südkorea

Süd-Korea

Else B. Herbst

BRD- West   6730 Neustadt/Weinstraße

Grünstr. 15

0170

Ingolf Koch
Ruhrstraße 11
5788 Winterberg-Niedersfeld
Germany

amnesty
international

Sektion der Bundesrepublik Deutschland e.V.

His Excellency
  Mr LEE Sahng-yeon
Ministry of Foreign Affaires
77 Sejong-no
Chongno-gu
SEOUL
Republic of Korea

Bezirk 3590   Gruppe 1588

30.7.1991

Your Excellency!

I think that you have already heard about amnesty international.
Amnesty international is an organization working for the respect
and the use of human rights in the whole world.That means refu-
sing death sentence and torture,demanding immediate release without any conditions for prisoners of conscience and working for
fair use of laws for everyone.amnesty international is independent from political affaires so that it can work against abuses
of human rights in all political systems.Since the foundation
30 years ago amnesty international took care of about 42000 cases
of offences against human rights.

  As we got information,there is another case of offence against
human rights.We regret to say that it takes place in your
country.The person who is restricted in making use of his rights
is

                Reverend Hong Keun-soo   洪근수   ,

pastor of the Hyang Rin Presbyterian Church in Seoul.Reverend
Hong Keun-soo was arrested on 20 February 1991 by members of the
Agency for National Security Planning.His office was searched and
several items were confiscated including eight tape recordings of
his lectures,a computer manuscript of his sermons and his 1990
church diary.Reverend Hong keun-soo remains in detention and
faces charges under Articles 7 and 3 of the National Security
Law.I think that I do not have to explain the contents of these
articles to You.

  The Agency for National Security Planning is reported to have
accused Revernd Hong Keun-soo in connection with:
-Delivering sermons praising North Korea.In one of his sermons
 he is reported to have said "There are some positive aspects to
 North Korea...In order to bring about national reunification,we
 must get to know the society that the people in North Korea have

Postgirokonto Köln (BLZ 370 100 50) Kto. Nr. 224046-502
BKD Duisburg (BLZ 350 601 90) Kto. Nr. 30.000
0171

built,and what they are saying".
-His comments during a television debate on KBS in September
 1988.He is alleged to have spoken in favour of reunification
 during this debate.
-His participation in the formation of the South Korean head-
 quaters of the Pan-National Alliance for the reunification of
 Korea and attendance at its inaugural meeting,and his plans to
 travel ti Panmunjom.
-Publication in 1989 of a collection of his writings entitled
 "Now is the time to Realize National Reunification".

   I think using articles 7 and 3 in the case of Hong Keun-soo
means an offence against the rights of freedom of expression and
freedom of association.

   amnesty international is concerned that Reverend Hong Keun-soo
is being held for the peaceful exercise of his freedom of expression and association.We regard him as a prisoner of conscience and we are calling for his immediate release.

   I hope that You will make use of Your authority to get Reverend Hong Keun-soo out of prison.If there are positive news about
the case please let me know because we would be very happy to
publicate them here in Germany.

            Yours respectfully and sincerely,

                   (Ingolf Koch,
                amnesty international)

0172

Ingolf Koch,Ruhrstraße 11,5788 Winterberg-5
Germany

0174

Ev. Erwachsenenbildung Niedersachsen

Einrichtung der Konföderation ev. Kirchen
in Niedersachsen für Erwachsenenbildung

regionale Zweigstelle Niedersachsen-Süd

Calsowstraße 1
3400 Göttingen
0551 / 45023
Fax   47655

Göttingen, den 1.8.91

Sehr geehrter Herr Roo, Tae - Woo,

wir würden uns freuen, wenn Sie sich - trotz knapper Zeit und der Notwendig-
keit der Übersetzung dieses Briefes - unserer folgenden Bitte annehmen könnten:

Aus Ihrem Land erhielten wir die traurige Nachricht, daß neben Hong, Sung-Dam
nun auch weitere 11 Künstler und Künstlerinnen des Nationalverbandes der Min-
jung-Kunstbewegung, Sektion Seoul, verhaftet worden sind. Unseres Wissens
liegt für diese Inhaftierung keine ausreichende Begründung vor. Wir wissen, daß
auch in Ihrem Land die Freiheit der Kunst bzw. Meinungsfreiheit gesetzlich ge-
währleistet ist. Wir wissen aber auch, daß dies grundlegende Menschenrecht
durch das Staatssicherheitsgesetz eingeschränkt wird. Diese Einschränkung wird
auch durch das Verfassungsgericht gesehen und kritisiert.

In Deutschland gilt Südkorea, trotz der Unruhen im Mai/Juni diesen Jahres, die
auch im deutschen Fernsehen zu verfolgen waren, als ein politisch stabiles Land,
das besonders aufgrund seines wirtschaftlichen Wachstums zu den Schwellen-
ländern gezählt wird.

Die deutsche Öffentlichkeit fragt sich allerdings, warum ein politisch stabiles Land
oppositionelle Künstler und Künstlerinnen inhaftiert. Ist Ihr Land tatsächlich durch
diese Künstler in seiner Existenz gefährdet, so daß Ihr Staatssicherheitsgesetz
als gerechtfertigt angesehen werden könnte?

Ungeachtet dieser Fragen setzt sich die deutsche Öffentlichket, besonders nach
ihren eigenen Erfahrungen während des Nationalsozialismus, für die Einhaltung
der Menschenrechte im eigenen Land, aber auch in anderen Ländern , ein.

So hoffen wir, daß Sie als Staatspräsident Ihren Einfluß für die 11 Inhaftierten
werden geltend machen.
Auch der Künstler Hong, Sung-Dam ist weiterhin in Haft. Für seine sofortige
Freilassung treten zahlreiche Ausstellungsbesucher mit ihrer Unterschrift ein.
Eine Wanderausstellung mit Werken Hong, Sung - Dams reist zur Zeit mit großem
Erfolg durch Deutschland.

0175

Sehr geehrter Herr Roo, Tae - Woo, wir möchten Sie also nochmals ein-
dringlich bitten, die genannten Inhaftierungen zu überprüfen und, so hoffen
wir, natürlich, sich für die Freilassung der Künstler und Künstlerinnen ein-
zusetzen.

Für Ihre Aufmerksamtkeit und Ihre Bemühungen bedanken wir uns im voraus
recht herzlich.

Mit freundlchen Grüßen

A. Hummerich, päd. Mitarbeiterin

0176

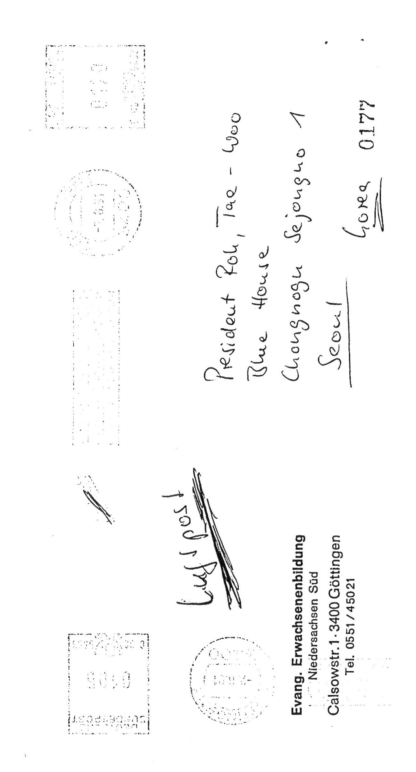

President Roh, Tae - Woo
Blue House
Chongnogu Sejongno 1
Seoul
Korea 0177

Evang. Erwachsenenbildung
Niedersachsen Süd
Calsowstr.1·3400 Göttingen
Tel. 0551/45021

An Seine Exzellenz
Präsident ROH Tae-woo

The Blue House
1 Sejong-no
Chongno-gu
Seoul
Republik Korea

Eure Exzellenz !

Viele Menschen in Österreich sorgen sich um die Menschenrechtssituation
in Ihrem Land. Ich habe während des vergangenen Jahres viele Informationen
über Nicht-Einhaltung von Menschenrechten in der Republik Korea erhalten.
Ich habe auch gehört, daß Sie und viele andere koreanische Politiker zahlreiche Briefe von besorgten Menschen auf der ganzen Welt erhalten haben.
Aber bisher haben diese Leute weder von Ihnen noch den anderen Politikern
auch nur eine einzige Antwort erhalten.
Sie können sich sicherlich vorstellen, wie enttäuscht ich über Ihren Mangel
an Interesse an Menschenrechten bin, da es für mich nur sehr schwer vor-
stellbar ist, daß Ihnen die Menschenrechtssituation in Ihrem Land nicht
wichtig erscheint.
Auch wenn Sie diesbezüglich anderer Meinung sind, so ist es bloß eine
Frage der Höflichkeit, auf Briefe von Menschen zu antworten, welche an
der Entwicklung größerer Sicherheit in Bezug auf Menschenrechte der Be-
wohner der Republik Korea interessiert sind.
Deshalb ersuche ich Sie, diese Briefe zu beantworten und alles in Ihrer
Macht stehende zu tun, um die Menschenrechte für jedermann in Ihrem Land
zu garantieren.
Hochachtungsvoll

0178

발 신 전 보

WGE-1538   910925 1636 FO

번 호 : _____   종별 : _____

수 신 : 주 독   대사. ~~총영사~~

발 신 : 장 관   (구일)

제 목 : DAAD 홍성담 초청 관련

연: 구일 202-750 (91.7.10)
계지

1. DAAD 는 공안사범으로 현재 구속중인 홍성담을 베를린 예술가 프로그램 장학생으로 3개월간 방독 초청한것으로 알려지고 있음.

2. 상기관련 주한독일 대사관측은 DAAD 로 부터 홍성담에게 장학 증서를 전달해 달라는 부탁을 받고 법무부에 장학증서 전달을 위한 홍성담씨 접견을 요청 하였는 바, 법무부는 관계규정 및 교화 목적상 접견 불가함을 설명하고, 가족에게 전달토록 고지(9.13) 하였다하니 향후 귀업무에 참고 바람.   끝.

(구주국장 권영민)

예 고 : 1991. 12. 31. 일반

예고문에의거재분류(1991.12.31.)
직위   성명 가ㅇ리

앙고재	91년 9월 25일	기안자 성명 김영희		과장 심의관		국장 전결		차관	장관

외신과통제

0179

법 무 부 인 권 과

1991.   .   .

아래 문건을 수신자에게 전달하여 주시기 바랍니다.

제 목 : <u>정보보고</u>

수 신 : <u>외무부 서기1과</u>

(수신처 FAX NO:)

발 신 : <u>   법무부 인권과   </u>

표지포함 총 ___ 매

0180

배 부 처	법 무 부								대 검		청와대		기 타 기 관					
	⊘⊘⊘⊘○○								⊘○		⊘○		⊘⊘⊘○○○○					
	장차법검 무찰 실국 관관장장								공 안 부 장		정책조사보과보 사정비서관실		제안외공법 1행 기무.보제 조.부.부.치.처					

정 보 보 고

1. 제 목

인권관련기사 진상보고

2. 출 처

인 권 과

(1991. 9. 25)

3. 내 용

1. 관련기사 요지

o 한겨레신문 9.25자

최근 내한한 국제사면위 영국지부 홍보책임자 댄 존스는
영국, 독일, 네덜란드 등 유럽 각국에서 홍성담외 작품
전시회가 100여회 개최되었으며,

✓ 독일학술교류처는 베를린예술가프로그램 장학생으로 동인을
초청했으며,

앞으로도 유럽예술계와 국제사면위원회에서 동인의 석방탄원
서명운동과 작품전시회를 계속 전개하리라고 언급하였다는 것임

2. 진 상

o 국제사면위 런던지부장 댄 존스는 9.9~9.19 사이 서울,
대구, 광주 등 지역 AI그룹 (주로 학계.종교계 종사자로
소규모이며 활동사항은 미미함) 방문, 한국지부 설치문제
등을 점검하는 한편,

0181 ~~0180~~

공안사범 구속자 가족 등과 접촉하여 자료 수집하였으며,

특히 9.14~9.18간 홍성담의 모 윤덕엽 가(광주시 소재)

에서 숙박한 바 있음 ('90.8. 초순 방한 경력)

o 국제사면위원회 등의 동인에 대한 석방탄원에 대하여는

정부차원에서 기히 대응한 바 있음

o 독일학술교류협회 초청장에 관하여

- 주한독일대사관 문화담당 스테파니 벡커는, 독일학술

교류협회로부터 홍성담에게 장학증서를 전달해 달라는

부탁을 받고, 당부에 장학증서 전달을 위한 홍성담 접견

을 요청하였는 바,

- 당부(교정국)는 스테파니 벡커에게 관계규정 및 교화

목적상 접견 불가함을 설명하고, 가족에게 전달하도록

고지 (9.13)

* 홍성담은 형기종료 출소후 독일에 유학할 예정임

- 3. 보도에 대한 대응조치 여부

동 언론기사에 대한 반박문 등 별도대처는 불요함

* 첨부 : 관련기사 사본 1부.

0182

네덜란드 암스테르담의 한 거리에 홍성담씨의 석방을 촉구하는 벽화를 제작하고 있는 네덜란드 젊은이들.

유럽 예술계 ▶ 국제사면위

홍성담씨 석방운동 '꾸준'

89년 비밀린 공동의장 홍성담(36)씨가 범양청년학생축전에 〈민족해방운동사〉 걸개그림 슬라이드를 보내 구속된 지 2년이 지났음에도 '19씨 석방을 촉구하는 유럽의 예술인·지식인과 국제사민위원회의 활동이 잦아들지 않고 더욱 활발해지고 있다.

최근 국제시민위 한국지부의 활동을 알려보기 위해 우리나라에 온 국제시민위 영국지부의 홍보책임가 밴 존스(51)는 "지금까지 기미 포스터·스티커 전시회의 장식하는 데 이용되기도 했다고 한다.

특히 지난 6월 탐래스교의 대표적 전시장간인 백텀립화랑에서 광주항쟁 희갑사진전과 함께 열린 홍성담판화전은 이 지역 어린이들을 위한 살아 있는 인권교육의 장으로 활용됐으며, 최근 세계 주요 양심수 예술인을 소개한 영국 텔레비전 프로그램에도 홍씨의 활동과 작품이 포함돼 많은 영국인들이 홍씨의 삶에 깊은 인상을 받았다고 밴

한 판화제작 과정이 주요 부분으로 들어 있는 중등학생들용 상내료 한 미술책용 발간할 예정으로 있다고 밝혔다.

한번 영국뿐 이나라 뒤워·네덜란드 등지에서도 홍씨의 석방을 촉구하는 행사와 활동이 다양하게 벌어지고 있다.

#독일하슐교류처는 홍씨가 구속되 있는 희실을 뻔히 알고 있음에도 최근 이 기관의 배를린 예술가프로그램 장리생으로, 홍씨를 초청하는 초청장을 보냈다.

작품전·언론소개 잦아 인권탄압 상징화
어린이 교육자료로 활용…벽화 제작도

을 포함, 1백여차례의 홍성남 작품전이 유럽 기지에서 있었다"며 앞으로도 각종 전시회와 석범탄원 서명운동이 줄기차게 계속될 것이라고 밝혔다.

밴 존스에 따르면 홍씨의 작품은 홍씨뿐 아니라 페루·소말리아·터키 등 세계 여러 나라의 각종 인권탄압사례를 고발하는 선전매체의 시각자료로도 활용되고 있으며, 지난 봄 영국 리버풀시 있었던 국제사면위 모임에서도 홍씨의 작품이

존스는 전했다. 〈리버스 다이제스토〉 영국판도 최근 국제사면위의 활동을 알리는 기사에 홍씨의 작품 〈이원규 열사도〉와 함께, 홍씨에 대한 내용을 게재한 바 있다.

"92년 문화도시로 지정된 에이레의 더블린이 내년 10월경 홍성담판화진을 갖는 한편 홍씨를 소개하는 라디오 프로그램을 방송할 계획"이라고 전하는 밴 존스는 국제사면위 영국지부도 을 11월경 홍씨의 지급을 응을

3개월의 독일 체류기간 동안 매위 3천미르크를 지불하겠다고 약속한 이 기관은 홍씨의 초청에 판한 사실이 이미 주한 독일대사관에 통고됐으며 비자 및 여권 문제와 관련해 대사관에 협조를 요청해 놓았다고 일러왔다.

네덜란드의 암스테르담에서는 최근 한 무리의 젊은이들이 홍씨의 석방을 촉구하는 벽화를 제작, 시민들에게 한국의 '예술탄압'을 소개하기도 했다.

〈이주헌 기자〉

(한겨레신문 '91.9.25 9면)

외 무 부

종 별 :

번 호 : HMW-0109

수 신 : 장 관(구일,문홍,기정동문)

발 신 : 주 함부르크총영사

제 목 : 홍성담 작품전시회

과 ~

일 시 : 91 1004 1630

시사항

7b

1. 국가보안법 위반으로 형집행중인 화가 홍 성담의 작품전시회가 당지 개신교단체 (EVANGELISCHHE AKADEMIE)협찬으로 당지에서 열리고 있는 바, 10.11.까지 열릴예정임

2. 당지 일간지 HAMBURG ABENDBLATT 지는 10.4자 문화면에 상기전시회 소개기사를 게재(홍의'전부적신명'사진 포함 4단기사)하였는 바, 요지 하기와 같음

0 현재 전시중인 홍의 '금지된작품'을 보면, 홍이 왜 한국정부의 눈의 가시인가를 알수있음

0. 한국의 반체제적인'민중문화운동'의 대표적 작가인 홍은 광주사태에도 참여, 선동적 작품을 제작했었음

0 독일의 저명한 작가, 학자, 정치인들의 홍을 위한탄원으로 홍의 형기는 금년초3년으로 감형된 바 있음.

끝. (총영사-국장)

구주국   1차보   문협국   외정실   안기부

91.10.05   07:56 WH

외신 1과 통제관

0184

주 독 대 사 관

1991.10.29.

주독(정)202- 1079

수 신 : 장 관

참 조 : 구주국장

제 목 : 이해학, 홍근수 목사 석방요구 독일인 서명

대 : 구일 202 - 27938

    1. 대호 관련 10.22 전부관 참사관은 Evangelische Kirche in Deutschland의 본 주재 사무소장 Hermann Kalina을 만나 이해학, 홍근수 양 목사의 실정법 위반 사실을 구체적으로 설명하고, 봉일전의 독일과 분단하의 한국은 그 상황이 상이함을 강조하였습니다.

이와 함께 6공화국의 인권개선 상황 특히 남·북 교류와 협력에 관한 법률제정의 내용을 상세히 설명하였으며, 피구속자가 종교인이란 이유로 정부가 특별한 관용을 베풀수는 없음을 지적하였습니다.

    2. 이에대해 Kalina 소장은 한국교회와 독일교회간의 긴밀한 관계에 따라 상기와 같은 석방요구 청원이 한국 및 독일정부에 제출되는 것으로 안다고 하며, 상기 아국 정부입장은 이해는 하나, 한·독간에 특별히 긴밀한 우호·협력 관계는 감안하여 아국정부가 이들 종교인에 대해 가급적 관용을 베풀 것을 요청하였습니다.

61535

1991.10. 2 9
주독일대사관

0185

3. 동 소장은 이어 자신으로서도 아국인권의 개선상황은 잘 알고
있으며, 기회가 있는데로 상기 아측설명을 독일 교회관계자에 설명하는 등
가능한 노력을 하겠다고 언급하였읍니다.   끝.

주   독   대

0186

정 리 보 존 문 서 목 록

기록물종류	일반공문서철	등록번호	2020040262	등록일자	2020-04-28
분류번호	742.14	국가코드		보존기간	영구
명 칭	인권관계 다자조약 유보철회, 1990-91				
생 산 과	국제법규과	생산년도	1990~1991	담당그룹	
내용목차	ㅇ 여성에 대한 모든 형태의 차별철폐에 관한 협약 제16조제1항 (다), (라), (바) 유보철회(조약 제1041호) - 제16조제1항 (사)호 유보 유지 ㅇ 시민적 및 정치적 권리에 관한 국제규약(B규약) 제23조제4항 유보철회(조약 제1042호)				

0001

"여성에 관한 모든 형태의 차별철폐에 관한 협약"중
일부 유보조항에 관한 유보이유

○ 아국은 84.12.27. 동 협약 비준시 제 9조와 제 16조 1항중 4개 세항을
   국적법, 민법 및 섭외사법의 일부조항에 저촉됨을 이유로 유보한바,
   유보조항의 내용 및 유보 사유는 아래와 같음.

유 보 조 항	유 보 사 유 (저촉되는 관련 국내법 조항)

○ 협약 제 9조
 	
  - 국적취득, 변경에 있어서의
    남녀의 동등한 권리
  - 부의 국적 변경으로 인한
    처의 국적 변경 강제금지
  - 자녀 국적 선택에 관한
    부모의 동등한 권리
	○ 국적법 제 2조
	
	  - 국적취득에 있어서의 부계 혈통주의
	    규정
	
	○ 국적법 제 8조
	
	  - 부 중심가족 단일국적주의 규정

○ 협약 제 16조 1항
 	
  (다) 혼인중 및 혼인해소 시의
      동등한 권리와 책임
	○ 민법 제 777조 (친족의 범위)
	  - 부는 8촌, 또는 4촌까지
	
	○ 민법 제 811조 (재혼금지 기간)
	  - 여자는 혼인종료후 6개월 이내에
	    혼인하지 못함.
	
	○ 민법 제 826조 (부부간의 의무)
	  - 처는 부의 가에 입적
	
	○ 민법 제 837조 (이혼과 자의 양육 책임)
	  - 당사자간에 약정이 없으면 부에게
	    양육 책임.
	
	○ 섭외사법 제 16,17,18조
	  - 혼인의 효력, 부부재산제, 이혼은
	    부의 본국법에 의함

0002

(라) 자녀문제에 있어서 부모로서의 동등한 권리와 책임	○ 민법 제781조 (자의 입적, 성과본)
	  - 부의 성과 본을 따르고 부의 가에 입적
	
	○ 민법 제909조 (친권자) 1항
	  - 부모의견 불일치시 부가 행사
	
	○ 민법 제909조 5항
	  - 부모이혼 또는 부사망시 모가 친가에 복적 또는 재혼한 경우 모는 전혼인중 출생자에 대한 친권 상실
	
	○ 섭외사법 제19조, 22조
	  - 친생자의 추정, 승인, 부인 및 친자간의 법률관계는 부 또는 부의 본국법을 우선 적용

(바) 아동의 보호, 후견, 재산관리 입양등과 관련하여 동등한 권리와 책임	○ 민법 제874조 (부부의 공동 입양)
	  - 처의 부재등으로 공동으로 할 수 없을 때, 부 일방이 쌍방 명의로 입양 및 피입양
	
	○ 민법 제932조 - 935조 (후견인의 순위)
	  - 남자, 최근친, 연장자의 순

(사) 가종성, 직업선택권과 관련하여 부부가 동등한 개인적 권리	○ 국내 관습상 제약 많음.

0003

The view of R.O.K. on the reservation
made upon ratification of the Convention
on the Elimination of All Forms of Discrimination
against Women

The Government of the Republic of Korea declares that it
shall not be bound by the provisions of article 9 and sub-
paragraphs (c), (d), (f) and (g) of paragraph 1 of article 16
of the convention as they conflict with some articles of
domestic laws i.e., the Law on Nationality, the Civil Code and
Conflict of Laws Act.

1.   Reservation concerning article 9

The R.O.K. Government expresses its reservation with
regard to the provisions in article 9 of the Convention
as they conflict with the article 2 and 8 of the Korean
Law on Nationality, which stipulate the child's acquisition
of his father's nationality and the wife's acquisition of
her husband's nationality.

2.   Reservation concerning article 16, paragraph (c)

The R.O.K. Government considers itself not bound by
article 16, paragraph (c) of the Convention as it runs
counter to the article 777, 811, 826, 837 of the Civil
Code and the article 16, 17, 18 of the Conflict of Laws Act,
the contents of which are as follows;

- 1 -

0004

A. Civil Code

Article 777 (Scope of Relatives) Legal efficacy arising
    due to relationship shall be effective upon the persons
    who fall under one of following Subparagraphs unless
    otherwise provided for in this Code or any other laws:

    1. Paternal relative by blood within eighth degree
        of relationship;
    2. Maternal relative by blood within fourth degree
        of relationship;
    3. Husband's paternal relative by blood within eighth
        degree of relationship;
    4. Husband's maternal relative by blood within fourth
        degree of relationship;
    5. Wife's parent;
    6. Spouse.

Article 811 (Period to Prohibit Re-marriage) A woman
    may not re-marry unless six (6) months have elapsed
    from the day of the termination of her previous
    marriage. It is, however, provided that if she gives
    birth after the termination of her previous matrimonial
    relation, this shall not apply.

Article 826 (Duties of Husband and Wife) (1) Husband and
    wife shall live together, and shall furnish support
    and aid each other. It is, however, provided that
    when husband and wife do not live together temporarily
    for a due reason, both party must tolerate it.

- 2 -

0005

(2) Cohabitation of husband and wife shall take place
at husband's place of dwelling or abode. It is, however,
provided that in the case of the proviso of Paragraph (3)
below, cohabitation shall take place at wife's place of
dwelling or abode.

(3) The wife shall have her name entered in husband's
family register. It is provided, however, that when the
wife is the head or the successor of headship of her
parent's family, the husband may have his name entered
in his wife's family register.

(4) In the case of the proviso of Paragraph (3) a child
born between husband and wife shall assume the mother's
surname and the origin of surname, and shall have his or her
name entered in mother's family register.

Article 837 (Divorce and Responsibility for Fostering and
    Education of their Children) (1) In case an agreement
    has not been made on matters concerning fostering and
    education of the children born between the parties, the
    father is responsible for fostering and education of their
    children.   (2) In case an agreement on the matters
    concerning fostering and education as set forth in Paragraph
    (1) has not been made or able to make, the court may, upon
    the application filed by the parties, decide the matters
    necessary for such fostering and education by taking into
    consideration of the age of their child or children,
    property status of the father and mother and any other
    circumstances thereof, and the court may change such matters
    or may take any other proper disposition at any time.

- 3 -

0006

(3) Except for matters relating to fostering and education, the provisions of Paragraph (2) shall not effect any change of the right and duty of the parent.

B. Conflict of Laws Act

Article 16 (Effect of Marriage) (1) The effect of a marriage shall be governed by the husband's national law.
(2) In a case where an alien has been adopted as a son by the heirless Korean national parents of a daughter and married the said daughter, the effect of the marriage shall be governed by the laws of the Republic of Korea.

Article 17 (Matrimonial Property System) (1) The matrimonial property system shall be governed by the husband's national law at the time of a marriage.
(2) In a case where an alien has been adopted as a son by heirless Korean national parents and married their daughter, the matrimonial property system shall be governed by the laws of the Republic of Korea.

Article 18 (Divorce) A divorce shall be governed by the husband's national law at the time when the facts which caused the divorce occurred. However, the court may not adjudicate a divorce if the facts which caused such divorce do not constitute cause for a divorce according to the laws of the Republic of Korea.

- 4 -

C007

3. Reservation concerning article 16, paragraph (d)

    The R.O.K. Government expresses its reservation to
article 16, paragraph (d) as they conflict with the article
781, 909 (1), 909(5) of the Civil Code, and the article 19,22
of the Conflict of Laws Act, the contents of which are as
follows;

A. Civil Code

    Article 781 (Entry into a Family Register and Surname
        and Origin of Surname, of a Child) (1) A child shall
        assume its father's surname and the origin of surname and
        shall have its name entered in its father's family register.
        (2) A child whose father is not recognizable shall assume
        its mother's surname and the origin of surname, and shall
        have its name entered in its mother's family register.
        (3) A child whose father and mother are not recognizable
        shall, with the approval of the court, establish a new
        surname and the origin of surname, and shall establish
        a new family. However, if the father or mother of a child
        become recognizable after a child has established a new
        surname and the origin of surname, the child shall assume
        its fatehr's or mother's surname.

    Article 909 (The Person in Parental Authority) (1) Parental
        power over a minor shall be exercised jointly by the father
        and mother. However, if no agreement can be reached, the
        father shall exercise the parental power.

- 5 -

(5) If father and mother are divorced, or the mother has
her register returned to her original family register or
the mother has re-married after the father of a child had died,
the mother shall not become the person in parental authority
over such child born to her during the existence of her
former marriage.

B. Conflict of Laws Act

Article 19 (Natural Parenthood) The presumption, recognition,
    or denial of natural Parenthood shall be governed by the
    mother's husband's national law at the time of birth of the
    child. If the husband has died before the birth of a child,
    such presumption, recognition or denial shall be governed
    by the husband's national law at the time of his death.

Article 22 (Legal Relation between the Parent and Child) The
    legal relation between the parent and child shall be
    governed by the father's national law and it shall be governed
    by the mother's national law if a child has no father.

4. Reservation concerning article 16, paragraph (f)

    The R.O.K. Government does not consider as binding upon
itself the article 16, paragraph (f) because they conflict with
the article 874, 932, 933, 934, 935 of the Civil Code, the
contents of which are as follows;

- 6 -

0009

Article 874 (Joint Adoption of Husband and Wife) (1) A
   person who has a wife may neither effect adoption nor be
   adopted except jointly with his spouse.
   (2) If adoption or being adopted can not be effected
   jointly due to the absence of wife or any other cause, the
   husband alone may effect adoption or may be adopted in the
   name of both.

Article 932 (Order in Which a Guardian over a Minor is to be
   Designated) If any guardian, pursuant to the provision of
   Article 931, has not been appointed at all, the spouse,
   lineal relative by blood, collateral relative by blood
   within the third degree of relationship and head of the
   family, of a minor shall become a guardian in its order.

Article 933 (Order in Which a Guardian over Incompetent, etc., is
   to be Appointed) When an adjudication of incompetency or
   limited-competency has been made, the spouse, lineal relative
   by blood, collateral relative by blood within the third
   degree of relationship and head of the family, of such
   adjudicated person shall become a guardian in its order.

Article 934 (Order in Which a Guardian over a Married Woman
   is to be Appointed) When a married woman is a minor, or
   has adjudicated as an incompetent or limited-competent, her
   spouse, the spous's lineal relative by blood, collateral
   relatives by blood within the third degree of relationship
   and head of the family of her spouse shall become a guardian
   in its order. However, when she returned to her parent's
   family register after the termination of her matrimonial
   relation, the order of appointment of guardian shall be
   governed by the provisions of Articles 932 and 933.

- 7 -

0010

Article 935 (Order in Which a Guardian is to be Appointed)

(1) When there are two or more lineal relatives by blood or collateral relatives by blood pursuant to the provisions of Articles 932 to 934, the first priority of appointment of guardian shall be placed upon the male relative, and where there are two or more male and female relatives by blood, the nearest relative shall have the first priority, and where there are two or more close relatives of same degree of relationship, the older relative shall have the first priority.

(2) Irrespective of Paragraph (1), when both the real father and mother of an adopted child and the adoptive father and mother are alive, the priority of appointment of guardian shall be placed on the adoptive father and mother, and in case where the degree of relationship between the relative by blood of his or her parent's family and the relative by blood of his or her adoptive family is same, the priority shall be placed on the relative blood of his or her adoptive family.

5. Reservation concerning article 16, paragraph (g)

The article 16, paragraph (g), which stiplulates the same personal rights as husband and wife, including the right to choose a family name, a profession and an occupation, conflicts with the customs and traditions of the Korean people.

- 8 -

C011

Because of the patriachal family system which has been
handed down from the old feudalistic society, the current
Family Law contains some tradition-bound provisions of the
family system in relation to

- the family headship system
- prohibition of marriage between the parties whose surname
  and place of family origin are same, and so on.

Since the family laws of any country are the codification
of the cultural and social traditions and age-old customs of
its society, revising the laws requires a general consensus
of the people.

Hence, the R.O.K. Government decides to reserve the
article 16, paragraph (g).

- 9 -

0012

57138

분류기호 문서번호	법규 20420-	기 안 용 지 (전화:)	시 행 상 특별취급	
보존기간	영구·준영구. 10. 5. 3. 1.	장 관		
수 신 처 보존기간				
시행일자	1990. 11. 19.			
보 조 기 관	국 장	전결	협 조 기 관	문 서 통 제
	심의관			
	과 장			
	기안책임자	김두영		발 인
경 유 수 신 참 조		법무부장관	발 신 명 의	
제 목		인권관계 다자조약 유보철회		

　　　1.　정부는 84.12.27. "여성에 대한 모든 형태의 차별철폐에

관한 협약"을 비준하였으며, 90.4.10. "시민적 및 정치적 권리에 관한

국제규약(B규약)"에 가입한 바 있습니다.

　　　2.　동 인권관계 다자협약의 비준 또는 가입시 정부는 국내법과

충돌되는 협약의 일부조항에 대하여 유보를 행하였던 바, "여성에 대한

모든 형태의 차별철폐에 관한 협약"의 제9조 및 제16조 제1항의 (다),

(라), (바), (사)호, 그리고 "시민적 및 정치적 권리에 관한 국제규약"

/ 계 속 / 　　　0013

1505-25(2-1) 일(1)갑
85. 9. 9. 승인　"내가아낀 종이 한장 늘어나는 나라살림"

190mm×268mm 인쇄용지 2급 60g/㎡
가 40-41 1990. 5. 28

(B규약)의 제14조 제5항과 제7항, 제22조 및 제23조 제4항이 동 유보

조항들입니다.

    3. 당부는 국내입법 및 제반여건의 변화에 부응하여 가능한

범위내에서 유보조치의 철회를 검토하고 있습니다.

    4. 이와관련, 91.1.1.부터 시행되는 개정민법의 내용에 반영된

가족법 사항과 관련된 일부조항, 즉 "여성에 대한 모든 형태의 차별철폐에

관한 협약" 제16조 제1항 (다), (라), (바), (사)호 및 "시민적 및 정치적

권리에 관한 국제규약"의 제23조 제4항의 경우, 유보사유가 해소된 것으로

판단되어 우선 동 조항에 대한 유보를 철회하고자 하는 바, 이에관한

귀부의 의견을 조속히 회시하여 주시기 바랍니다.

    5. 아울러 여타 조항에 관하여도 국내법의 변경이나 정책적

고려에 의하여 유보의 철회가 필요하다고 판단되는 사항이 있는 경우,

그 내용을 ~~아울러~~ 통보하여 주시기 바랍니다.

    6. 본건 관련 공문은 다음과 같습니다.

    가. 시민적 및 정치적 권리에 관한 국제규약 유보

    대: 인권 20420-3956(89.3.23.)

    인권 20420-8435(89.6.23.)

/ 계 속 /   0014

1505-25(2-2) 일(1)을   "내가아낀 종이 한장 늘어나는 나라살림"   190mm×268mm 인쇄용지 2급 60g/㎡
85. 9. 9.승인   가 40-41 1990. 5. 28

연 : 법규 20420-1439(89.1.17.)
법규 20420-20366(89.5.19.)
법규 20420-21645(89.5.29.)
나. 여성에 대한 모든 형태의 차별철폐에 관한 협약 유보
담부 법규 743-22142(84.6.7.) 및 국무총리 주재 여성
정책 심의위원회 제3차 회의(84.8.30.) 참조. 끝.

0015

대 한 민 극
외 무 부

(720-4045)

198/90. 11. 19.

법규 20420-

수신 법무부장관

제목 인권관계 다자조약 유보철회

1. 정부는 84.12.27. "여성에 대한 모든 형태의 차별철폐에 관한 협약"을 비준하였으며, 90.4.10. "시민적 및 정치적 권리에 관한 국제규약(B규약)"에 가입한 바 있습니다.

2. 동 인권관계 다자협약의 비준 또는 가입시 정부는 국내법과 충돌되는 협약의 일부조항에 대하여 유보를 행하였던 바, "여성에 대한 모든 형태의 차별철폐에 관한 협약"의 제9조 및 제16조 제1항의 (다), (라), (바), (사)호 그리고 "시민적 및 정치적 권리에 관한 국제규약" (B규약)의 제14조 제5항과 제7항, 제22조 및 제23조 제4항이 동 유보 조항들입니다.

3. 당부는 국내입법 및 제반여건의 변화에 부응하여 가능한 범위내에서 유보조치의 철회를 검토하고 있습니다.

4. 이와관련, 91.1.1.부터 시행되는 개정민법의 내용에 반영된 가족법 사항과 관련된 일부조항, 즉 "여성에 대한 모든 형태의 차별철폐에 관한 협약" 제16조 제1항 (다), (라), (바), (사)호 및 "시민적 및 정치적 권리에 관한 국제규약"의 제23조 제4항의 경우, 유보사유가 해소된 것으로 판단되어 우선 동 조항에 대한 유보를 철회하고자 하는바, 이에관한 귀부의 의견을 조속히 회시하여 주시기 바랍니다.

0016

5. 아울러 其타 조항에 관하여도 국내법의 변경이나 정책적
고려에 의하여 유보의 철회가 필요하다고 판단되고 사항이 있는 경우,
그 내용을 통보하여 주시기 바랍니다.

6. 본건 관련 공문은 다음과 같습니다.

　　가. 시민적 및 정치적 권리에 관한 국제규약 유보

　　　　대: 인권 20420-3956 (89.3.23.)

　　　　　　인권 20420-8435 (89.6.23.)

　　　　연: 법규 20420-1439 (89.1.17.)

　　　　　　법규 20420-20366(89.5.19.)

　　　　　　법규 20420-21645(89.5.29.)

　　나. 여성에 대한 모든 형태의 차별철폐에 관한 협약 유보

　　　　당부 법규 743-22142(84.6.7.)및 국무총리 주재 여성
　　　　정책 심의위원회 제3차 회의(84.8.30.)참조. 끝.

외　　　무　　　부　　　장　　　관

　국제기구조약국장

0017

법　　　무　　　부

인권 20420- **16139** 503-7045   1990. 12. 10.

수신 외무부장관

제목 인권관계 다자조약 유보철회 검토의견 송부

　　1. 법규 20420-57138 ('90.11.19)와 관련입니다.

　　2. 개정민법의 시행에 따라 귀부에서 요청한 "여성에 대한 모든
형태의 차별철폐에 관한 협약" 제16조 제1항 (다),(라),(바),(사)호
및 "시민적 및 정치적 권리에 관한 국제규약" 제23조 제4항의 유보철회
여부에 대한 당부 검토의견을 별첨과 같이 송부합니다.

　　첨부 : 인권관계 다자조약 유보철회 검토의견 1부. 끝.

법　　　무　　　부　　　장　　　관

34747   C018

인권관계 다자조약 유보철회에 대한 당부 검토의견
==

1. 여성에 대한 모든 형태의 차별철폐에 관한 협약중 제16조 제1항의
   (다),(라),(바),(사)호에 대하여

   ㅇ (다),(라),(바)호

   개정민법 ('91.1.1(법률 제4199호) 시행)은 친족의 범위를
   남녀평등관념에 입각, 합리적으로 조정하고 상속제도 및 친권행사,
   이혼 등 제반 가족법 관계에서의 남녀불평등 요소를 해소시켰으므로
   유보를 철회함이 상당함

   ㅇ (사)호

   동 규정중 가족의 성(姓)을 자유로이 선택할 권리는 개정민법에
   의하더라도 자(子)는 부(父)의 성(姓)과 본(本)을 따르고
   부가(父家)에 입적함이 원칙이고 (개정민법 제781조 제1항)
   부(父)를 알 수 없는 경우에만 모(母)의 성과 본을 따르게 되어
   있고 (동법 제781조 제2항), 또한 처도 부의 가(家)에 입적
   하는 것을 원칙으로 하고 처가 호주 또는 호주승계인인 경우에만
   예외적으로 부가 처의 가에 입적하기로 규정되어 있으므로
   (동법 제826조 제3항) 이 부분에 한해서는 우리의 관습 및
   법제와 맞지 아니하여 이를 유보함이 상당하다고 사료됨

0019

2. 시민적 및 정치적 권리에 관한 국제규약중 제23조 제4항에 대하여

   동 조항에 대하여는 유보이유가 된 민법조항들이 '91.1.1자로
   남녀동등권이 인정되는 방향으로 개정되었으므로 유보를 철회함이
   상당함

3. 기타 유보조항중 여성에 대한 모든 형태의 차별철폐에 관한 협약
   제9조 및 시민적·정치적 권리에 관한 국제규약 제14조 제7항
   등에 대하여는   현재 유보조치를 철회할만한 입법이나 조치가
   되어 있지 아니하므로 계속 유보함이 타당함

0020

1. 撤回對象條項

   ○ 女性에 대한 모든 形態의 差別撤廢에 관한 協約
     - 第16條 第1項 (다), (라), (바)號

   ○ 市民的 및 政治的 權利에 관한 國際規約
     - 第23條 第4項

2. 撤回對象 條項의 內容 및 留保事由

   가. 內容

      (1) 女性에 대한 모든 形態의 差別撤廢 協約
          第16條 第1項 (다), (라), (바)號

      ○ 婚姻과 家族關係에 있어서 差別을 撤廢하기 위하여
        當事國에게 適切한 措置義務 賦課
        (다)號: 婚姻中 및 婚姻解消時의 同等한 權利와
                責任
        (라)號: 子女問題에 있어서 父母로서 同等한
                權利와 責任

- 8 -

0021

(바)號: 兒童의 保護, 後見, 財産管理, 入養等과
關聯하여 同等한 權利와 責任

나. 市民的 및 政治的 權利에 관한 國際規約 第23條 第4項
　o 婚姻中 및 婚姻解消時 同等한 權利와 責任

나. 留保事由

　o 父系血統主義에 立脚, 男性爲主로 規定되어 있던 改正前
我國 民法上의 家族法制와 衝突

　o 衝突되는 主要 關聯 國內民法 規定(改正前)
　　－ 夫中心의 家族生活關係
　　　· 同居場所는 夫의 住所 또는 居所(第826條 第2項)
　　　· 夫婦共同入養時 夫의 一方的 決定權(第874條 第2項)
　　　· 生活費 夫 負擔(第833條)
　　－ 子女에 대한 父權利 中心
　　　· 父母 意見不一致時 父의 親權行使(第909條 第1項)
　　　· 離婚後 夫의 子에 대한 養育責任(第837條 第1項)
　　－ 父系中心의 親族範圍
　　　· 8寸以内 父系血族 4寸以内 母系血族(第777條)

3. 留保撤回 事由

　o 91.1.1.부터 施行되는 改正民法이 上記 留保條項의 内容을
受容, 衝突 事由를 解消

－ 9 －

0022

o 改正民法 主要內容

   - 夫婦共同의 家族生活 關係

      · 同居場所 夫婦協議(第826條 第2項), 夫婦共同入養時
        協議(第874條 第2項), 生活費 共同負擔(第833條),
        離婚時 財産分割 請求權(第839條의 2, 新設)

   - 子女에 대한 父母의 同等한 權利

      · 共同親權行使(第909條 第2項), 離婚後 養育協議
        (第837條 第1項), 離婚後 面接交涉權(第837條의
        2, 新設)

   - 同一한 親族範圍

      · 8寸以內 血族 및 4寸以內 姻戚(第777條)

4. 留保가 繼續되는 條項(未撤回)

가. 女性에 대한 모든 形態의 差別撤廢에 관한 協約:
    第9條 및 第16條 第1項 (사)號

(國   文)

第9條(國籍關係)

1. 當事國은 女性이 國籍을 取得, 變更 또는 保有함에
   있어 男性과 同等한 權利를 賦與하여야 한다.
   當事國은 특히 外國人과의 結婚 또는 婚姻中 夫에
   의한 國籍의 變更으로 妻의 國籍이 自動的으로
   變更되거나, 妻가 無國籍으로 되거나 또는 夫의 國籍이
   妻에게 強制되지 아니하도록 確保하여야 한다.

- 10 -

0023

2. 當事國은 子女의 國籍에 관하여 男性과 同等한 權利를
   女性에게 賦與하여야 한다.

第16條 第1項 (사)號(家族의 姓)
(사) 家族姓 및 職業을 選擇할 權利를 包含하여 夫婦
    로서의 同一한 個人的 權利

(英 文)

Convention on the Elimination of All Forms of Discrimination against Women

Article 9

1. States Parties shall grant women equal rights with men to acquire, change or retain their nationality. They shall ensure in particular that neither marriage to an alien nor change of nationality by the husband during marriage shall automatically change the nationality of the wife, render her stateless or force upon her the nationality of the husband.

2. States Parties shall grant women equal rights with men with respect to the nationality of their children.

Alticle 16, Paragraph 1

(g) The same personal rights as husband and wife,
including the right to choose a family name, a
profession and an occupation;

나. 市民的 및 政治的 權利에 관한 國際規約:
第14條 第5項 및 第7項, 第22條

(國 文)

第14條 第5項, 第7項(上訴權保障, 二重處罰禁止)

5. 有罪判決을 받은 모든 사람은 法律에 따라 그 判決 및
宣告에 대하여 上級 法院에서 再審을 받을 權利를 가진다.

7. 어느 누구도 各國의 法律 및 刑事節次에 따라 이미
確定的으로 有罪 또는 無罪宣告를 받은 行爲에 관하여서는
다시 裁判 또는 處罰을 받지 아니한다.

第22條(結社의 自由)

1. 모든 사람은 자기의 利益을 保護하기 위하여 勞動組合을
結成하고 이에 加入하는 權利를 包含하여 다른 사람과의
結社의 自由에 대한 權利를 갖는다

2. 이 權利의 行使에 대하여는 法律에 의하여 規定되고,
國家安保, 公共의 安全, 公共秩序, 公衆保健 또는 道德의
보호 또는 他人의 權利 및 自由의 保護를 위하여

- 12 -

0025

民主社會에서 必要한 것이외의 어떠한 制限도 과하여
져서는 아니된다. 이 條는 軍隊와 警察의 構成員이
이 權利를 行使하는 데 대하여 合法的인 制限을 賦課하는
것을 防害하지 아니한다.

3. 이 條의 어떠한 規定도 結社의 自由 및 團結權의 保護에
   관한 1948年의 國際勞動機構協約의 當事國이 同 協約에
   規定하는 保障을 沮害하려는 立法措置를 取하도록 하거나
   또는 이를 沮害하려는 方法으로 法律을 適用할 것을 許容
   하는 것은 아니다.

(英 文)

International Covenant on Civil and Political Rights

Article 14

5. Everyone convicted of a crime shall have the right
   to his conviction and sentence being reviewed by a
   higher tribunal according to law.

7. No one shall be liable to be tried or punished
   again for an offence for which he has already been
   finally convicted or acquitted in accordance with
   the law and penal procedure of each country.

- 13 -

0026

Article 22

1. Everyone shall have the right to freedom of
    association with others, including the right to
    form and join trade unions for the protection of
    his interests.

2. No restrictions may be placed on the exercise of
    this right other than those which are prescribed
    by law and which are necessary in a democratic
    society in the interests of national security or
    public safety, public order(ordre public), the
    protection of public health or morals or the
    protection of the rights and freedoms of others.
    This article shall not prevent the imposition of
    lawful restrictions on members of the armed forces
    and of the police in their exercise of this right.

3. Nothing in this article shall authorize States
    Parties to the International Labour Organisation
    Convention of 1948 concerning Freedom of Association
    and Protection of the Right to Organize to take
    legislative measures which would prejudice, or to
    apply the law in such a manner as to prejudice,
    the guarantees provided for in that Convention.

- 14 -

0027

5. 留保撤回와 關聯된 民法 新·舊 條文對比表

從　　前	現　　行
第777條(親族의 範圍)　親族關係로 인한 法律上 效力은 本法 또는 다른 法律에 特別한 規定이 없는 한 다음 各號에 該當하는 者에 미친다. 1.　8寸以内의 父系血族 2.　4寸以内의 母系血族 3.　夫의 8寸以内의 父系血族 4.　夫의 4寸以内의 母系血族 5.　妻의 父母 6.　配偶者	第777條(親族의 範圍)　親族關係로 인한 法律上 效力은 本法 또는 다른 法律에 特別한 規定이 없는 한 다음 各號에 該當하는 者에 미친다. 1.　8寸이내의 血族 2.　4寸이내의 姻戚 3.　配偶者
第826條(夫婦間의 義務) ② 夫婦의 同居는 夫의 住所나 居所에서 한다. 그러나, 第3項 但書의 경우에는 妻의 住所나 居所에서 한다.	第826條(夫婦間의 義務) ② 夫婦의 同居場所는 夫婦의 協議에 따라 정한다. 그러나 協議가 이루어지지 아니하는 경우에는 當事者의 請求에 의하여 家庭法院이 이를 정한다.
第833條(生活費用)　夫婦의 共同生活에 必要한 費用의 負擔은 當事者間에 特別한 約定이 없으면 夫가 이를 負擔한다.	第833條(生活費用)　夫婦의 共同生活에 必要한 費用은 當事者間에 特別한 約定이 없으면 夫婦가 共同으로 負擔한다.
第837條(離婚과 子의 養育責任) ① 當事者間에 그 子의 養育에 관한 事項은 協定하지 아니한 때에는 그 養育의 責任은 父에게 있다.	第837條(離婚과 子의 養育責任) ① 當事者는 그 子의 養育에 관한 事項을 協議에 의하여 정한다.

－　15　－

0028

從　　　前	現　　　行
〈新設〉	第837條의 2(面接交涉權)　①子를 직접 養育하지 아니하는 父母中 一方은 面接交涉權을 가진다.
〈新設〉	第839條의 2(財産分割請求權) ① 協議上 離婚한 者의 一方은 다른 一方에 대하여 財産分割을 請求할 수 있다.
第874條(夫婦의 共同入養) ② 妻의 不在 기타 事由로 인하여 共同으로 할 수 없는 때에는 夫 一方이 夫婦雙方의 名義로 養子를 할 수 있고 養子가 될 수 있다.	第874條(夫婦의 共同入養) ② 配偶者 있는 者가 養子가 될 때에는 다른 一方의 同意를 얻어야 한다.
第909條(親權者)　① 未成年者인 子에 대한 親權은 父母가 共同으로 行使한다. 다만, 父母의 意見이 一致하지 아니하는 境遇에는 父가 行使한다.	第909條(親權者) ② 親權은 父母가 婚姻중인 때는 父母가 共同으로 이를 행사한다. 그러나 父母의 의견이 一致하지 아니하는 경우에는 當事者의 請求에 依하여 家庭法院이 이를 定한다.

-　16　-

유 보 철 회 검 토

1990. 12.

공람	국제법규과	90년 쓰산	담 당	과 장	심의관	국 장
			검두명			

국 제 법 규 과

0030

유보철회 검토

I. 유보철회 관행

　1. 타국의 관행

　　가. 미국

　　　ㅇ 유보철회를 위한 특별한 국내절차를 갖고 있지 않으나,
　　　　특허협력조약(Patent Cooperation Treaty)의 경우 75년
　　　　상원의 요청으로 유보부로 가입하였음을 감안, 84년 유보
　　　　철회시 상원의 조언과 동의를 요청 유보를 철회한바 있음.

　　나. 일본

　　　ㅇ 유보철회를 이미 국회의 승인을 얻은 조약 범위내의 행위
　　　　라고 보고, 외교관계 처리의 일환으로 별도의 국회의 승인을
　　　　얻지 않고 행정부가 처리함.

　2. 아국의 관행

　　ㅇ 유보철회문제가 거의 제기되지 않았던 관계로 확립된 철회
　　　관행은 없음.

　　ㅇ 특허청의 요청에 따라 90.9.1.자로 특허협력조약 제2장에 대한
　　　유보철회시에는 유보조항의 내용이 국내법으로 전면 수용되었음에
　　　비추어, 외무부장관 명의의 세계지적소유권기구 사무국장 앞
　　　공한을 발송하고 국내적으로는 이를 외무부 고시로 관보에
　　　게재, 유보를 철회함.

CC31

Ⅱ. 아국의 실례의 문제점

ㅇ 아국의 특허협력조약에 대한 유보철회 방식은 절차상 다소 하자가
  있었던 것으로 사료됨.

ㅇ 즉 헌법 제6조 제1항의 "헌법에 의하여 체결·공포된 조약과
  일반적으로 승인된 국제법규는 국내법과 같은 효력을 가진다."는
  규정에 비추어 유보가 철회된 조항도 국내법과 같은 효력을 갖게됨.

ㅇ 따라서 유보철회조항이 국내법과 동일한 효력을 갖는다고 볼 때 그
  효력을 발하는 절차도 동일하여야 할 것이며, 국무회의 심의와
  대통령재가를 거쳐야 한다고 볼수 있음.

Ⅲ. 향후 유보철회 국내절차 방안

1. 공포방식

가. 국무회의 심의 및 대통령재가를 득하여 공포하는 방안
  - 조약체결 절차에 준하여 정식으로 국무회의의 심의 및
    대통령재가를 득하여 공포함.

나. 대통령재가만을 득하여 공포하는 방안
  - 비준·가입시에 조약안에 대하여 국무회의 심의를 거쳤음을
    감안, 국무회의 심의는 생략하고 대통령의 재가만을 득하여
    조약공포 형식으로 관보에 게재함.
  - 국무회의 심의 생략문제에 관하여는 총무처 및 법제처와
    협의를 진행시켜야 할 것으로 봄.

다. 장·단점
  - 절차상으로는 완벽하나 처리에 많은 시간이 소요됨.

0032

2. 고시방식

　가.　대통령 재가를 득한 후 고시하는 방안
　　　- 조약체결권자인 대통령의 원칙재가를 득하되 관보게재는
　　　　외무부고시의 형식을 취함.

　나.　외무부 고시방안
　　　- 특허협력조약의 경우처럼 외무부장관 재가와 함께 외무부
　　　　고시로 관보에 게재함.

　다.　장·단점
　　　- 절차상 하자는 있으나 신속한 처리가 가능함.

0033

61909

기 안 용 지
(전화 :   )

분류기호 문서번호	법규 20420-		시 행 상 특별취급	
보존기간	영구·준영구. 10. 5. 3. 1.	장		관
수 신 처 보존기간				
시행일자	1990. 12. 18.			

보조기관	국 장	전결	협조기관	조약과장: 소	문 서 통 제	처입 90.12.18
	심의관					
	과 장				발 송 인	
기안책임자	김두영					

경 유		발신명의	
수 신	법제처장		
참 조			

제 목	인권관계 다자조약 유보철회

　　1. 정부는 84.12.27. "여성에 대한 모든 형태의 차별철폐에

관한 협약"을 비준하였으며, 90.4.10 "시민적 및 정치적 권리에 관한

국제규약"(B 규약)에 가입한 바 있습니다.

　　2. 동 인권관계 다자조약의 비준 또는 가입시 정부는 국내법과

충돌되는 일부조항에 대하여 유보를 행하였던 바, "여성에 대한 모든

형태의 차별철폐에 관한 협약"의 제9조 및 제16조 제1항의 (다), (라),

(바), (사)호, 그리고 "시민적 및 정치적 권리에 관한 국제규약"(B규약)

의 제14조 제5항과 제7항, 제22조 및 제23조 제4항이 동 유보조항들입니다.

1505-25(2-1) 일(1)갑
85. 9. 9. 승인　　"내가아낀 종이 한장 늘어나는 나라살림"　　190mm×268mm 인쇄용지 2급 60g/㎡
가 40-41 1990. 5. 28
0034

3. 동 유보조항중 "여성에 대한 모든 형태의 차별철폐에 관한

협약" 제16조 제1항 (다), (라), (바)호 및 "시민적 및 정치적 권리에

관한 국제규약"(B규약) 제23조 제4항의 경우, 91.1.1.부터 개정민법

시행으로 유보의 사유가 해소됨에 따라 개정민법 발효 이후에 적절한

시점에서 유보철회 조치를 취하고자 하는 바, 국무회의 심의 필요여부

등 이에 대한 귀처의 의견을 조속 회보하여 주시기 바랍니다.

첨부: 1. 여성에 대한 모든 형태의 차별철폐에 관한 협약(국·영문)

    2. 시민적 및 정치적 권리에 관한 국제규약(국·영문). 끝.

    3. 법무부 검토 의견서 사본. 끝

0035

1505-25(2-2) 일(1)을   "내가아낀 종이 한장 늘어나는 나라살림"   190㎜×268㎜ 인쇄용지 2급 60g/㎡
85. 9. 9.승인   가 40-41 1990. 5. 28

대 한 민 국
의 무 부

(720 - 4045)

198 90. 12. 18.

법규 20420-

수신 법제처장

제목 인권관계 다자조약 유보철회

　　1. 정부는 84.12.27. "여성에 대한 모든 형태의 차별철폐에
관한 협약"을 비준하였으며, 90.4.10. "시민적 및 정치적 권리에
관한 국제규약"(B규약)에 가입한 바 있습니다.

　　2. 동 인권관계 다자조약의 비준 또는 가입시 정부는 국내법과
충돌되는 일부조항에 대하여 유보를 행하였던 바, "여성에 대한 모든
형태의 차별철폐에 관한 협약"의 제9조 및 제16조 제1항의 (다),
(라), (바), (사)호, 그리고 "시민적 및 정치적 권리에 관한 국제규약"
(B규약)의 제14조 제5항과 제7항, 제22조 및 제23조 제4항이 동
유보조항들입니다.

　　3. 동 유보조항중 "여성에 대한 모든 형태의 차별철폐에 관한
협약" 제16조 제1항 (다), (라), (바)호 및 "시민적 및 정치적 권리에
관한 국제규약"(B규약) 제23조 제4항의 경우, 91.1.1.부터 개정민법
시행으로 유보의 사유가 해소됨에 따라 개정민법 발효 이후에 적절한
시점에서 유보철회 조치를 취하고자 하는 바, 국무회의 심의 필요여부
등 이에 대한 귀처의 의견을 조속 회보하여 주시기 바랍니다.

C036

첨부: 1. 여성에 대한 모든 형태의 차별철폐에 관한 협약(국·영문)

2. 시민적 및 정치적 권리에 관한 국제규약(국·영문)

3. 법무부 검토 의견서 사본. 끝.

외   무   부   장   관

국제기구조약국장

0037

외무부고시를 통한 유보철회 절차 검토

90.12.19.
국제법규과

1. 선례

o 아국의 다자조약에 대한 유보철회의 최초의 선례는 90.9.1.자로 행한
특허협력조약(Patent Cooperation Treaty) 제2장에 대한 유보의 철회임.

o 동 유보철회시 유보조항의 내용과 문안이 국내법에 거의 전적으로
수용되었음을 이유로 외무부장관 재가만으로 외무부고시로서 관보에
게재, 유보를 철회함.

2. 인권관계 다자조약에 대한 유보철회 추진

o "여성에 대한 모든 형태의 차별철폐에 관한 협약" 제16조 제1항
(다), (라), (바)호 및 "시민적 및 정치적 권리에 관한 국제규약"
제23조 제4항에 대한 유보철회 국내절차 관련, 상기 선례에 따라
외무부고시로서 처리하는 방안이 일단 고려됨.

o 그러나 외무부고시 형식을 통한 국내적 유보철회 절차는 아래와
같은 사유로 위법적인 행정행위인 것으로 사료됨.

(가) 유보철회주체

- 유보의 철회는 유보된 조항에 대하여는 새로운 가입이 되며
조약전체로 볼때는 부분적 가입에 해당하는 바, 조약의
체결·비준권이 대통령의 권한(헌법 제73조)임에 비추어
유보철회의 주체는 당연히 대통령이며 명시적 위임이 없는한
외무부장관은 철회의 주체가 될 수 없음.

0038

260   한국 인권문제 민주화 관련 기타 자료 2

(나) 절차

- 유보의 철회는 조약에 대한 부분적 가입으로서 유보가 철회되는 조항은 조약에 대한 부분적 가입안이 된다고 볼 수 있는 바, 헌법 제98조 제3호가 조약안을 법률안 등과 함께 국무회의 심의사항으로 열거하고 있음에 비추어 유보철회는 국무회의 심의사항에 속한다고 할 수 있음. 다만 조약안 심의시 유보철회문제를 동시에 심의하였을 경우에는 차후 유보철회 심의를 생략할 수 있을 것임.

- 따라서 외무부고시로서 국무회의 심의를 거치지 않고 처리된 유보철회는 절차상 위법임.

(다) 공포

- 조약이 효력을 갖기 위하여는 법령 등 공포에 관한 법률에 따라 고시가 아닌 공포의 형식을 취하여야 함. 즉 고시로서는 법률효과가 발생하지 아니함.

- 따라서 국내적으로 고시를 통해 유보철회를 공고할 경우, 당해 유보철회가 대외적으로는 효력을 갖는다고 하더라도, 국내적으로는 철회된 조항의 원용이 불가함.

o 이상과 같은 사유로 상기 2개 인권관계 다자조약에 대한 유보의 철회는 국무회의 심의, 대통령재가, 공포의 절차를 취하기로 함.

0039

3. 향후 유보철회 절차 방안

   가. 정식절차

      ○ 조약안과 같이 국무회의 심의, 대통령재가, 공포의 절차를 밟음.

      ○ 국회동의를 구하는 문제는 유보가 철회되는 조항의 내용이
        헌법 제60조 제1항에 규정된 조약에 속하는지 여부로 결정하여야
        할 것임. 그러나 현실적으로 국내법상 유보사유가 해소되지
        않은 상황에서 유보철회 추진 가능성은 거의 없다는 점에서
        국회동의 필요성도 거의 없을 것으로 봄.

   나. 약식절차

      ○ 조약안 심의과정에서 유보문제를 심의할 시 향후 국내법과
        충돌사유가 해소될 경우 유보를 철회한다는 점을 명시, 유보
        철회시에는 국무회의 심의는 생략하고 대통령재가, 공포의
        절차를 취함.

4. 참고사항

   ○ 이상은 90.12.15.(토) 인권관계 다자조약에 대한 유보철회 조치
     추진과 관련 외무부 고시를 통한 철회방안에 대하여 문제점이
     제기된 후, 90.12.17.(월)-18.(화) 양일간 국제법규과와 조약과가
     논의한 사항임.

0040

다자조약 유보철회 국내절차 검토

90.12.20.
국제법규과

1. 문제의 제기

o 다자조약에 대하여 유보를 철회한 예가 거의 전무하였던 관계로
  유보철회 국내절차에 관한 관행이 확립되지 않고 있음.

2. 인권관계 다자조약에 대한 유보철회 추진

o "여성에 대한 모든 형태의 차별철폐에 관한 협약" 제16조 제1항
  (다), (라), (바)호 및 "시민적 및 정치적 권리에 관한 국제규약"
  제23조 제4항에 대한 유보철회 국내절차를 추진함에 있어서 아래
  사항들이 고려되어야 할 것으로 봄.

(가) 유보철회주체

- 유보의 철회는 유보된 조항에 대하여는 새로운 가입이 되며
  조약전체로 볼때는 부분적 가입에 해당하는 바, 조약의
  체결·비준권이 대통령의 권한(헌법 제73조)임에 비추어
  유보철회의 주체는 대통령이됨.

(나) 절차

- 유보의 철회는 조약에 대한 부분적 가입으로서 유보가 철회
  되는 조항은 조약에 대한 부분적 가입안이 된다고 볼 수
  있는 바, 헌법 제89조 제3호가 조약안을 법률안 등과 함께
  국무회의 심의사항으로 열거하고 있음에 비추어 유보철회는
  국무회의 심의사항에 속한다고 할 수 있음.

0041

다만 조약안 심의시 유보철회문제를 동시에 심의하였을
경우에는 차후 유보철회 심의를 생략할 수 있을 것임.

(다) 공포

- 조약이 효력을 갖기 위하여는 법령 등 공포에 관한 법률에
따라 공포의 형식을 취하여야 함. 따라서 부분적 조약
가입인 유보철회도 법적 효력을 갖기 위하여는 공포되어야 함.

o 이상에 비추어 상기 2개 인권관계 다자조약에 대한 유보의 철회는
국무회의 심의, 대통령재가, 공포의 절차를 취하여야 한다고 봄.

3. 향후 유보철회 절차 방안

가. 정식절차

o 조약안과 같이 국무회의 심의, 대통령재가, 공포의 절차를 밟음.

o 국회동의를 구하는 문제는 유보가 철회되는 조항의 내용이
헌법 제60조 제1항에 규정된 조약에 속하는지 여부로 결정하여야
할 것임. 그러나 현실적으로 국내법상 유보사유가 해소되지
않은 상황에서 유보철회 추진 가능성은 거의 없다는 점에서
국회동의 필요성도 없을 것으로 봄.

나. 약식절차

o 조약안 심의과정에서 유보문제를 심의할 시 향후 국내법과
충돌사유가 해소될 경우 유보를 철회한다는 점을 명시, 유보
철회시에는 국무회의 심의는 생략하고 대통령재가, 공포의
절차를 취함.

0042

외 무 부

1990 년 12 월 21일

인권관계 다자조약 유보철회
==============================

1. 건의 내용
   ○ "여성에 대한 모든 형태의 차별철페에
      관한 협약" 제16조 제1항 (다)、(라)、
      (바)호 및 "시민적 및 정치적 권리에
      관한 국제규약" 제23조 제4항에 대한
      유보철회안 국무회의 상정

2. 유보철회 이유
   ○ 91.1.1.부터 시행되는 개정민법이 상기
      유보조항의 내용을 수용함으로써 유보사유가
      해소

0043

국제법규과 (720-4045)

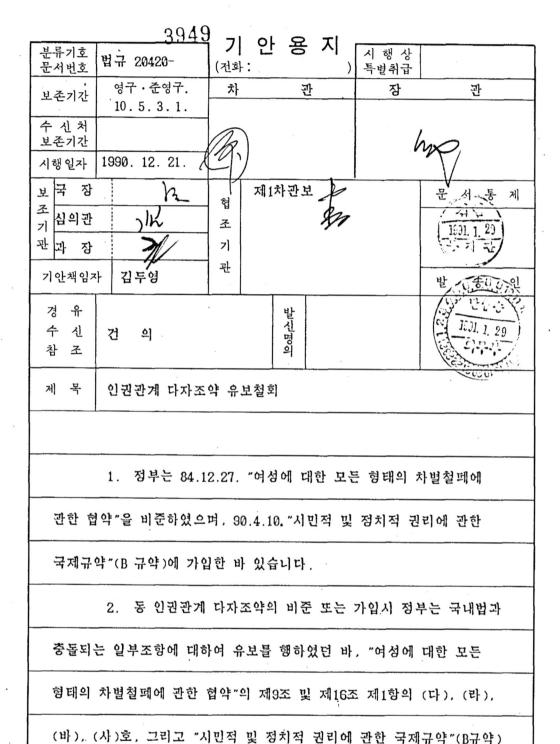

<table>
<tr><td rowspan="7">분류기호
문서번호</td><td>법규 20420-</td><td colspan="2">기 안 용 지
(전화 :   )</td><td>시 행 상
특별취급</td><td></td></tr>
</table>

3949

분류기호 문서번호	법규 20420-	기 안 용 지 (전화 :)		시 행 상 특별취급	
보존기간	영구·준영구. 10. 5. 3. 1.	차 관		장 관	
수 신 처 보존기간					
시행일자	1990. 12. 21.		제1차관보	문 서 통 제	
보 조 기 관	국 장	협 조 기 관			1991. 1. 29
	심의관				
	과 장			발 송 인	
기안책임자	김두영			1991. 1. 29	
경 유 수 신 참 조	건 의	발신명의			
제 목	인권관계 다자조약 유보철회				

    1.　정부는 84.12.27. "여성에 대한 모든 형태의 차별철폐에

관한 협약"을 비준하였으며, 90.4.10. "시민적 및 정치적 권리에 관한

국제규약"(B 규약)에 가입한 바 있습니다.

    2.　동 인권관계 다자조약의 비준 또는 가입시 정부는 국내법과

충돌되는 일부조항에 대하여 유보를 행하였던 바, "여성에 대한 모든

형태의 차별철폐에 관한 협약"의 제9조 및 제16조 제1항의 (다), (라),

(바), (사)호, 그리고 "시민적 및 정치적 권리에 관한 국제규약"(B규약)

의 제14조 제5항과 제7항, 제22조 및 제23조 제4항이 동 유보조항들입니다.

1505-25(2-1) 일(1)갑　　　　　　　　　　　　　　　　　190㎜×268㎜ 인쇄용지 2급 60g/㎡
85. 9. 9. 승인　　"내가아낀 종이 한장 늘어나는 나라살림"　　가 40-41 1990. 5. 28

0044

3. 동 유보조항중 "여성에 대한 모든 형태의 차별철폐에 관한

협약" 제16조 제1항 (다), (라), (바)호 및 "시민적 및 정치적 권리에

관한 국제규약"(B규약) 제23조 제4항의 경우, 91.1.1.부터 개정민법

시행으로 유보사유가 해소됨에 따라 동 개정민법 발효 이후에 아래와

같이 유보철회 조치를 취할 것을 건의하오니 재가하여 주시기 바랍니다.

- 아   래 -

가. 동 유보철회안을 별안과 같이 국무회의에 상정함.

나. 국무회의 심의를 거쳐 대통령 재가를 득한 후 국제연합사무총장에게

   유보철회 의사를 통보함.

첨부: 국무회의 안건(안). 끝.

0045

(별 안)
수신 : 국무회의 의장
참조 : 총무처장관
제목 : 국무회의 상정안건 제출
아래 안건을 국무회의에 상정하고자 하오니 심의하여 주시기
바랍니다.
－ 아 래 －
1. 안건제목 : 가. "여성에 대한 모든 형태의 차별철폐에 관한 협약"
제16조 제1항 (다), (라), (바)호에 대한 유보철회
나. "시민적 및 정치적 권리에 관한 국제규약" 제23조
제4항에 대한 유보철회
2. 유인물 부수 : 각 45부(별첨). 끝.

0046

1505－25(2－2) 일(1)을 "내가 아낀 종이 한장 늘어나는 나라살림"   190mm×268mm 인쇄용지 2급 60g/㎡
85. 9 . 9 . 승인   가 40－41 1990. 5. 28

議案番號	第 號
議 決 年 月 日	19 . . . (第 回)

議 決 事 項

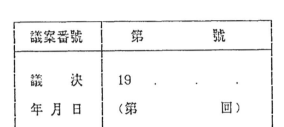

"女性에 대한 모든 形態의 差別撤廢에 관한 協約" 第16條
第1項 (다), (라), (바)號에 대한 留保撤回

提 出 者	國務委員 李 相 玉 (外務部長官)
提出年月日	19 . . .

法 制 處 審 査 畢

0047

1. 의결주문

정부는 1984년 12월 27일 "여성에 대한 모든 형태의 차별철폐에 관한 협약" 비준시에 행한 동 협약 제16조 제1항 (다), (라) 및 (바)호에 대한 유보를 철회함.

2. 제안이유

1991년 1월 1일부터 개정민법 시행으로 유보사유가 해소되어 유보를 철회하고자 함.

3. 주요골자

가. 유보조항의 내용

혼인중 및 혼인해소시의 동등한 권리와 책임, 자녀문제에 관한 동등한 권리와 책임 및 아동의 보호, 후견, 재산관리, 입양에 관한 동등한 권리와 책임을 보장하기 위하여 당사국은 여성에 대한 차별 철폐 조치를 취하여야 함.

나. 유보사유

아국의 민법상 친족의 범위, 친권행사, 이혼후 양육책임, 공동입양, 상속 등과 관련된 조항이 부계혈통주의에 입각, 남성위주로 규정되어 있어 협약비준 당시 동 국내법 관계규정이 유보대상조항과 저촉되었음.

다. 유보철회 사유

91.1.1.부터 시행되는 개정민법에서 혼인중 및 혼인해소시에 남·녀간 차별적 요소가 수정됨에 따라 상기 유보조항의 내용과 아국 법제와의 저촉문제가 해소됨.

4. 주요토의 과제

없음.

0048

5. 참고사항

가. 입법 및 예산조치 : 별도조치 필요없음.

나. 관계부처 합의 : 법무부, 법제처와 합의되었음.

다. 기타

(1) 협약 채택 및 발효경위

1979.12.18. 채택

1981.9.3. 발효

1983.5.25. 아국서명

1984.12.27. 아국비준

1985.1.26. 아국에 대하여 발효

(2) 협약중 유보철회조항 : 제16조 제1항 (다), (라), (바)호

(국 문)

1. 당사국은 혼인과 가족관계에 관한 문제에 있어 여성에 대한 차별을 철폐하기 위한 모든 적절한 조치를 취하여야 하며, 특히 남녀 평등의 기초위에 다음을 보장하여야 한다.

(다) 혼인중 및 혼인을 해소할 때의 동일한 권리와 책임

(라) 부모의 혼인상태를 불문하고 자녀에 관한 문제에 있어 부모로서의 동일한 권리와 책임 ; 모든 경우에 있어서 자녀의 이익이 최우선적으로 고려되어야 함.

(바) 아동에 대한 보호, 후견, 재산관리 및 자녀입양 또는 국내법제상 존재하는 개념중에 유사한 제도와 관련하여 동일한 권리와 책임 ; 모든 경우에 있어서 아동의 이익이 최우선적으로 고려되어야 함.

0049

(영 문)

1. States Parties shall take all appropriate measures to eliminate discrimination against women in all matters relating to marriage and family relations and in particular shall ensure, on a basis of equality of men and women:

(c) The same rights and responsibilities during marriage and at its dissolution;

(d) The same rights and responsibilities as parents, irrespective of their marital status, in matters relating to their children; in all cases the interests of the children shall be paramount;

(f) The same rights and responsibilities with regard to guardianship, wardship, trusteeship and adoption of children, or similar institutions where these concepts exist in national legislation; in all cases the interests of the children shall be paramount;

0050

議案番號	第　　　　號		議
議　　決 年 月 日	19　．　．　． （第　　　回）		決 事 項

"市民的 및 政治的 權利에 관한 國際規約" 第23條 第4項에 대한

留　保　撤　回

提 出 者	國務委員　李 相 玉 （外務部長官）
提出年月日	19　．　．　．

法 制 處 審 査 畢

0051

1. 의결주문

정부는 1990년 4월 10일 "시민적 및 정치적 권리에 관한 국제규약"
가입시에 행한 동 규약 제23조 제4항에 대한 유보를 철회함.

2. 제안이유

1991년 1월 1일부터 개정민법 시행으로 유보사유가 해소되어 유보를
철회하고자함.

3. 주요골자

가. 유보조항의 내용

혼인중 및 혼인해소시 부부의 동등한 권리와 책임을 확보하기 위한
당사국의 적절한 조치의무를 규정함.

나. 유보사유

아국의 민법상 혼인중 및 혼인해소시 부부의 권리 및 책임에 관한
관계규정이 남성중심으로 규정되어 있어, 협약비준당시 동 국내법
관계규정이 유보대상조항과 저촉되었음.

다. 유보철회 사유

91.1.1.부터 시행되는 개정민법에서 혼인중 및 혼인해소시에
남·녀간 차별적 요소가 수정됨에 따라 상기 유보조항의 내용과
아국 법제와의 저촉문제가 해소됨.

4. 주요토의과제
없음.

5. 참고사항

가. 입법 및 예산조치 : 별도조치 필요없음.

나. 관계부처 합의 : 법무부, 법제처와 합의되었음.

다. 기타

    (1) 규약 채택 및 발효 경위

        1966.12.16. 채택

        1976.3.23. 발효

        1990.4.10. 아국 가입

        1990.7.10. 아국에 대하여 발효

    (2) 협약중 유보철회조항 : 제23조 제4항

        (국 문)

        이 규약의 당사국은 혼인기간중 및 혼인해소시에 혼인에 대한

        배우자의 권리 및 책임의 평등을 확보하기 위하여 적절한

        조치를 취한다. 혼인해소의 경우에는 자녀에 대한 필요한

        보호를 위한 조치를 취한다.

        (영 문)

        States Parties to the present Covenant shall take appropriate

        steps to ensure equality of rights and responsibilities

        of spouses as to marriage, during marriage and at its

        dissolution. In the case of dissolution, provision shall

        be made for the necessary protection of any children.

0053

외 무 부

1991 년 1 월 3 일

인권관계 다자조약에 대한 유보철회 관련 전화협의

1. 통화자: 법제처 제1국 조영규사무관

2. 일 시: 91.1.3. 11:30-35

3. 통화요지

   o 유보철회 관련 의견요청에 관해 사안의 성격상
     서면회신은 불요하다는 것이 법제관이나 국장의
     견해임

   o 즉 법제처에 의견을 구하지 않고 외무부가
     독자적으로 판단처리할 수 있는 사안이라고
     봄.

0054

국제법규과 (720-4045)

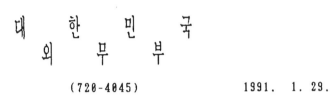

대 한 민 국
외 무 부

(720-4045)   1991. 1. 29.

법규 20420- 3p4p

수신 국무회의의장

참조 총무처장관

제목 국무회의상정 안건 제출

        아래 안건을 국무회의에 상정하고자 하오니 심의하여 주시기
바랍니다.

                    - 아   래 -

    1. 안건의 제목: 가. "여성에 대한 모든 형태의 차별철폐에 관한
                            협약" 제16조 제1항 (다), (라), (바)호에
                            대한 유보철회

                    나. "시민적 및 정치적 권리에 관한 국제규약"
                            제23조 제4항에 대한 유보철회

    2. 유인물 부수: 45부(별첨). 끝.

                    외   무   부   장   관

                                            0055

提 案 説 明 　제1안

"女性에 대한 모든 形態의 差別撤廢에 관한 協約" 第16條 第1項
(다), (라), (바)號와 "市民的 및 政治的 權利에 관한 國際規約"
第23條 第4項에 대한 留保撤回

1991. 2.

國際機構條約局
國際法規課

0056

（議案 第　　　　　號입니다）

　　우리 政府는 1984年 12月 27日 ″女性에 대한 모든 形態의 差別
撤廢에 관한 協約″을 批准하며 행한 留保中 同 協約 第16條 第1項
（다）, （라）및 （바）號에 대한 留保와, 1990年 4月 10日 ″市民的 및
政治的 權利에 관한 國際規約″에 대한 加入時에 행한 留保中 同
規約 第23條 第4項에 대한 留保를 撤回하고자 이 案件을 提出
하였습니다.

　　以上 2個 人權關係 多者條約에 대한 批准 또는 加入時에 우리
政府는 國內法規와 衝突되는 一部條項들에 대하여 關聯部處間의
合議를 거쳐 可能限한 最小限의 範圍內에서 留保를 행한바 있습니다.

　　이번에 留保撤回 對象이된 ″女性에 대한 모든 形態의 差別撤廢에
관한 協約″ 第16條 第1項의 （다）, （라）, （바）號는 婚姻과 家族關係에
있어서 女性에 대한 差別을 없애기 위한 當事國의 適切한 措置義務를
規定한 條項으로서, 婚姻中 및 婚姻解消時, 子女問題, 兒童의 保護,
後見, 財産管理, 入養 等과 關聯하여 夫婦의 同等한 權利와 責任을
確保할 義務를 當事國에게 賦課하고 있습니다.
한편 ″市民的 및 政治的 權利에 관한 國際規約″ 第23條 第4項 역시
婚姻中 및 婚姻解消時에 配偶者의 同等한 權利와 責任 確保에 관하여
當事國이 適切한 措置를 取하도록 規定하고 있습니다.

0057

家族生活關係에서 男女의 平等을 規定한 以上 2個 條項의 內容은
父系血統主義에 立脚, 男性爲主로 規定되어 있던 改正前 우리 民法
親族相續編의 多數條項들과 상충되어 批准 또는 加入時에 留保事由가
된바 있습니다.

그러나 우리 民法上의 男女不平等 條項은 1989年 第147回 定期
國會에서 夫婦의 權利와 責任이 同等해지는 方向으로 改正되었으며,
同 改正民法이 今年 1月 1日부터 施行됨에 따라, 國內法과 衝突에
따른 留保事由가 解消되었습니다.

以上 2個 人權關係 多者條約에 대한 留保撤回와 關聯하여
法務部, 法制處와 合議하였습니다.

審議, 議決하여 주시기 바랍니다.

0058

提 案 說 明

"女性에 대한 모든 形態의 差別撤廢에 관한 協約" 第16條 第1項 (다),
(라), (바)號와 "市民的 및 政治的 權利에 관한 國際規約" 第23條
第4項에 대한 留保撤回

1991. 2.

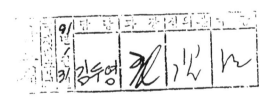

國 際 機 構 條 約 局
國 際 法 規 課

0059

(議案 第 116 號와 第 117 號입니다)

지난 1984年 12月 27日 "女性에 대한 모든 形態의 差別撤廢에 관한 協約" 批准時 우리나라 政府가 행한 留保中 協約 第16條 第1項 (다), (라) 및 (바)號에 대한 留保와, 1990年 4月 10日 "市民的 및 政治的 權利에 관한 國際規約" 加入時 행한 留保中 規約 第23條 第4項에 대한 留保를 撤回하고자 이 案件을 提出하였습니다.

이러한 條項들은 婚姻과 家族關係에서 男女의 平等을 規定하고 있어 男系中心으로 되어있던 從前 우리民法의 關係規定과 抵觸되었습니다.

그러나 우리나라 民法 親族相續編의 男女差別的 要素들이 修正되어 今年 1月 1日부터 施行됨에 따라 國內法과의 抵觸에 따른 留保事由가 解消되었으므로 이를 撤回하고자 합니다.

本件과 關聯하여 法務部, 法制處와 合議하였습니다.

審議, 議決하여 주시기 바랍니다.

0060

提 案 說 明

"大韓民國 政府와 사우디아라비아王國 政府간의
韓國醫療團 活動에 관한 協定" 締結과
"女性差別撤廢에 관한 協約" 및
"市民的 및 政治的 權利에 관한 國際規約" 留保撤回

1991. 2.

國 際 機 構 條 約 局

(議案 第115, 116, 117號입니다.)

　　먼저 議案 第115號에 대하여 말씀드리면,

　　本 議案은 지난 1월 22일 리야드에서 署名된 우리 政府와 사우디
아라비아王國 政府간 "사우디아라비아王國 領域안에서의 韓國醫療團의
活動에 관한 協定"의 正式發效를 위한 國內節次의 完結에 관한 것입니다.

　　이 協定은 國軍醫療支援團의 사우디 派遣이 1월 23일로 豫定됨에 따라
醫療團 地位問題에 대한 사우디 政府와의 協定締結이 時急함을 勘案하여
大統領 裁可를 얻어 事前 署名하게 된 것이며, 동 協定은 協定發效에
必要한 國內節次를 모두 마친후 正式 發效하게 되어 있으므로, 署名후
國務會議에 上程하게 된 점을 諒解하여 주시기 바랍니다.

　　이 協定의 締結目的은 國際聯合의 國際平和努力에 同參하여 우리나라의
國際的 位相을 提高시키고, 韓.美 安保協力關係 및 對아랍국 友好關係를
增進하기 위하여 사우디에 派遣된 우리 醫療團의 活動과 地位에 관한 法的
基盤을 마련하는 데 있습니다.

　　醫療團 地位協定의 主要內容을 말씀드리면,

0062

우리 政府는 사우디 政府의 要請에 따라 醫療團을 사우디에 派遣하며,
醫療團은 사우디 政府의 決定에 따라 撤收하나 우리 政府도 사우디
政府와의 協議를 거쳐 30일전의 事前 通告후 醫療團을 撤收시킬 權利를
갖고 있는 것으로 되어 있습니다.

醫療團員에 대한 指揮權은 우리 醫療團長이 행사하되, 사우디軍
最高司令官의 戰略指針을 尊重하도록 되어 있으며,

醫療團員은 外交使節團의 行政 및 技能職員과 同一한 免除를 享有하고,
모든 關稅와 稅金으로부터 免除되며, 사우디 政府는 醫療團員의 任務遂行중
發生된 사우디側의 人命이나 財産上 損害나 傷害에 대한 報償을 우리 政府에
請求하지 않도록 規定하고 있습니다.

또한 우리 政府와 사우디 政府는 이 協定의 履行을 確保하기 위하여
共同協議委員會를 設置하고, 사우디 政府는 醫療團 活動에 必要한 用役과
物資를 提供하도록 되어 있습니다.

이 協定의 締結에 따르는 別途의 立法措置나 豫算措置는 必要하지
않으나, 醫療團의 派遣에 관하여는 지난 1월 22일 國會의 同意를 얻은 바
있으며, 이 協定에 관하여는 國防部 및 法制處와 合議하였습니다.

0063

다음으로는 議案 第116號와 第117號에 대하여 말씀드리겠습니다.

지난 1984년 12월 27일 "女性에 대한 모든 形態의 差別撤廢에 관한 協約" 批准時 우리나라 政府가 行한 留保中 協約 第16條 第1項 (다), (라) 및 (바)號에 대한 留保와, 1990년 4월 10일 "市民的 및 政治的 權利에 관한 國際規約" 加入時 行한 留保中 規約 第23條 第4項에 대한 留保를 撤回하고자 이 案件을 提出하였습니다.

이러한 條項들은 婚姻과 家族關係에서 男女의 平等을 規定하고 있어 男系中心으로 되어있던 從前 우리民法의 關係規定과 抵觸되었습니다.

그러나 우리나라 民法 親族相續編의 男女差別的 要素들이 修正되어 今年 1월 1일부터 施行됨에 따라 國內法과의 抵觸에 따른 留保事由가 解消되었으므로 이를 撤回하고자 합니다.

本件과 關聯하여 法務部, 法制處와 合議하였습니다.

以上 3개 案件을 審議, 議決하여 주시기 바랍니다.

0064

"女性에 대한 모든 形態의 差別撤廢에 관한 協約" 第16條

第1項 (다), (라), (바)號와 "市民的 및 政治的 權利에

관한 國際規約" 第23條 第4項에 대한 留保撤回 檢討

1991. 2.

國 際 機 構 條 約 局

國 際 法 規 課

Ⅰ. 撤回對象條項

o 女性에 대한 모든 形態의 差別撤廢에 관한 協約
  - 第16條 第1項 (다), (라), (바)號

o 市民的 및 政治的 權利에 관한 國際規約
  - 第23條 第4項

Ⅱ. 撤回對象 條項의 內容 및 留保事由

1. 內容

가. 女性에 대한 모든 形態의 差別撤廢 協約
   第16條 第1項 (다), (라), (바)號

   o 婚姻과 家族關係에 있어서 差別을 撤廢하기 위하여
     當事國에게 適切한 措置義務 賦課
     (다)號: 婚姻中 및 婚姻解消時의 同等한 權利와
             責任
     (라)號: 子女問題에 있어서 父母로서 同等한
             權利와 責任
     (바)號: 兒童의 保護, 後見, 財産管理, 入養等과
             關聯하여 同等한 權利와 責任

나. 市民的 및 政治的 權利에 관한 國際規約 第23條 第4項
   o 婚姻中 및 婚姻解消時 同等한 權利와 責任

- 1 -

0066

2. 留保事由

    ○ <u>父系血統主義에 立脚, 男性爲主로 規定되어 있던 改正前 我國 民法上의 家族法制와 衝突</u>

    ○ <u>衝突되는 主要 關聯 國內民法 規定(改正前)</u>
        - 夫中心의 家族生活關係
            · 同居場所는 夫의 住所 또는 居所(第826條 第2項)
            · 夫婦共同入養時 夫의 一方的 決定權(第874條 第2項)
            · 生活費 夫 負擔(第833條)
        - 子女에 대한 父權利 中心
            · 父母 意見不一致時 父의 親權行使(第909條 第1項)
            · 離婚後 夫의 子에 대한 養育責任(第837條 第1項)
        - 父系中心의 親族範圍
            · 8寸以內 父系血族 4寸以內 母系血族(第777條)

Ⅲ. 留保撤回 事由

    ○ <u>91.1.1.부터 施行되는 改正民法이 上記 留保條項의 內容을 受容, 衝突 事由를 解消</u>

    ○ <u>改正民法 主要內容</u>
        - 夫婦共同의 家族生活 關係
            · 同居場所 夫婦協議(第826條 第2項), 夫婦共同入養時 協議(第874條 第2項), 生活費 共同負擔(第833條), 離婚時 財産分割 請求權(第839條의 2. 新設)

- 2 -

0067

- 子女에 대한 父母의 同等한 權利
  · 共同親權行使(第909條 第2項), 離婚後 養育協議
    (第837條 第1項), 離婚後 面接交涉權(第837條의
    2, 新設)
- 同一한 親族範圍
  · 8寸以內 血族 및 4寸以內 姻戚(第777條)

Ⅳ. 留保가 繼續되는 條項(未撤回)

1. 女性에 대한 모든 形態의 差別撤廢에 관한 協約:
   第9條 및 第16條 第1項 (사)號

(國 文)

第9條(國籍關係)

1. 當事國은 女性이 國籍을 取得, 變更 또는 保有함에
   있어 男性과 同等한 權利를 賦與하여야 한다.
   當事國은 특히 外國人과의 結婚 또는 婚姻中 夫에
   의한 國籍의 變更으로 妻의 國籍이 自動的으로
   變更되거나, 妻가 無國籍으로 되거나 또는 夫의 國籍이
   妻에게 强制되지 아니하도록 確保하여야 한다.

2. 當事國은 子女의 國籍에 관하여 男性과 同等한 權利를
   女性에게 賦與하여야 한다.

第16條 第1項 (사)號(家族의 姓)

(사) 家族姓 및 職業을 選擇할 權利를 包含하여 夫婦
    보서의 同一한 個人的 權利

- 3 -

0068

(英 文)

Convention on the Elimination of All Forms of Discrimination against Women

Article 9

1. States Parties shall grant women equal rights with men to acquire, change or retain their nationality. They shall ensure in particular that neither marriage to an alien nor change of nationality by the husband during marriage shall automatically change the nationality of the wife, render her stateless or force upon her the nationality of the husband.

2. States Parties shall grant women equal rights with men with respect to the nationality of their children.

Alticle 16. Paragraph 1

(g) The same personal rights as husband and wife, including the right to choose a family name, a profession and an occupation;

2. 市民的 및 政治的 權利에 관한 國際規約

第14條 第5項 및 第7項, 第22條

（國 文）

第14條 第5項, 第7項（上訴權保障, 二重處罰禁止）

5. 有罪判決을 받은 모든 사람은 法律에 따라 그 判決 및
宣告에 대하여 上級 法院에서 再審을 받을 權利를 가진다.

7. 어느 누구도 各國의 法律 및 刑事節次에 따라 이미
確定的으로 有罪 또는 無罪宣告를 받은 行爲에 관하여서는
다시 裁判 또는 處罰을 받지 아니한다.

第22條（結社의 自由）

1. 모든 사람은 자기의 利益을 保護하기 위하여 勞動組合을
結成하고 이에 加入하는 權利를 包含하여 다른 사람과의
結社의 自由에 대한 權利를 갖는다

2. 이 權利의 行使에 대하여는 法律에 의하여 規定되고,
國家安保, 公共의 安全, 公共秩序, 公衆保健 또는 道德의
보호 또는 他人의 權利 및 自由의 保護를 위하여
民主社會에서 必要한 것이외의 어떠한 制限도 과하여
져서는 아니된다. 이 條는 軍隊와 警察의 構成員이
이 權利를 行使하는 데 대하여 合法的인 制限을 賦課하는
것을 防害하지 아니한다.

- 5 -

0070

3. 이 條의 어떠한 規定도 結社의 自由 및 團結權의 保護에
   관한 1948年의 國際勞動機構協約의 當事國이 同 協約에
   規定하는 保障을 沮害하려는 立法措置를 取하도록 하거나
   또는 이를 沮害하려는 方法으로 法律을 適用할 것을 許容
   하는 것은 아니다.

(英 文)

International Covenant on Civil and Political Rights

Article 14

5. Everyone convicted of a crime shall have the right
   to his conviction and sentence being reviewed by a
   higher tribunal according to law.

7. No one shall be liable to be tried or punished
   again for an offence for which he has already been
   finally convicted or acquitted in accordance with
   the law and penal procedure of each country.

Article 22

1. Everyone shall have the right to freedom of
   association with others, including the right to
   form and join trade unions for the protection of
   his interests.

- 6 -

0071

2. No restrictions may be placed on the exercise of this right other than those which are prescribed by law and which are necessary in a democratic society in the interests of national security or public safety, public order(ordre public), the protection of public health or morals or the protection of the rights and freedoms of others. This article shall not prevent the imposition of lawful restrictions on members of the armed forces and of the police in their exercise of this right.

3. Nothing in this article shall authorize States Parties to the International Labour Organisation Convention of 1948 concerning Freedom of Association and Protection of the Right to Organize to take legislative measures which would prejudice, or to apply the law in such a manner as to prejudice, the guarantees provided for in that Convention.

```
┌─────────────────────────────────┐
│  人權關係 多者條約 留保撤回 關聯   │
│                                  │
│  豫想質疑·答辯 및 參考資料         │
└─────────────────────────────────┘
```

1991. 2.

國 際 機 構 條 約 局

國 際 法 規 課

0073

目　　　　次

1. 留保가 撤回될 條項의 內容과 撤回 事由

ㅇ 이번에 留保를 撤回하게될 "女性에 대한 모든 形態의 差別撤廢에 관한
   協約" 第16條 第1項의 (다), (라), (바)號는 婚姻과 家族關係에 있어서
   女性에 대한 差別을 撤廢하기 위한 當事國의 適切한 措置義務를 規定한
   條項으로서 婚姻中 및 婚姻解消時의 夫婦의 同等한 權利 및 責任과 子女
   問題, 兒童의 保護, 後見, 財産管理, 入養 等과 關聯하여 夫婦의 同等한
   權利와 責任을 確保할 義務를 當事國에게 賦課하고 있습니다.

ㅇ 한편 "市民的 및 政治的 權利에 관한 國際規約" 第23條 第4項 역시
   婚姻中 및 婚姻解消時에 配偶者의 同等한 權利와 責任 確保를 위해
   當事國이 適切한 措置를 取하도록 規定하고 있습니다.

ㅇ 以上의 條項들은 男系中心으로 되어 있던 改正前 우리民法 親族相續編의
   規定들과 抵觸되어 留保를 하였으나, 男女差別的 要素를 修正한 改正民法이
   91.1.1부터 施行됨에 따라, 留保事由가 解消되어 撤回하게 된것입니다.

0075

- 1 -

留保撤回 條項 條文

○ 女性에 대한 모든 形態의 差別撤廢에 관한 協約

第16條 第1項 (다), (라), (바)號

1. 當事國은 婚姻과 家族關係에 관한 모든 問題에 있어 女性에 대한 差別을 撤廢하기 위한 모든 適切한 措置를 취하여야 하며, 특히 男女平等의 基礎위에 다음을 保障하여야 한다.

(다) 婚姻中 및 婚姻解消時의 同一한 權利와 責任

(라) 父母의 婚姻狀態를 不問하고 子女에 관한 問題에 있어 父母로서의 同一한 權利와 責任; 모든 경우에 있어서 子女의 利益이 最優先的으로 考慮되어야 함.

(바) 兒童에 대한 保護, 後見, 財産管理 및 子女入養 또는 國內法制上 存在하는 槪念중에서 類似한 制度와 관련하여 同一한 權利와 責任; 모든 경우에 있어서 兒童의 利益이 最優先的으로 考慮되어야 함.

○ 市民的 및 政治的 權利에 관한 國際規約

第23條 第4項

4. 이 規約의 當事國은 婚姻期間中 및 婚姻解消時에 婚姻에 대한 配偶者의 權利 및 責任을 確保하기 위하여 適切한 措置를 취한다. 婚姻解消의 경우에는 子女에 대한 必要한 保護를 위한 措置를 취한다.

- 2 -

0076

2. 今番 留保撤回 以後에도 繼續 留保하는 條項과 그 事由는?

o "女性에 대한 모든 形態의 差別撤廢에 관한 協約"의 第9條 및 第16條 第1項의 (사)號와 "市民的 및 政治的 權利에 관한 國際規約" 第14條 第5項 및 第7項과 第22條에 대한 留保는 繼續됩니다.

o 이 條項들은 女性差別撤廢協約上 國籍의 取得과 變更 그리고 家族姓의 選擇에 관한 男女間의 同等한 權利를 規定한 것이며, 人權規約上 上訴權保障, 二重處罰禁止, 結社의 自由에 관한 規定들로서 우리 政府는 國內法規와의 抵觸을 理由로 同 條項들을 留保한 바 있습니다.

o 우리 政府가 批准 또는 加入할 當時에 留保의 事由가 되었던 國內關係法規들이 現在도 그대로 維持되고 있으므로, 그러한 條項들에 대한 留保는 繼續하여야 할 것입니다.

- 3 -

0077

留保繼續 條項 條文

○ 女性에 대한 모든 形態의 差別撤廢에 관한 協約

第9條(國籍關係)

1. 當事國은 女性이 國籍을 取得, 變更 또는 保有함에 있어 男性과 同等한 權利를 賦與하여야 한다. 當事國은 특히 外國人과의 結婚 또는 婚姻中 夫에 의한 國籍의 變更으로 妻의 國籍이 自動的으로 變更되거나, 妻가 無國籍으로 되거나 또는 夫의 國籍이 妻에게 强制되지 아니하도록 確保하여야 한다.

2. 當事國은 子女의 國籍에 관하여 男性과 同等한 權利를 女性에게 賦與하여야 한다.

第16條 第1項 (사)號(家族의 姓)

(사) 家族姓 및 職業을 選擇할 權利를 包含하여 夫婦로서의 同一한 個人的 權利

○ 市民的 및 政治的 權利에 관한 國際規約

第14條 第5項(上訴權保障) 및 第7項(二重處罰禁止)

5. 有罪判決을 받은 모든 사람은 法律에 따라 그 判決 및 宣告에 대하여 上級 法院에서 再審을 받을 權利를 가진다.

7. 어느 누구도 各國의 法律 및 刑事節次에 따라 이미 確定的으로 有罪 또는 無罪宣告를 받은 行爲에 관하여서는 다시 裁判 또는 處罰을 받지 아니한다.

- 4 -

第22條(結社의 自由)

1. 모든 사람은 자기의 利益을 保護하기 위하여 勞動組合을 結成하고 이에 加入하는 權利를 包含하여 다른 사람과의 結社의 自由에 대한 權利를 갖는다.

2. 이 權利의 行使에 대하여는 法律에 의하여 規定되고, 國家安保, 公共의 安全, 公共秩序, 公衆保健 또는 道德의 보호 또는 他人의 權利 및 自由의 保護를 위하여 民主社會에서 必要한 것이외의 어떠한 制限도 과하여져서는 아니된다. 이 條는 軍隊와 警察의 構成員이 이 權利를 行使하는 데 대하여 合法的인 制限을 賦課하는 것을 防害하지 아니한다.

3. 이 條의 어떠한 規定도 結社의 自由 및 團結權의 保護에 관한 1948年의 國際勞動機構協約의 當事國이 同 協約에 規定하는 保障을 沮害하려는 立法措置를 取하도록 하거나 또는 이를 沮害하려는 方法으로 法律을 適用한 것을 許容하는 것은 아니다.

- 5 -

3. 留保撤回의 効力

ㅇ 多者條約에 대하여 留保를 撤回하게 되면, 留保가 撤回되는 條項은
留保撤回國에 대하여 當然히 効力을 가지게 되며, 同時에 當該條約의
他當事國들과의 關係에도 適用되게 되어 對外的인 効力을 가지게 됩니다.

ㅇ 通常 多者條約에의 留保는 國內法規와의 抵觸으로 인하여 行하게 되는
것임을 감안 할 때, 抵觸事由가 解消되는 時點과 동시에 撤回도 이루어지는
것이 理想的이라고 할 수는 있으나, 國內法의 發効 以後 適切한 時點에
法律關係를 調整하는 것이 現實的이라고 사료됩니다.

ㅇ 今番에 留保를 撤回하게되는 規定들의 경우, 그 內容이 家族生活에 관한
것으로 國內的 施行에 關聯된 것들인 바, 國民들의 實生活에서는 91.1.1.
부터 改正民法이 適用됨으로써 協約當該 條項 留保의 未撤回로 인하여
어떠한 不利益도 받지 아니하며, 또한 對外關係에 있어서도 協約內容의
不履行 問題는 發生하지 않습니다.

4. 留保撤回 案件의 國務會議 上程 理由

ㅇ 留保의 撤回는 留保가 撤回되는 條項에 대한 새로운 加入行爲로서 條約 全體로 볼때는 部分的인 加入에 該當합니다.

ㅇ 이러한 意味에서 留保撤回案은 當該條約에 대한 部分的 加入案이 된다고 볼 수 있으며, 우리憲法 第89條 第3號가 條約案을 法律案 等과 함께 國務會議 審議事項으로 規定하고 있음에 비추어, 部分的 條約加入案인 留保撤回案은 國務會議의 審議事項에 속하는 것입니다.

1. 撤回對象條項

ㅇ 女性에 대한 모든 形態의 差別撤廢에 관한 協約
  - 第16條 第1項 (다), (라), (바)號

ㅇ 市民的 및 政治的 權利에 관한 國際規約
  - 第23條 第4項

2. 撤回對象 條項의 內容 및 留保事由

가. 內容

  (1) 女性에 대한 모든 形態의 差別撤廢 協約
      第16條 第1項 (다), (라), (바)號

  ㅇ 婚姻과 家族關係에 있어서 差別을 撤廢하기 위하여
     當事國에게 適切한 措置義務 賦課
     (다)號: 婚姻中 및 婚姻解消時의 同等한 權利와
            責任
     (라)號: 子女問題에 있어서 父母로서 同等한
            權利와 責任

- 8 -

0082

(비)號: 兒童의 保護, 後見, 財産管理, 入養等과
關聯하여 同等한 權利와 責任

나. 市民的 및 政治的 權利에 관한 國際規約 第23條 第4項
  ○ 婚姻中 및 婚姻解消時 同等한 權利와 責任

나. 留保事由

  ○ 父系血統主義에 立脚, 男性爲主로 規定되어 있던 改正前
    我國 民法上의 家族法制와 衝突

  ○ 衝突되는 主要 關聯 國內民法 規定(改正前)
    - 夫中心의 家族生活關係
      · 同居場所는 夫의 住所 또는 居所(第826條 第2項)
      · 夫婦共同入養時 夫의 一方的 決定權(第874條 第2項)
      · 生活費 夫 負擔(第833條)
    - 子女에 대한 父權利 中心
      · 父母 意見不一致時 父의 親權行使(第909條 第1項)
      · 離婚後 夫의 子에 대한 養育責任(第837條 第1項)
    - 父系中心의 親族範圍
      · 8寸以內 父系血族 4寸以內 母系血族(第777條)

3. 留保撤回 事由

  ○ 91.1.1.부터 施行되는 改正民法이 上記 留保條項의 內容을
    受容, 衝突 事由를 解消

- 9 -

0083

○ 改正民法 主要内容

　　- 夫婦共同의 家族生活 關係

　　　・ 同居場所 夫婦協議(第826條 第2項), 夫婦共同入養時
　　　　協議(第874條 第2項), 生活費 共同負擔(第833條),
　　　　離婚時 財産分割 請求權(第833條의 2. 新設)

　　- 子女에 대한 父母의 同等한 權利

　　　・ 共同親權行使(第909條 第2項), 離婚後 養育協議
　　　　(第837條 第1項), 離婚後 面接交涉權(第837條의
　　　　2. 新設)

　　- 同一한 親族範圍

　　　・ 8寸以內 血族 및 4寸以內 姻戚(第777條)

4. 留保가 繼續되는 條項(未撤回)

가. 女性에 대한 모든 形態의 差別撤廢에 관한 協約:
　　第9條 및 第16條 第1項 (사)號

(國 文)

第9條(國籍關係)

1. 當事國은 女性이 國籍을 取得. 變更 또는 保有함에
　　있어 男性과 同等한 權利를 賦與하여야 한다.
　　當事國은 특히 外國人과의 結婚 또는 婚姻中 夫에
　　의한 國籍의 變更으로 妻의 國籍이 自動的으로
　　變更되거나. 妻가 無國籍으로 되거나 또는 夫의 國籍이
　　妻에게 强制되지 아니하도록 確保하여야 한다.

- 10 -

0084

2. 當事國은 子女의 國籍에 관하여 男性과 同等한 權利를
   女性에게 賦與하여야 한다.

第16條 第1項 (사)號(家族의 姓)

(사) 家族姓 및 職業을 選擇할 權利를 包含하여 夫婦
    로서의 同一한 個人的 權利

(英 文)

Convention on the Elimination of All Forms of Discrimination
against Women

Article 9

1. States Parties shall grant women equal rights with
   men to acquire, change or retain their nationality.
   They shall ensure in particular that neither marriage
   to an alien nor change of nationality by the husband
   during marriage shall automatically change the
   nationality of the wife, render her stateless or
   force upon her the nationality of the husband.

2. States Parties shall grant women equal rights with men
   with respect to the nationality of their children.

- 11 -

0085

Alticle 16. Paragraph 1

(g) The same personal rights as husband and wife,
    including the right to choose a family name, a
    profession and an occupation;

나. 市民的 및 政治的 權利에 관한 國際規約:
第14條 第5項 및 第7項, 第22條

(國 文)

第14條 第5項, 第7項(上訴權保障, 二重處罰禁止)

5. 有罪判決을 받은 모든 사람은 法律에 따라 그 判決 및
   宣告에 대하여 上級 法院에서 再審을 받을 權利를 가진다.

7. 어느 누구도 各國의 法律 및 刑事節次에 따라 이미
   確定的으로 有罪 또는 無罪宣告를 받은 行爲에 관하여서는
   다시 裁判 또는 處罰을 받지 아니한다.

第22條(結社의 自由)

1. 모든 사람은 자기의 利益을 保護하기 위하여 勞動組合을
   結成하고 이에 加入하는 權利를 包含하여 다른 사람과의
   結社의 自由에 대한 權利를 갖는다

2. 이 權利의 行使에 대하여는 法律에 의하여 規定되고,
   國家安保, 公共의 安全, 公共秩序, 公衆保健 또는 道德의
   보호 또는 他人의 權利 및 自由의 保護를 위하여

- 12 -

0086

民主社會에서 必要한 것이외의 어떠한 制限도 과하여
져서는 아니된다. 이 條는 軍隊와 警察의 構成員이
이 權利를 行使하는 데 대하여 合法的인 制限을 賦課하는
것을 防害하지 아니한다.

3. 이 條의 어떠한 規定도 結社의 自由 및 團結權의 保護에
   관한 1948年의 國際勞動機構協約의 當事國이 同 協約에
   規定하는 保障을 沮害하려는 立法措置를 取하도록 하거나
   또는 이를 沮害하려는 方法으로 法律을 適用할 것을 許容
   하는 것은 아니다.

(英 文)

International Covenant on Civil and Political Rights

Article 14

5. Everyone convicted of a crime shall have the right
   to his conviction and sentence being reviewed by a
   higher tribunal according to law.

7. No one shall be liable to be tried or punished
   again for an offence for which he has already been
   finally convicted or acquitted in accordance with
   the law and penal procedure of each country.

13

0087

Article 22

1. Everyone shall have the right to freedom of
   association with others, including the right to
   form and join trade unions for the protection of
   his interests.

2. No restrictions may be placed on the exercise of
   this right other than those which are prescribed
   by law and which are necessary in a democratic
   society in the interests of national security or
   public safety, public order(ordre public), the
   protection of public health or morals or the
   protection of the rights and freedoms of others.
   This article shall not prevent the imposition of
   lawful restrictions on members of the armed forces
   and of the police in their exercise of this right.

3. Nothing in this article shall authorize States
   Parties to the International Labour Organisation
   Convention of 1948 concerning Freedom of Association
   and Protection of the Right to Organize to take
   legislative measures which would prejudice, or to
   apply the law in such a manner as to prejudice,
   the guarantees provided for in that Convention.

-- 14 --

0088

5. 留保撤回와 關聯된 民法 新·舊 條文對比表

從　　前	現　　行
第777條(親族의 範圍) 親族關係로 인한 法律上 效力은 本法 또는 다른 法律에 特別한 規定이 없는 한 다음 各號에 該當하는 者에 미친다. 1. 8寸以内의 父系血族 2. 4寸以内의 母系血族 3. 夫의 8寸以内의 父系血族 4. 夫의 4寸以内의 母系血族 5. 妻의 父母 6. 配偶者	第777條(親族의 範圍) 親族關係로 인한 法律上 效力은 本法 또는 다른 法律에 特別한 規定이 없는 한 다음 各號에 該當하는 者에 미친다. 1. 8寸이내의 血族 2. 4寸이내의 姻戚 3. 配偶者
第826條(夫婦間의 義務) ② 夫婦의 同居는 夫의 住所나 居所에서 한다. 그러나, 第3項 但書의 경우에는 妻의 住所나 居所에서 한다.	第826條(夫婦間의 義務) ② 夫婦의 同居場所는 夫婦의 協議에 따라 定한다. 그러나 協議가 이루어지지 아니하는 경우에는 當事者의 請求에 의하여 家庭法院이 이를 定한다.
第833條(生活費用) 夫婦의 共同生活에 必要한 費用의 負擔은 當事者間에 特別한 約定이 없으면 夫가 이를 負擔한다.	第833條(生活費用) 夫婦의 共同生活에 必要한 費用은 當事者間에 特別한 約定이 없으면 夫婦가 共同으로 負擔한다.
第837條(離婚과 子의 養育責任) ① 當事者間에 그 子의 養育에 관한 事項은 協定하지 아니한 때에는 그 養育의 責任은 父에게 있다.	第837條(離婚과 子의 養育責任) ① 當事者는 그 子의 養育에 관한 事項을 協議에 의하여 定한다.

- 15 -

0089

인권관계 다자조약 유보철회, 1990-91 311

從　　　前	現　　　行
〈新設〉	第837條의 2(面接交渉權)　①子를 직접 養育하지 아니하는 父母中 一方은 面接交渉權을 가진다.
〈新設〉	第839條의 2(財產分割請求權) ① 協議上 離婚한 者의 一方은 다른 一方에 대하여 財產分割을 請求할 수 있다.
第874條(夫婦의 共同入養) ② 妻의 不在 기타 事由로 인하여 共同으로 할 수 없는 때에는 夫 一方이 夫婦雙方의 名義로 養子를 할 수 있고 養子가 될 수 있다.	第874條(夫婦의 共同入養) ② 配偶者 있는 者가 養子가 될 때에는 다른 一方의 同意를 얻어야 한다.
第909條(親權者)　① 未成年者인 子에 대한 親權은 父母가 共同으로 行使한다. 다만, 父母의 意見이 一致하지 아니하는 境遇에는 父가 行使한다.	第909條(親權者) ② 親權은 父母가 婚姻중인 때는 父母가 共同으로 이를 행사한다. 그러나 父母의 의견이 一致하지 아니하는 경우에는 當事者의 請求에 依하여 家庭法院이 이를 定한다.

외 무 부

1991년 2월 11일

인권관계 다자조약에 대한 유보철회

1. 건의내용

　o 종전 민법규정과 저촉되어 비준 및 가입시 유보한
　　아래 협약 관계 조항들에 대하여 국내민법이 개정
　　되어 유보사유가 해소되었으므로 동유보를 철회함.

　　- "여성에 대한 모든 형태의 차별 철폐에 관한
　　　협약" 제16조 제1항 (다)、(라)、(바)호
　　　(5개 유보조항중 3개 철회)
　　- "시민적 및 정치적 권리에 관한 국제규약"
　　　제23조 제4항
　　　(4개 유보조항중 1개 철회)

2. 유보철회 방식

　o 외무부 장관 명의의 유보철회 공한을 국제연합
　　사무총장에게 전달하고、이를 관보에 공포함.

국제법규과 (720-4045)　　0091

분류기호 문서번호	법규 20420-	기 안 용 지 (전화 :)		시 행 상 특별취급	
보존기간	영구·준영구. 10. 5. 3. 1.	차 관		장 관	
수 신 처 보존기간					
시행일자	1991. 2. 12.		제1차관보	문 서 통 제	
보 조 기 관	국 장	협 조 기 관			
	심의관				
	과 장				
기안책임자	김두영			발 송 인	
경 유 수 신 참 조	내부결재	발 신 명 의			

제 목   인권관계 다자조약에 대한 유보철회

"여성에 대한 모든 형태의 차별철폐에 관한 협약" 제16조 제1항

(다),(라),(바)호와 "시민적 및 정치적 권리에 관한 국제규약" 제23조

제4항에 대한 대한민국 정부의 유보를 철회하기 위하여 아래와 같은

조치를 취할 것을 건의하오니 재가하여 주시기 바랍니다. 상기 유보

철회에 관하여는 1991년 2월 7일 제7회 국무회의의 심의를 거친 바

있습니다.

- 아   래 -

　1. 별첩1과 같이 외무부장관 명의의 유보철회 공한을

국제연합사무총장에게 송부함.   0092

2. 유보철회 사실을 별첩 2와 같이 공포함.

첨부: 1. 유보철회 공한 각1부.

2. 유보철회 공포안 각1부.

3. 국무회의 의결안 각1부. 끝.

0093

1991년 2월   일

귀하,

　　본인은 1979년 12월 18일 채택된 "여성에 대한 모든 형태의
차별철폐에 관한 협약"에 대한 대한민국정부의 비준서에 포함되어
있는 제16조 제1항의 (다), (라), (바)호에 대한 유보를 1991년
　월　　일자로 철회함을 귀하에게 통보하는 영광을 가집니다.

　　귀하에게 본인 최고의 경의를 표하는 바입니다.

　　　　　　　　　　　　　　　　　　　　　외무부장관
　　　　　　　　　　　　　　　　　　　　　이 상 옥

국제연합
사무총장
하비에르 페레스 데 꾸에야르

0094

(Draft)

February 1991

Excellency,

I have the honour to notify you that the Government of the Republic of Korea withdraws as of   1991 the reservations contained in its instrument of ratification to sub-paragraphs (c), (d) and (f) of paragraph 1 of Article 16 of the Convention on the Elimination of All Forms of Discrimination against Women adopted on 18 December 1979.

Accept, Excellency, the assurances of my highest consideration.

LEE Sang-Ock
Minister

His Excellency
  Mr. Javier Perez de Cuellar
    Secretary-General
      United Nations
        New York.

0095

1991년 2월   일

귀하,

　　본인은 1966년 12월 16일 채택된 "시민적 및 정치적 권리에 관한
국제규약"에 대한 대한민국정부의 가입서에 포함된 제23조 제4항에
대한 유보를 1991년   월   일자로 철회함을 귀하에게 통보하는
영광을 가집니다.

　　귀하에게 본인 최고의 경의를 표하는 바입니다.

외무부장관
이 상 옥

국제연합
사무총장
하비에르 뻬레스 데 꾸에야르

0096

(Draft)

February 1991

Excellency,

I have the honour to notify you that the Government of the
Republic of Korea withdraws as of   1991 the reservation
contained in its instrument of accession to paragraph 4 of Article
23 of the International Covenant on Civil and Political Rights
adopted on 16 December 1966.

Accept, Excellency, the assurances of my highest consideration.

LEE Sang-Ock
Minister

His Excellency
  Mr. Javier Perez de Cuellar
    Secretary-General
    United Nations
    New York.

0097

공   포   안

　　정부가 1984년 12월 27일 "여성에 대한 모든 형태의 차별
철폐에 관한 협약" 비준시 행한 유보내용중 동 협약 제16조 제1항
(다),(라),(바)호에 대한 유보의 철회에 관하여 1991년 2월 7일
제7회 국무회의의 심의를 거치고 1991년　월　일 국제연합사무
총장에게 통고함으로써 동 유보가 1991년 3 월 /5 일자로 철회됨을
이에 공포한다.

　　　　대　　통　　령　　노　　　태　　　우

1991년　월 일

　　　　국　무　총　리　　　　　노　　　재　　　봉

　　　　국　무　위　원　　　　　　이　　　상　　　옥
　　　　　(외무부장관)

조약 제 /04/ 호
"여성에 대한 모든 형태의 차별철폐에 관한 협약"
제16조 제1항 (다),(라),(바)호
(이하 본문 별첨)

0098

공 포 안

　　정부가 1990년 4월 10일 "시민적 및 정치적 권리에 관한
국제규약"에 가입시 행한 유보내용중 제23조 제4항에 대한 유보의
철회에 관하여 1991년 2월 7일 제7회 국무회의의 심의를 거치고
1991년　월　일 국제연합사무총장에게 통고함으로써 동 유보가
1991년 3 월 15일자로 철회됨을 이에 공포한다.

　　　　대　　통　　령　　　노　　태　　우

1991년　월　일

　　　　국　무　총　리　　　　　노　　재　　봉

　　　　국　무　위　원　　　　　　이　상　옥
　　　　　（외무부장관）

조약 제 1042 호
"시민적 및 정치적 권리에 관한 협약" 제23조 제4항
（이하 본문 별첨）

0099

45

議案番號	第 116 號
議 決 年 月 日	1991. 2. 7. (第 7 回)

議決事項

" 女性에 대한 모든 形態의 差別撤廢에
관한 協約 "第16條 第1項 (다), (라),
(바)號에 대한 留保撤回

提 出 者	國務委員 李 相 玉 (外 務 部 長 官)
提出年月日	1991. . .

法 制 處 審 査 畢

0100

1. 議決主文

政府는 1984年 12月 27日 "女性에 대한 모든 形態의 差別撤廢에 관한 協約" 批准時에 행한 同 協約 第16條 第1項 (다), (라) 및 (바) 號에 대한 留保를 撤回함.

2. 提案理由

1991年 1月 1日부터 改正民法 施行으로 留保事由가 解消되어 留保를 撤回하고자 함.

3. 主要骨子

가. 留保條項의 內容

婚姻中 및 婚姻解消時의 同等한 權利와 責任, 子女問題에 관한 同等한 權利와 責任 및 兒童의 保護, 後見, 財産管理, 入養에 관한 同等한 權利와 責任을 保障하기 위하여 當事國은 女性에 대한 差別撤廢 措置를 취하여야 함.

나. 留保事由

我國의 民法上 親族의 範圍, 親權行使, 離婚後

- 1 -

0101

養育責任, 共同入養, 相續 등과 關聯된 條項이
父系血統主義에 立脚, 男性爲主로 規定되어 있어
協約批准 當時 同 國內法 關係規定이 留保對象
條項과 抵觸되었음.

다. 留保撤回 事由

1991年1月1日부터 施行되는 改正民法에서 婚姻中
및 婚姻解消時에 男·女間 差別的 要素가 修正됨
에 따라 上記 留保條項의 內容과 我國 法制와의
抵觸問題가 解消됨.

4. 主要 討議課題

없 음.

5. 參考事項

가. 立法 및 豫算措置 : 別途措置 必要없음.

나. 關係部處 合議 : 法務部, 法制處와 合議되었음.

다. 其 他
 (1) 協約 採擇 및 發效 經緯
   1979.12.18. 採擇
   1981. 9. 3. 發效

0102

1983. 5.25. 我國署名

1984.12.27. 我國批准

1985. 1.26. 我國에 대하여 發效

(2) 協約中 留保撤回條項 : 第16條 第1項 (다) , (라) , (바) 號

(國 文)

1. 當事國은 婚姻과 家族關係에 관한 問題에 있어 女性에 대한 差別을 撤廢하기 위한 모든 適切한 措置를 취하여야 하며, 特히 男女 平等의 基礎위에 다음을 保障하여야 한다.

(다) 婚姻中 및 婚姻을 解消할 때의 同一한 權利와 責任

(라) 父母의 婚姻狀態를 不問하고 子女에 關한 問題에 있어 父母로서의 同一한 權利와 責任 ; 모든 境遇에 있어서 子女의 利益이 最優先的으로 考慮되어야 함.

(바) 兒童에 대한 保護, 後見, 財産管理 및 子女入養 또는 國內法制上 存在하는 概念中에

- 3 -

0103

類似한 制度와 關聯하여 同一한 權利와 責任 ;
모든 境遇에 있어서 兒童의 利益이 最優先的으로
考慮되어야 함.

（英 文）

1. States Parties shall take all appropriate measures to eliminate
discrimination against women in all matters relating to marriage
and family relations and in particular shall ensure, on a basis of
equality of men and women:

(c) The same rights and responsibilities during marriage and
at its dissolution;

(d) The same rights and responsibilities as parents, irrespective
of their marital status, in matters relating to their children; in
all cases the interests of the children shall be paramount;

(f) The same rights and responsibilities with regard to guardianship, wardship, trusteeship and adoption of children, or similar
institutions where these concepts exist in national legislation; in
all cases the interests of the children shall be paramount;

0104

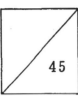
45

議案番號	第 117 號
議　決年 月 日	1991. 2 .7 .（第 7 回）

議決事項

" 市民的 및 政治的 權利에 관한 國際規約 "

第23條 第4項에 대한 留保撤回

提 出 者	國務委員 李 相 玉（外 務 部 長 官）
提出年月日	1991.　.　.

法 制 處 審 査 畢

0105

1. 議決主文

政府는 1990年 4月 10日 "市民的 및 政治的 權利에 관한 國際規約" 加入時에 행한 同 規約 第23條 第4項에 대한 留保를 撤回함.

2. 提案理由

1991年 1月 1日부터 改正民法 施行으로 留保事由가 解消되어 留保를 撤回하고자 함.

3. 主要骨子

가. 留保條項의 內容
婚姻中 및 婚姻解消時 夫婦의 同等한 權利와 責任을 確保하기 위한 當事國의 適切한 措置義務를 規定함.

나. 留保事由
我國의 民法上 婚姻中 및 婚姻解消時 夫婦의 權利 및 責任에 관한 關係規定이 男性中心으로 規定되어 있어, 協約批准當時 同 國內法 關係規定이 留保對象條項과 抵觸되었음.

－1－

0106

다. 留保撤回 事由

　　1991年1月1日부터 施行되는 改正民法에서 婚姻中
　　및 婚姻解消時에 男·女間 差別的 要素가 修正
　　됨에 따라 上記 留保條項의 內容과 我國 法制
　　와의 抵觸問題가 解消됨.

4. 主要 討議課題

　　없 음.

5. 參考事項

가. 立法 및 豫算措置 : 別途措置 必要없음

나. 關係部處 合議 : 法務部 , 法制處와 合議되었음.

다. 其 他
　(1) 規約 採擇 및 發效 經緯
　　　1966.12.16. 採擇
　　　1976. 3.23. 發效
　　　1990. 4.10. 我國 加入
　　　1990. 7.10. 我國에 대하여 發效

0107

(2) 規約中　留保撤回條項：第23條　第4項

（國　文）

이　規約의　當事國은　婚姻期間中　및　婚姻解消時에
婚姻에　대한　配偶者의　權利　및　責任의　平等을
確保하기　위하여　適切한　措置를　취한다.　婚姻解消
의　境遇에는　子女에　대한　必要한　保護를　위한
措置를　취한다.

（英　文）

States Parties to the present Covenant shall take appropriate steps
to ensure equality of rights and responsibilities of spouses as to
marriage, during marriage and at its dissolution. In the case of
dissolution, provision shall be made for the necessary protection of
any children.

- 3 -

0108

인권관계 다자조약에 대한 유보철회

1. 건의내용

   o 종전 민법규정과 저촉되어 비준 및 가입시 유보한 아래 협약 관계 조항들에 대하여 국내민법이 개정 되어 유보사유가 해소되었으므로 동유보를 철회함.

   - "여성에 대한 모든 형태의 차별 철폐에 관한 협약" 제16조 제1항 (다)·(라)·(바)호
     (5개 유보조항중 3개 철회)

   - "시민적 및 정치적 권리에 관한 국제규약" 제23조 제4항
     (4개 유보조항중 1개 철회)

2. 유보철회 방식

   o 외무부 장관 명의의 유보철회 공한을 국제연합사무 총장에게 전달하고, 이를 관보에 공포함.

부처명 : 외 무 부

0109

분류기호 문서번호	법규 20420-	(전화번호 :)		대 통 령
처리기한		외무부장관	국무총리	
시행일자	1991. 2. 12.			노에우
보존연한		mq	平	

관 련 기 관 협 조 여 부				대통령재가일 91.2.25.
협 조 기 관				

수 신	내부결재	발 신		통 제

제 목	인권관계 다자조약에 대한 유보철회

"여성에 대한 모든 형태의 차별철폐에 관한 협약" 제16조 제1항

(다), (라), (바)호와 "시민적 및 정치적 권리에 관한 국제규약" 제23조

제4항에 대한 대한민국 정부의 유보를 철회하기 위하여 아래와 같은 조치를

취할 것을 건의하오니 재가하여 주시기 바랍니다. 상기 유보 철회에

관하여는 1991년 2월 7일 제7회 국무회의의 심의를 거친 바 있습니다.

- 아   레 -

1. 별첨1과 같이 외무부장관 명의의 유보철회 공한을 국제연합사무총장

에게 송부함.

0110

1205-27(2-1) 일(2)
1984. 3. 21. 승인

190mm×268mm 인쇄용지(특급) 70g/㎡

2. 유보철회 사실을 별첨 2와 같이 공포함.

첨부: 1. 유보철회 공한 각1부.

2. 유보철회 공포안 각1부.

3. 국무회의 의결안 각1부. 끝.

0111

1205 - 27 (2 - 2) A(1)
1982. 7. 30. 승인

190mm×268mm인쇄용지특급70g/㎡
(조 달 청   20,000매 인 쇄)

1991년 2월   일

귀하,

　　본인은 1979년 12월 18일 채택된 "여성에 대한 모든 형태의
차별철폐에 관한 협약"에 대한 대한민국정부의 비준서에 포함되어
있는 제16조 제1항의 (다), (라), (바)호에 대한 유보를 1991년
　월　　일자로 철회함을 귀하에게 통보하는 영광을 가집니다.

　　귀하에게 본인 최고의 경의를 표하는 바입니다.

　　　　　　　　　　　　　　　　　　　　　외무부장관
　　　　　　　　　　　　　　　　　　　　　이 상 옥

국제연합
사무총장
하비에르 뻬레스 데 꾸에야르

0112

(Draft)

February 1991

Excellency,

I have the honour to notify you that the Government of the Republic of Korea withdraws as of   1991 the reservations contained in its instrument of ratification to sub-paragraphs (c), (d) and (f) of paragraph 1 of Article 16 of the Convention on the Elimination of All Forms of Discrimination against Women adopted on 18 December 1979.

Accept, Excellency, the assurances of my highest consideration.

LEE Sang-Ock
Minister

His Excellency
  Mr. Javier Perez de Cuellar
    Secretary-General
      United Nations
        New York.

0113

1991년 2월   일

귀하,

　　본인은 1966년 12월 16일 채택된 "시민적 및 정치적 권리에 관한
국제규약"에 대한 대한민국정부의 가입서에 포함된 제23조 제4항에
대한 유보를 1991년   월   일자로 철회함을 귀하에게 통보하는
영광을 가집니다.

　　귀하에게 본인 최고의 경의를 표하는 바입니다.

외무부장관
이 상 옥

국제연합
사무총장
하비에르 뻬레스 데 꾸에야르

0114

(Draft)

Excellency,

I have the honour to notify you that the Government of the Republic of Korea withdraws as of   1991 the reservation contained in its instrument of accession to paragraph 4 of Article 23 of the International Covenant on Civil and Political Rights adopted on 16 December 1966.

Accept, Excellency, the assurances of my highest consideration.

LEE Sang-Ock
Minister

His Excellency
Mr. Javier Perez de Cuellar
Secretary-General
United Nations
New York.

0115

공 포 안

정부가 1984년 12월 27일 "여성에 대한 모든 형태의 차별
철폐에 관한 협약" 비준시 행한 유보내용중 동 협약 제16조 제1항
(다),(라),(바)호에 대한 유보의 철회에 관하여 1991년 2월 7일
제7회 국무회의의 심의를 거치고, 1991년   월   일 국제연합사무
총장에게 통고함으로써 동 유보가 1991년   월   일자로 철회됨을
이에 공포한다.

대   통   령   노   태   우

1991년   월 일

국 무 총 리   노   재   봉

국 무 위 원   이   상   옥
    (외무부장관)

조약 제   호
"여성에 대한 모든 형태의 차별철폐에 관한 협약"
제16조 제1항 (다),(라),(바)호
(이하 본문 별첨)

0116

공　　포　　안

　　정부가 1990년 4월 10일 "시민적 및 정치적 권리에 관한
국제규약"에 가입시 행한 유보내용중 제23조 제4항에 대한 유보의
철회에 관하여 1991년 2월 7일 제7회 국무회의의 심의를 거치고
1991년　　월　　일 국제연합사무총장에게 통고함으로써 동 유보가
1991년　　월　　일자로 철회됨을 이에 공포한다.

　　　　대　　　통　　　령　　　노　　　태　　　우

1991년　　월　일

　　　　국　무　총　리　　　　　노　　재　　봉

　　　　국　무　위　원　　　　　이　　상　　옥
　　　　　（외무부장관）

　　조약 제　　　호
　　"시민적 및 정치적 권리에 관한 협약" 제23조 제4항
　　（이하 본문 별첨）

0117

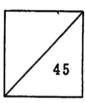

45

議案番號	第 116 號
議 決 年 月 日	1991. 2. 7. （第 7 回）

議決事項

"女性에 대한 모든 形態의 差別撤廢에
관한 協約"第16條 第1項 （다）,（라）,
（바）號에 대한 留保撤回

提 出 者	國務委員 李 相 玉 （外 務 部 長 官）
提出年月日	1991. . .

法 制 處 審 查 畢

0118

1. 議決主文

政府는 1984年 12月 27日 "女性에 대한 모든 形態의 差別撤廢에 관한 協約" 批准時에 행한 同協約 第16條 第1項 (다), (라) 및 (바) 號에 대한 留保를 撤回함.

2. 提案理由

1991年 1月 1日부터 改正民法 施行으로 留保事由가 解消되어 留保를 撤回하고자 함.

3. 主要骨子

가. 留保條項의 內容

婚姻中 및 婚姻解消時의 同等한 權利와 責任, 子女問題에 관한 同等한 權利와 責任 및 兒童의 保護, 後見, 財産管理, 入養에 관한 同等한 權利와 責任을 保障하기 위하여 當事國은 女性에 대한 差別撤廢 措置를 취하여야 함.

나. 留保事由

我國의 民法上 親族의 範圍, 親權行使, 離婚後

- 1 -

0119

養育責任, 共同入養, 相續 등과 關聯된 條項이
父系血統主義에   立脚, 男性爲主로 規定되어 있어
協約批准 當時 同 國內法 關係規定이 留保對象
條項과 抵觸되었음.

다. 留保撤回 事由

   1991年1月1日부터 施行되는 改正民法에서 婚姻中
   및 婚姻解消時에 男·女間 差別的 要素가 修正됨
   에 따라 上記 留保條項의 內容과 我國 法制와의
   抵觸問題가 解消됨.

4. 主要 討議課題

   없 음.

5. 參考事項

가. 立法 및 豫算措置 : 別途措置 必要없음.

나. 關係部處 合議 : 法務部, 法制處와 合議되었음.

다. 其 他
   (1) 協約 採擇 및 發效 經緯
      1979.12.18. 採擇
      1981. 9. 3. 發效

0120

1983. 5.25. 我國署名

1984.12.27. 我國批准

1985. 1.26. 我國에 대하여 發效

(2) 協約中 留保撤回條項 : 第16條 第1項 (다) , (라) ,

(바) 號

(國 文)

1. 當事國은 婚姻과 家族關係에 관한 問題에
   있어 女性에 대한 差別을 撤廢하기 위한
   모든 適切한 措置를 취하여야 하며, 特히
   男女 平等의 基礎위에 다음을 保障하여야
   한다.

   (다) 婚姻中 및 婚姻을 解消할 때의 同一한
   權利와 責任

   (라) 父母의 婚姻狀態를 不問하고 子女에 關한
   問題에 있어 父母로서의 同一한 權利와 責任;
   모든 境遇에 있어서 子女의 利益이 最優先的
   으로 考慮되어야 함.

   (바) 兒童에 대한 保護, 後見, 財産管理 및
   子女入養 또는 國內法制上 存在하는 概念中에

0121

- 3 -

類似한 制度와 關聯하여 同一한 權利와 責任 ;
모든 境遇에 있어서 兒童의 利益이 最優先的으로
考慮되어야 함.

（英　文）

1. States Parties shall take all appropriate measures to eliminate
discrimination against women in all matters relating to marriage
and family relations and in particular shall ensure, on a basis of
equality of men and women:

(c) The same rights and responsibilities during marriage and
at its dissolution;

(d) The same rights and responsibilities as parents, irrespective
of their marital status, in matters relating to their children; in
all cases the interests of the children shall be paramount;

(f) The same rights and responsibilities with regard to guardianship, wardship, trusteeship and adoption of children, or similar
institutions where these concepts exist in national legislation; in
all cases the interests of the children shall be paramount;

0122

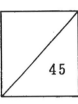

議案番號	第 117 號	議決事項
議 決 年 月 日	1991. 2. 7. (第 7 回)	

> "市民的 및 政治的 權利에 관한 國際規約"
>
> 第23條 第4項에 대한 留保撤回

提 出 者	國務委員 李 相 玉 (外 務 部 長 官)
提出年月日	1991. . .

法 制 處 審 査 畢

0123

1. 議決主文

政府는 1990年4月10日 "市民的 및 政治的 權利에 관한 國際規約"加入時에 행한 同 規約 第23條 第4項에 대한 留保를 撤回함.

2. 提案理由

1991年1月1日부터 改正民法 施行으로 留保事由가 解消되어 留保를 撤回하고자 함.

3. 主要骨子

가. 留保條項의 內容
婚姻中 및 婚姻解消時 夫婦의 同等한 權利와 責任을 確保하기 위한 當事國의 適切한 措置義務를 規定함.

나. 留保事由
我國의 民法上 婚姻中 및 婚姻解消時 夫婦의 權利 및 責任에 관한 關係規定이 男性中心으로 規定되어 있어, 協約批准當時 同 國內法 關係規定이 留保對象條項과 抵觸되었음.

— 1 —

0124

다. 留保撤回 事由

1991年1月1日부터 施行되는 改正民法에서 婚姻中
및 婚姻解消時에 男·女間 差別的 要素가 修正
됨에 따라 上記 留保條項의 內容과 我國 法制
와의 抵觸問題가 解消됨.

4. 主要 討議課題

없 음.

5. 參考事項

가. 立法 및 豫算措置 : 別途措置 必要없음

나. 關係部處 合議 : 法務部 , 法制處와 合議되었음.

다. 其 他

(1) 規約 採擇 및 發效 經緯

1966.12.16. 採擇

1976. 3.23. 發效

1990. 4.10. 我國 加入

1990. 7.10. 我國에 대하여 發效

0125

(2) 規約中　留保撤回條項 : 第23條　第4項

（國　文）

이　規約의　當事國은　婚姻期間中　및　婚姻解消時에
婚姻에　대한　配偶者의　權利　및　責任의　平等을
確保하기　위하여　適切한　措置를　취한다. 婚姻解消
의　境遇에는　子女에　대한　必要한　保護를　위한
措置를　취한다.

（英　文）

States Parties to the present Covenant shall take appropriate steps
to ensure equality of rights and responsibilities of spouses as to
marriage, during marriage and at its dissolution. In the case of
dissolution, provision shall be made for the necessary protection of
any children.

6408

기 안 용 지

분류기호 문서번호	법규 20420-			시 행 상 특별취급	
보존기간	영구·준영구. 10. 5. 3. 1.		장 관		
수 신 처 보존기간					
시행일자	1991. 2. 27.				
보조기관	국 장	전결	협조기관		문 서 통 제
	심의관				1.01. 2. 27
	과 장				
기안책임자		김두영			1.01. 2. 27
경유 수신 참조	주유엔대사		발신명의		
제 목	인권관계 다자조약에 대한 유보철회				

1. "여성에 대한 모든 형태의 차별철폐에 관한 협약"

제16조 제1항 (다)、(라)、(바)호와 "시민적 및 정치적 권리에 관한

국제규약" 제23조 제4항에 대한 유보를 철회하는 공한을 별첨과 같이

송부하오니 유엔사무총장에게 적의 전달하고、 그 결과를 지급 보고하여

주시기 바랍니다.

2. 동 유보철회건은 1991년 2월 7일 제7회 국무회의 심의를

거쳐 1991년 2월 25일 차로 대통령 재가를 득하였음을 참고하시기

바랍니다.   0127

/ 계 속 /

1505-25(2-1)일(1)갑
85. 9. 9. 승인   "내가아낀 종이 한장 늘어나는 나라살림"

190mm×268mm 인쇄용지 2급 60g/㎡
가 40-41 1990. 5. 28

첨부 : 1. 유보철회 공한 및 사본 각1부. 끝.

　　　 2. 국무회의 의결안 2부.

0128

대 한 민 국
외 무 부

1991. 2 . 27.

법규 20420-

수신 주유엔대사

제목 인권관계 다자조약에 대한 유보철회

1. "여성에 대한 모든 형태의 차별철폐에 관한 협약" 제16조
제1항 (다),(라),(바)호와 "시민적 및 정치적 권리에 관한 국제규약"
제23조 제4항에 대한 유보를 철회하는 공한을 별첨과 같이 송부하오니
유엔사무총장에게 적의 전달하고, 그 결과를 지급 보고하여 주시기 바랍니다.

2. 동 유보철회건은 1991년 2월 7일 제7회 국무회의 심의를 거쳐
1991년 2월 25일자로 대통령 재가를 득하였음을 참고하시기 바랍니다.

첨부: 1. 유보철회 공한 및 사본 각1부.
      2. 국무회의 의결안 2부.   끝.

외   무   부   장   관

국제기구조약국장

0129

MINISTRY OF FOREIGN AFFAIRS
REPUBLIC OF KOREA

27 February 1991

Excellency,

I have the honour to notify you that the Government
of the Republic of Korea withdraws as of 15 March 1991 the
reservations contained in its instrument of ratification to
sub-paragraphs (c), (d) and (f) of paragraph 1 of Article
16 of the Convention on the Elimination of All Forms of
Discrimination against Women adopted on 18 December 1979.

Accept, Excellency, the assurances of my highest
consideration.

LEE Sang-Ock
Minister

His Excellency
   Mr. Javier Perez de Cuellar
      Secretary-General
         United Nations
            New York

0130

MINISTRY OF FOREIGN AFFAIRS
REPUBLIC OF KOREA

27 February 1991

Excellency,

I have the honour to notify you that the Government
of the Republic of Korea withdraws as of 15 March 1991 the
reservation contained in its instrument of accession to
paragraph 4 of Article 23 of the International Covenant on
Civil and Political Rights adopted on 16 December 1966.

Accept, Excellency, the assurances of my highest
consideration.

LEE Sang-Ock
Minister

His Excellency
    Mr. Javier Perez de Cuellar
        Secretary-General
            United Nations
            New York.

0131

발 신 전 보

	분류번호	보존기간

번 호 : WUN-0453   910307 1320 CT   종별 :

수 신 : 주 유엔   대사. 총영사

발 신 : 장 관 (법규)

제 목 : 인권관계 다자조약 유보철회

연 : 법규 20420-6408 (91. 2. 27.)

표제건 조치 결과 보고바람.

(국제기구조약국장 문동석)

보 안 통 제	03

앙 고 재	91 년 3 월 ? 일	국 제 기 구 조 약 과	기안자 성명 정병화	과 장	심의관	국 장 전결	차 관	장 관	외신과통제

0132

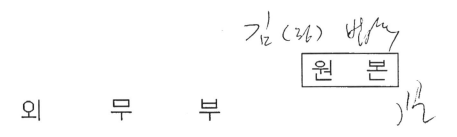

외 무 부

원 본

종 별 :

번 호 : UNW-0529

일 시 : 91 0307 1900

수 신 : 장 관(법규)(사본:노창희대사)

발 신 : 주 유엔 대사

제 목 : 인권관계 다자조약 유보철회

대:법규 20420-6408, WUN-0453

1. 대호건 아측 서한의 유보철회 발효시기 (91.3.15)와 관련 대호 공한 전달시기에 관하여 유엔조약국측과 협의중인바, 명 3.8.중 조약국측의 공식의견을 접수후 봉보조치 예정임.

2. 유엔 조약국측에 의하면 봉상적으로 유보철회의 경우 철회 봉보서 접수 일자에 발효하게 되어있으나, 당사국이 특정일자를 발효시기로 하기를 희망할경우 이에 따라 발효일자를 조정가능하다고함. 시민적 및 정칙적 권리에 관한규약의 경우 유보철회 발효시기 조항이 없으므로 당사국 요청수락에 문제가 없다고함.

3. 그러나 여성차별 철폐협약은 28조 3항에서 철회봉보서 접수일자를 발효일자로 한다고 규정하고있어, 아측이 철회봉보서를 발효희망시기 (3.15)에 앞서 제출할경우 해석에따라 문제가 있을수도 있다고함.

4. 조약국측은 상기 3항관련, 철회서 접수일시가 발효희망 시기로 유권해석될 경우 (1) 유보철회서를 일단 유엔에서 접수후 발효희망시기 (3.15)까지 처리하지 않는방안 (2) 아측이 3.15.에 철회서를 접수시키는 방안등이 있으나, 어떠한 경우에도 해당국의 희망을 충분히 감안하여, 도움이되는 방향으로 협조할것이라고 함.끝

(대사대리 신기복-국장)

국기국 ② 대사

PAGE 1

91.03.08   11:27 WG

외신 1과 통제관

0133

원 본

외 무 부

종　별 :

번　호 : UNW-0540　　　　　　　　　　　　일　시 : 91 0308 1900

수　신 : 장 관(법규)(사본:노창희대사)

발　신 : 주 유엔 대사

제　목 : 인권관계 다자조약 유보철회

연: UNW-0529

1. 유엔 조약국측은 금 3.8. 연호 3항 여성차별철폐 협약 규정과 아국의 발효희망시기와의 충돌을 피하기 위하여 아국이 3.15 이전 유보철회서를 송부하는 경우에도 3.15 공식접수, 동일자로 발효하는 것으로 간주한다는 입장을 당관에 알려옴.

2. 이에따라 대호 유보철회 서한 2건을 당관 명의 공한에 첨부, 금 3.8. 유엔사무국에 송부하였음.끝

(대사대리 신기복-국장)

국기국　　　국기국

외신 1과 통제관
0134

356　한국 인권문제 민주화 관련 기타 자료 2

10462

기 안 용 지

분류기호 문서번호	법규 20420-	(전화 :)	시 행 상 특별취급	
보존기간	영구·준영구. 10.5.3.1.		장 관	
수 신 처 보존기간				
시행일자	1991· 3· 11·			문 서 통 제

보 조 기 관	국 장		협 조 기 관		문 서 통 제
	심의관				
	과 장				
기안책임자		김두영			발

경 유 수 신 참 조	총무처장관 기획관리실장	발 신 명 의	

제 목	국제인권규약에 대한 유보철회 공포의뢰

1· 정부의 "시민적 및 정치적 권리에 관한 국제규약"

제23조 제4항에 대한 유보의 철회가 1991년 3월 8일 국제연합

사무총장에게 통고되어 1991년 3월 15일자로 발효될 예정인 바,

동 유보철회를 "법령등 공포에 관한 법률" 제11조에 의거 별첨안과

같이 공포하여 주시기 바랍니다.

2· 동 유보철회건은 1991년 2월 7일 제7회 국무회의의

심의를 거쳐 1991년 2월 25일 대통령 재가를 득하였습니다.

첨부 : 동 공포안 3부· 끝·

0135

1505-25(2-1) 일(1)갑
85. 9. 9. 승인   "내가아낀 종이 한장 늘어나는 나라살림"   190mm×268mm 인쇄용지 2급 60g/㎡
가 40-41 1990. 3. 30

공   포   안

정부가 1990년 4월 10일 "시민적 및 정치적 권리에 관한
국제규약"에 가입시 행한 유보내용중 제23조 제4항에 대한 유보의
철회에 관하여 1991년 2월 7일 제7회 국무회의의 심의를 거치고
1991년 3월 8일 국제연합사무총장에게 통고함으로써 동 유보가
1991년 3월 15일자로 철회됨을 이에 공포한다.

    대   통   령   노   태   우

1991년   월   일

    국 무 총 리   노   재   봉

    국 무 위 원   이   상   옥
        (외무부장관)

조약 제 1042 호
"시민적 및 정치적 권리에 관한 협약" 제23조 제4항
(이하 본문 별첨)

0136

시민적 및 정치적 권리에 관한 국제규약 제23조 제4항

(국 문)

이 협약의 당사국은 혼인기간중 및 혼인해소시에 혼인에 대한
배우자의 권리 및 책임의 평등을 확보하기 위하여 적절한 조치를
취한다. 혼인해소의 경우에는 자녀에 대한 필요한 보호를 위한
조치를 취한다.

(영 문)

States Parties to the present Covenant shall take appropriate
steps to ensure equality of rights and responsibilities of
spouses as to marriage, during marriage and at its dissolution.
In the case of dissolution, provision shall be made for the
necessary protection of any children.

0137

10463

<table>
<tr><td colspan="2">분류기호
문서번호</td><td>법규 20420-</td><td colspan="2">기 안 용 지
(전화 :　　　)</td><td>시 행 상
특별취급</td><td></td></tr>
<tr><td colspan="2">보존기간</td><td>영구·준영구.
10.5.3.1.</td><td colspan="3" align="center">장　　　　　관</td><td></td></tr>
<tr><td colspan="2">수 신 처
보존기간</td><td></td><td colspan="4" rowspan="2" align="center">ㄴ</td></tr>
<tr><td colspan="2">시행일자</td><td>1991. 3. 11.</td></tr>
</table>

지 급

| 분류기호
문서번호 | 법규 20420- | 기 안 용 지
(전화 :   ) | 시 행 상
특별취급 | |

제 목　여성차별 철폐협약에 대한 유보철회 공포의뢰

1. 정부의 "여성에 대한 모든 형태의 차별철폐에 관한 협약"

제16조 제1항 (다)、(라)、(바)호에 대한 유보의 철회가 1991년

3월 15일 국제연합사무총장에게 통고되어 동일자로 발효될 예정인바

동유보철회를 "법령등 공포에 관한 법률" 제11조에 의거 별첨안과

같이 공포하여 주시기 바랍니다.

2. 동 유보철회건은 1991년 2월 7일 제7회 국무회의의

심의를 거쳐 1991년 2월 25일 대통령 재가를 득하였습니다.

／ 계　속 ／　　　　　0138

1505-25(2-1) 일(1)갑
85. 9. 9. 승인　　"내가아낀 종이 한장 늘어나는 나라살림"

190mm×268mm 인쇄용지 2급 60g/m²
가 40-41 1990. 3. 30

3. 상기협약 제28조 제3항에 따라 유보의 철회는 국제연합

사무총장에게 통고가 접수된 날에 발효함을 첨언합니다.

첨부: 동 공포안 3부. 끝.

0139

1505-25(2-2) 일(1)을
85. 9. 9. 승인   "내가아낀 종이 한장 늘어나는 나라살림"   190mm×268mm 인쇄용지 2급 60g /㎡
가 40-41 1988. 7. 11.

공 포 안

정부가 1984년 12월 27일 "여성에 대한 모든 형태의 차별철폐에 관한 협약" 비준시 행한 유보내용중 동 협약 제16조 제1항 (다),(라),(바)호에 대한 유보의 철회에 관하여 1991년 2월 7일 제7회 국무회의의 심의를 거치고, 1991년 3월 15일 국제연합사무총장에게 통고함으로써 동 유보가 1991년 3월 15일자로 철회됨을 이에 공포한다.

대   통   령   노   태   우

1991년   월   일

국 무 총 리   노   재   봉

국 무 위 원   이   상   옥
    (외무부장관)

조약 제 1041 호
"여성에 대한 모든 형태의 차별철폐에 관한 협약"
제16조 제1항 (다),(라),(바)호
(이하 본문 별첨)

0140

여성에 대한 모든 형태의 차별 철폐에 관한 협약

제16조 제1항 (다),(라),(바)호

(국 문)

1. 당사국은 혼인과 가족관계에 관한 문제에 있어 여성에 대한
   차별을 철폐하기 위한 모든 적절한 조치를 취하여야 하며,
   특히 남녀 평등의 기초위에 다음을 보장하여야 한다.

   (다) 혼인중 및 혼인을 해소할 때의 동일한 권리와 책임

   (라) 부모의 혼인상태를 불문하고 자녀에 관한 문제에 있어
        부모로서의 동일한 권리와 책임; 모든 경우에 있어서
        자녀의 이익이 최우선적으로 고려되어야 함.

   (바) 아동에 대한 보호, 후견, 재산관리 및 자녀입양 또는
        국내법제상 존재하는 개념중에 유사한 제도와 관련하여
        동일한 권리와 책임; 모든 경우에 있어서 아동의 이익이
        최우선적으로 고려되어야 함.

(영 문)

1. States Parties shall take all appropriate measures to
   eliminate discrimination against women in all matters
   relating to marriage and family relations and in particular
   shall ensure, on a basis of equality of men and women:

   (c) The same rights and responsibilities during marriage
       and at its dissolution;

0141

(d) The same rights and responsibilities as parents,
irrespective of their marital status, in matters
relating to their children; in all cases the interests
of the children shall be paramount;

(f) The same rights and responsibilities with regard to
guardianship, wardship, trusteeship and adoption of
children, or similar institutions where these concepts
exist in national legislation; in all cases the
interests of the children shall be paramount;

0142

보 도 자 료

외 무 부

제   호   문의전화: 720-2408~10   보도일시: 91. 3. 13.   10:00 시

제 목 : 인권관계 다자조약에 대한 유보철회

국제법규과

가. 정부는 1991년 3월 15일자로 "여성에 대한 모든 형태의 차별 철폐에 관한
협약" 제16조 제1항 (다),(라),(바)호와 "시민적 및 정치적 권리에 관한
국제규약" 제23조 제4항에 대한 유보를 철회하게 됩니다.
이번 유보철회조치로 상기 조항들이 철회일자부로 우리나라에 대하여
새로이 적용되게 되었습니다.

나. 혼인과 가족생활관계에서 남녀평등을 규정한 이 조항들에 대하여는
남계중심으로 되어 있던 개정전 우리 민법 친족상속편의 일부 규정들과
저촉되어 각각 비준 및 가입시에 유보를 하였으나, 남녀차별적요소를
수정한 개정민법이 1991.1.1.부터 시행됨에 따라 유보사유가 해소
되었으므로 이를 철회하게 되었습니다.

다. 정부로서는 앞으로도 기 가입한 국제조약의 일부 유보조항에 대하여는
국내법의 개정 등으로 유보사유가 해소될 시에는 신속한 철회조치를
취하며 여타 미가입 인권조약의 가입을 적극 추진함으로써 국민의 인권
신장 노력을 강화해 나갈 방침입니다.

첨부: 유보철회 참고자료

91
3
11 김두영

0143

보 도 자 료

외 무 부

제 <u>91-67</u> 호　　문의전화 : 720-2408~10　　보도일시 : <u>01 . 3 . 14 . 10 : 00</u> 시

제 목 :　인권관계 다자조약에 대한 유보철회

<u>국제법규과</u>

가.　정부는 1991년 3월 15일자로 "여성에 대한 모든 형태의 차별 철폐에 관한
　　　협약" 제16조 제1항 (다),(라),(바)호와 "시민적 및 정치적 권리에 관한
　　　국제규약" 제23조 제4항에 대한 유보를 철회하게 됩니다.
　　　이번 유보철회조치로 상기 조항들이 철회일자부로 우리나라에 대하여
　　　새로이 적용되게 되었습니다.

나.　혼인과 가족생활관계에서 남녀평등을 규정한 이 조항들에 대하여는
　　　남계중심으로 되어 있던 개정전 우리 민법 친족상속편의 일부 규정들과
　　　저촉되어 각각 비준 및 가입시에 유보를 하였으나, 남녀차별적요소를
　　　수정한 개정민법이 1991.1.1.부터 시행됨에 따라 유보사유가 해소
　　　되었으므로 이를 철회하게 되었습니다.

　　　첨부:　유보철회 참고자료

0144

유보철회 참고자료

Ⅰ. 철회대상조항

○ 여성에 대한 모든 형태의 차별철폐에 관한 협약
   - 제16조 제1항 (다), (라), (바)호

○ 시민적 및 정치적 권리에 관한 국제규약
   - 제23조 제4항

Ⅱ. 철회대상 조항의 내용 및 유보사유

1. 내용

가. 여성에 대한 모든 형태의 차별철폐에 관한 협약 제16조 제1항 (다), (라), (바)호

○ 당사국은 혼인과 가족관계에 관한 모든 문제에 있어 여성에 대한 차별을 철폐하기 위한 모든 적절한 조치를 취하여야 하며, 특히 남녀평등의 기초위에 다음을 보장 하여야 한다.

(다) 혼인중 및 혼인해소시의 동일한 권리와 책임

(라) 부모의 혼인상태를 불문하고 자녀에 관한 문제에 있어 부모로서의 동일한 권리와 책임; 모든 경우에 있어서 자녀의 이익이 최우선적으로 고려되어야 함.

(바) 아동에 대한 보호, 후견, 재산관리 및 자녀입양 또는 국내법제상 존재하는 개념중에서 유사한 제도와 관련하여 동일한 권리와 책임; 모든 경우에 있어서 아동의 이익이 최우선적으로 고려되어야 함.

0145

o States Parties shall take all appropriate measures to
   eliminate discrimination against women in all matters
   relating to marriage and family relations and in particular
   shall ensure, on a basis of equality of men and women:

   (c) The same rights and responsibilities during marriage
        and at its dissolution;

   (d) The same rights and responsibilities as parents,
        irrespective of their marital status, in matters
        relating to their children; in all cases the
        interests of the children shall be paramount;

   (f) The same rights and responsibilities with regard to
        guardianship, wardship, trusteeship and adoption of
        children, or similar institutions where these concepts
        exist in national legislation; in all cases the
        interests of the children shall be paramount;

나. 시민적 및 정치적 권리에 관한 국제규약 제23조 제4항
   o 이 규약의 당사국은 혼인기간중 및 혼인해소시에 혼인에
      대한 배우자의 권리 및 책임의 평등을 확보하기 위하여
      적절한 조치를 취한다. 혼인해소의 경우에는 자녀에 대한
      필요한 보호를 위한 조치를 취한다.

   o States Parties to the present Covenant shall take
      appropriate steps to ensure equality of rights and
      responsibilities of spouses as to marriage, during
      marriage and at its dissolution. In the case of
      dissolution, provision shall be made for the necessary
      protection of any children.

0146

2. 유보사유

    o 부계혈통주의에 입각, 남성위주로 규정되어 있던 개정전 아국
        민법상의 가족법제와 충돌

    o 충돌되는 주요 관련 국내민법 규정(개정전)
        - 부(夫)중심의 가족생활관계
           · 동거장소는 부(夫)의 주소 또는 거소(제826조 제2항)
           · 부부공동입양시 부의 일방적 결정권(제874조 제2항)
           · 생활비 부 부담(제833조)
        - 자녀에 대한 부(父)권리 중심
           · 부모 의견불일치시 부의 친권행사(제909조 제1항)
           · 이혼후 부의 자에 대한 양육책임(제837조 제1항)
        - 부계중심의 친족범위
           · 8촌이내 부계혈족 4촌이내 모계혈족(제777조)

Ⅲ. 유보철회 사유

    o 91.1.1.부터 시행되는 개정민법이 상기 유보조항의 내용을 수용,
        충돌 사유를 해소
    o 개정민법 주요내용
        - 부부공동의 가족생활 관계
           · 동거장소 부부협의(제826조 제2항), 부부공동입양시 협의
               (제874조 제2항), 생활비 공동부담(제833조), 이혼시 재산
               분할 청구권(제839조의 2, 신설)
        - 자녀에 대한 부모의 동등한 권리
           · 공동친권행사(제909조 제2항), 이혼후 양육협의(제837조
               제1항), 이혼후 면접교섭권(제837조의 2, 신설)

0147

- 동일한 친족범위

  · 8촌이내 혈족 및 4촌이내 인척(제777조)

IV. 채택 및 발효경위

1. 여성에 대한 모든 형태의 차별철폐에 관한 협약

   1979.12.18. 유엔총회 협약 채택

   1981.9.3.   협약발효

   1983.5.25.   한국서명

   1984.12.27. 한국비준

   1985.1.26.   한국에 대하여 발효

2. 시민적 및 정치적 권리에 관한 국제규약

   1966.12.16. 유엔총회 규약 채택

   1976.3.23.   규약발효

   1990.4.10.   한국가입

   1990.7.10.   한국에 대하여 발효

0148

분류기호 문서번호	법규 20420-	**기 안 용 지** (전화 :)		시 행 상 특별취급		
보존기간	영구·준영구. 10. 5. 3. 1.	장 관				
수 신 처 보존기간						
시행일자	1991. 3. 13.					
보 조 기 관	국 장 전견 심의관 川 과 장	협 조 기 관		문 서 통 제 1991. 3. 13		
	기안책임자 정병화			발 인 1991. 3. 13		
경 유 수 신 참 조	국회사무총장	발신 명의				
제 목	국제인권규약 유보철회					

1. 정부가 1990년 4월 10일 "시민적 및 정치적 권리에 관한

국제규약" 가입시 행한 유보내용중 동 규약 제23조 제4항에 대한 유보의철회가

1991년 3월 8일 국제연합 사무총장에게 통고되어 1991년 3월 15일자로 아국에

대하여 발효될 예정임을 알려드립니다.

　　2. 혼인과 가족생활관계에서 남녀평등을 규정한 이 조항들에 대하여는

남녀차별적 요소를 수정한 개정민법이 1991·1·1·부터 시행됨에 따라 유보사유가

해소되어 이를 철회하게 되었음을 첨언합니다.

　　첨부 : 동 규약 유보철회 조항 국·영문 1부. 끝.　　　0149

대 한 민 국
외 무 부

(720-4045)   1991. 3 . 13.

법규 20420-

수신 국회사무총장

제목 국제인권규약 유보철회

　　1. 정부가 1990년 4월 10일 "시민적 및 정치적 권리에 관한
국제규약" 가입시 행한 유보내용중 동 규약 제23조 제4항에 대한 유보의
철회가 1991년 3월 8일 국제연합 사무총장에게 통고되어 1991년 3월 15일자로
아국에 대하여 발효될 예정임을 알려드립니다.

　　2. 혼인과 가족생활관계에서 남녀평등을 규정한 이 조항들에
대하여는 남녀차별적 요소를 수정한 개정민법이 1991. 1. 1.부터 시행됨에
따라 유보사유가 해소되어 이를 철회하게 되었음을 첨언합니다.

첨부: 동 규약 유보철회 조항 국·영문 1부. 끝.

　　　　외 　 무 　 부 　 장 　 관

　　　　　국제기구조약국장

0150

10911

기 안 용 지

분류기호 문서번호	법규 20420-	(전화 :)	시 행 상 특별취급	

보존기간	영구·준영구. 10. 5. 3. 1.		장	관
수 신 처 보존기간	.			
시행일자	1991. 3. 13.			

보 조 기 관	국 장	전결	협 조 기 관		문 서 통 제
	심의관				검열 1991. 3. 13
	과 장				
기안책임자		정병화			발 인 발송 1991. 3. 13

경 유 수 신 참 조	국회사무총장、정무제2장관	발 신 명 의	

제 목	여성차별철폐협약 유보철회

　　　　1. 정부가 1984년 12월 27일 "여성에 대한 모든 형태의 차별

철폐에 관한 협약" 비준시 행한 유보내용중 동 협약 제16조 제1항 (다)、

(라)、(바)호에 대한 유보의 철회가 1991년 3월 15일 국제연합사무총장에게

통고되어 동일자로 아국에 대하여 발효될 예정임을 알려드립니다.

　　　　2. 혼인과 가족생활관계에서 남녀평등을 규정한 이 조항들에

대하여는 남녀차별적 요소를 수정한 개정민법이 1991.1.1.부터 시행됨에

따라 유보사유가 해소되어 이를 철회하게 되었음을 첨언합니다.

　　　　첨부: 동 협약 유보철회 조항 국·영문 1부. 끝.　　　　0151

대 한 민 국
외 무 부

(720-4045)   1991 . 3 . 13 .

법규 20420-

수신 국회사무총장

제목 여성차별철폐협약 유보철회

   1. 정부가 1984년 12월 27일 "여성에 대한 모든 형태의 차별
철폐에 관한 협약" 비준시 행한 유보내용중 동 협약 제16조 제1항 (다)、
(라)、(바)호에 대한 유보의철회가 1991년 3월 15일 국제연합사무총장에게
통고되어 동일자로 아국에 대하여 발효될 예정임을 알려드립니다.

   2. 혼인과 가족생활관계에서 남녀평등을 규정한 이 조항들에
대하여는 남녀차별적 요소를 수정한 개정민법이 1991.1.1.부터 시행됨에
따라 유보사유가 해소되어 이를 철회하게 되었음을 첨언합니다.

첨부: 동 협약 유보철회 조항 국·영문 1부. 끝.

                외   무   부   장   관
                국제기구조약국장

                                          0152

대 한 민 국
외 무 부

(720-4045)   1991. 3. 13.

법규 20420-

수신 정무제2장관

제목 여성차별철폐협약 유보철회

1. 정부가 1984년 12월 27일 "여성에 대한 모든 형태의 차별
철폐에 관한 협약" 비준시 행한 유보내용중 동 협약 제16조 제1항 (다),
(라), (바)호에 대한 유보의철회가 1991년 3월 15일 국제연합사무총장에게
통고되어 동일자로 아국에 대하여 발효될 예정임을 알려드립니다.

2. 혼인과 가족생활관계에서 남녀평등을 규정한 이 조항들에
대하여는 남녀차별적 요소를 수정한 개정민법이 1991.1.1.부터 시행됨에
따라 유보사유가 해소되어 이를 철회하게 되었음을 첨언합니다.

첨부: 동 협약 유보철회 조항 국·영문 1부. 끝.

외   무   부   장   관

국제기구조약국장

0153

발 신 전 보

	분류번호	보존기간

번   호 : WGV-0305   910313 1636 FK 종별 : _____

수   신 : 주 제네바   대사.//총영사

발   신 : 장 관 (법규)

제   목 : 인권관계 다자조약에 대한 유보철회

1. 정부의 "시민적 및 정치적 권리에 관한 국제규약" 제23조 제4항과
   "여성에 대한 모든 형태의 차별철폐에 관한 협약" 제16조 제1항
   (다),(라),(바)호에 대한 유보의 철회가 각각 91.3.8., 91.3.15.자로
   유엔사무총장에게 통고되어 ~~공히~~ 91.3.15.자로 발효될 예정이니
   참고바람.

2. 동 유보철회 관련 자료는 차파편 송부 예정임.

·   (국제기구조약국장 문동석)

	보 안 통 제	

앙고재	국제기구과	기안자 성명	과 장	심의관	국 장		차 관	장 관		외신과통제
91년3월13일		정병화			전결					

0154

조　　약

정부가 1984년12월27일 "여성에 대한 모든 형태의 차별철폐에 관한 협약" 비준시 행한 유보내용 중 동 협약 제16조제1항 (다), (라), (바)호에 대한 유보의 철회에 관하여 1991년 2 월 7 일 제7회 국무회의의 심의를 거치고, 1991년 3 월15일 국제연합사무총장에게 통고함으로써 동 유보가 1991년 3 월15일자로 철회됨을 이에 공포한다.

대 통 령 노 태 우 ㊞
1991년 3 월15일

국 무 총 리 노 재 봉
국 무 위 원
외무부장관 이 상 옥

◉조약 제1,041호
여성에대한모든형태의차별철폐
에관한협약제16조제1항(다),(라),
(바)호

1. 당사국은 혼인과 가족관계에 관한 문제에 있어 여성에 대한 차별을 철폐하기 위한 모든 적절한 조치를 취하여야 하며, 특히 남녀 평등의 기초 위에 다음을 보장하여야 한다.

(다) 혼인중 및 혼인을 해소할 때의 동일한 권리와 책임

(라) 부모의 혼인상태를 불문하고 자녀에 관한 문제에 있어 부모로서의 동일한 권리와 책임: 모든 경우에 있어서 자녀의 이익이 최우선적으로 고려되어야 함.

(바) 아동에 대한 보호, 후견, 재산관리 및 자녀 입양 또는 국내법제상 존재하는 개념중에 유사한 제도와 관련하여 동일한 권리와 책임: 모든 경우에 있어서 아동의 이익이 최우선적으로 고려되어야 함.

1. States Parties shall take all appropriate measures to eliminate discrimination against women in all matters relating to marriage and family relations and in particular shall ensure, on a basis of equality of men and women:

(c) The same rights and responsibilities during marriage and at its dissolution;

(d) The same rights and responsibilities as parents, irrespective of their marital status, in matters relating to their children; in all cases the interests of the children shall be paramount;

(f) The same rights and responsibilities with regard to guardianship, wardship, trusteeship and adoption of children, or similar institutions where these concepts exist in national legislation; in all cases the interests of the children shall be paramount;

정부가 1990년 4 월10일 "시민적 및 정치적 권리에 관한 국제규약"에 가입시 동규약 제14조제5항에 대한 유보의 철회를 1991년 2 월 7 일 제7회 국무회의의 심의를 거치고, 1991년 3 월15일 국제연합사무총장에게 1991년 3 월15일자로 철회하였다.

대 통 령
1991년 3 월15일

국 무
국 무
외 무

States Parties t
steps to ensure
spouses as to m
In the case of
necessary prote

대 통 령

국무회의의 심의를 거친
개정정령을 이에 공포한다
대 통 령
1991년 3 월15일
국 무
국 무
총 리

대통령령 제13,327호
특허청과그소속기
그소속기관직제중 다음
제2조 "관리국·심사국"을
으로 하고, "차장밑에
각 1인"을 "청장밑
기획관리관 및 비상계
제2조 다음과 같이 신
제1조(공보담당관) ①공
별정직국가공무원 으
공보담당관은 공보사무에
제41항중 "출원과 등

기 안 용 지

분류기호 문서번호	법규 20420-	(전화 :)	시 행 상 특별취급	
보존기간	영구·준영구. 10. 5. 3. 1.	장 관		
수 신 처 보존기간				문 서 통 제
시행일자	1991. 3. 15.			
보 조 기 관	국 장 ｜전 결 심의관 과 장	협 조 기 관		
	기안책임자 ｜ 정병화			발 송 인
경 유 수 신 참 조	주제네바 대사	발 신 명 의		
제 목	인권관계 다자조약 유보철회 관련자료송부			

연 : WGV-0305 (91.3.13.)

연호 "여성에 대한 모든 형태의 차별철폐에 관한 협약" 제16조

제1항 (다)·(라)·(바)호와 "시민적 및 정치적 권리에 관한 국제규약"

제23조 제4항에 대한 유보철회와 관련하여 1991·2·7·자 국무회의 의결안

문서를 별첨과 같이 송부합니다.

첨부 : 국무회의 의결안 문서 2부. 끝.

0156

1505-25(2-1) 일(1)잡
85. 9. 9. 승인   "내가아낀 종이 한장 늘어나는 나라살림"   190mm×268mm 인쇄용지 2급 60g/㎡
가 40-41 1990. 3. 30

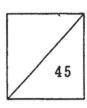

45

議案番號	第 116 號
議 決 年 月 日	1991. 2. 7. (第 7 回)

議決事項

"女性에 대한 모든 形態의 差別撤廢에
관한 協約" 第16條 第1項 (다), (라),
(바)號에 대한 留保撤回

提 出 者	國務委員 李 相 玉 (外 務 部 長 官)
提出年月日	1991. . .

法 制 處 審 査 畢

0157

1. 議決主文

政府는 1984年12月27日 "女性에 대한 모든 形態의 差別撤廢에 관한 協約"批准時에 행한 同 協約 第16條 第1項 (다), (라) 및 (바) 號에 대한 留保를 撤回함.

2. 提案理由

1991年1月1日부터 改正民法 施行으로 留保事由가 解消되어 留保를 撤回하고자 함.

3. 主要骨子

가. 留保條項의 內容

婚姻中 및 婚姻解消時의 同等한 權利와 責任, 子女問題에 관한 同等한 權利와 責任 및 兒童의 保護, 後見, 財産管理, 入養에 관한 同等한 權利와 責任을 保障하기 위하여 當事國은 女性에 대한 差別撤廢 措置를 취하여야 함.

나. 留保事由

我國의 民法上 親族의 範圍, 親權行使, 離婚後

- 1 -

0158

養育責任 , 共同入養 , 相續 등과 關聯된 條項이 父系血統主義에 立脚 , 男性爲主로 規定되어 있어 協約批准 當時 同 國內法 關係規定이 留保對象 條項과 抵觸되었음.

다. 留保撤回 事由

1991年1月1日부터 施行되는 改正民法에서 婚姻中 및 婚姻解消時에 男·女間 差別的 要素가 修正됨에 따라 上記 留保條項의 內容과 我國 法制와의 抵觸問題가 解消됨.

4. 主要 討議課題

없 음.

5. 參考事項

가. 立法 및 豫算措置 : 別途措置 必要없음.

나. 關係部處 合議 : 法務部 , 法制處와 合議되었음.

다. 其 他
   (1) 協約 採擇 및 發效 經緯
      1979.12.18. 採擇
      1981. 9. 3. 發效

0159

1983. 5.25. 我國署名

1984.12.27. 我國批准

1985. 1.26. 我國에 대하여 發效

(2) 協約中 留保撤回條項：第 16 條 第 1 項 (다), (라), (바) 號

（國　文）

1. 當事國은 婚姻과 家族關係에 관한 問題에 있어 女性에 대한 差別을 撤廢하기 위한 모든 適切한 措置를 취하여야 하며, 特히 男女 平等의 基礎위에 다음을 保障하여야 한다.

(다) 婚姻中 및 婚姻을 解消할 때의 同一한 權利와 責任

(라) 父母의 婚姻狀態를 不問하고 子女에 關한 問題에 있어 父母로서의 同一한 權利와 責任 ; 모든 境遇에 있어서 子女의 利益이 最優先的으로 考慮되어야 함.

(바) 兒童에 대한 保護, 後見, 財産管理 및 子女入養 또는 國內法制上 存在하는 槪念中에

- 3 -

0160

類似한 制度와 關聯하여 同一한 權利와 責任 ;
모든 境遇에 있어서 兒童의 利益이 最優先的으로
考慮되어야 함.

（英 文）

1. States Parties shall take all appropriate measures to eliminate discrimination against women in all matters relating to marriage and family relations and in particular shall ensure, on a basis of equality of men and women:

(c) The same rights and responsibilities during marriage and at its dissolution;

(d) The same rights and responsibilities as parents, irrespective of their marital status, in matters relating to their children; in all cases the interests of the children shall be paramount;

(f) The same rights and responsibilities with regard to guardian-ship, wardship, trusteeship and adoption of children, or similar institutions where these concepts exist in national legislation; in all cases the interests of the children shall be paramount;

0161

대한민국정부

관보는 공문서로서의 효력을 갖는다.

선 람	기 관 의 장

제11770호 1991. 3. 15. (금)

정부시책소개

(이면 계속)

회 람							

발행총무처(편집☎720−4331 보급☎754−4332)

1201-4A 1981.12.18. 승인
190×268 신문용지 54g/㎡

0162

조 약

정부가 1984년12월27일 "여성에 대한 모든 형태의 차별철폐에 관한 협약" 비준시 행한 유보내용 중 동 협약 제16조제1항 (다), (라), (바)호에 대한 유보의 철회에 관하여 1991년 2월 7일 제7회 국무회의의 심의를 거치고, 1991년 3월15일 국제연합사무총장에게 통고함으로써 동 유보가 1991년 3월15일자로 철회됨을 이에 공포한다.

　대 통 령　노 태 우 ㊞
　1991년 3월15일
　　　국무총리　노 재 봉
　　　국무위원
　　　외무부장관　이 상 옥

◉조약 제1,041호
여성에대한모든형태의차별철폐
에관한협약제16조제1항(다),(라),
(바)호

1. 당사국은 혼인과 가족관계에 관한 문제에 있어 여성에 대한 차별을 철폐하기 위한 모든 적절한 조치를 취하여야 하며, 특히 남녀 평등의 기초위에 다음을 보장하여야 한다.

(다) 혼인중 및 혼인을 해소할 때의 동일한 권리와 책임

(라) 부모의 혼인상태를 불문하고 자녀에 관한 문제에 있어 부모로서의 동일한 권리와 책임 : 모든 경우에 있어서 자녀의 이익이 최우선적으로 고려되어야 함.

(바) 아동에 대한 보호, 후견, 재산관리 및 자녀 입양 또는 국내법제상 존재하는 개념중에 유사한 제도와 관련하여 동일한 권리와 책임 : 모든 경우에 있어서 아동의 이익이 최우선적으로 고려되어야 함.

1. States Parties shall take all appropriate measures to eliminate discrimination against women in all matters relating to marriage and family relations and in particular shall ensure, on a basis of equality of men and women:

(c) The same rights and responsibilities during marriage and at its dissolution;

(d) The same rights and responsibilities as parents, irrespective of their marital status, in matters relating to their children; in all cases the interests of the children shall be paramount;

(f) The same rights and responsibilities with regard to guardianship, wardship, trusteeship and adoption of children, or similar institutions where these concepts exist in national legislation; in all cases the interests of the children shall be paramount;

4

0163

정부가 1990년 4월 10일 "시민적 및 정치적 권리에 관한 국제규약"에 가입시 행한 유보내용중 제23조제4항에 대한 유보의 철회에 관하여 1991년 2월 7일 제7회 국무회의의 심의를 거쳐고 1991년 3월 8일 국제연합사무총장에게 통고함으로써 동 유보가 1991년 3월 15일자로 철회됨을 이에 공포한다.

대통령 노 태 우 ⑩
1991년 3월 15일
국무총리 노 재 봉
국무위원
외무부장관 이 상 옥

⊙조약 제1,042호
시민적및정치적권리에관한협약
제23조제4항

이 협약의 당사국은 혼인기간중 및 혼인해소시에 혼인에 대한 배우자의 권리 및 책임의 평등을 확보하기 위하여 적절한 조치를 취한다. 혼인해소의 경우에는 자녀에 대한 필요한 보호를 위한 조치를 취한다.

States Parties to the present Covenant shall take appropriate steps to ensure equality of rights and responsibilities of spouses as to marriage, during marriage and at its dissolution. In the case of dissolution, provision shall be made for the necessary protection of any children.

5

0164

기 안 용 지

(전화 :   )

분류기호 문서번호	법규 20420-		시 행 상 특별취급	
보존기간	영구·준영구. 10. 5. 3. 1.	장 관		
수 신 처 보존기간				
시행일자	1991. 3. 16.	ん		

보 조 기 관	국 장	기결	협 조 기 관		문 서 통 제	
	심의관	)に				
	과 장	13				
기안책임자	정병화			발 송 인	

경 유 수 신 참 조	주영대사	발 신 명 의	

제 목	인권관계 다자조약 유보철회

　　1. 정부는 혼인과 가족생활관계에서 남계 위주로 규정된 국내민법과의

상충으로 인하여 "여성에 대한 모든형태의 차별철폐에 관한 협약" 제16조

제1항 (다)、(라)、(바)호 및 "시민적 및 정치적 권리에 관한 국제규약"

제23조 제4항에 대하여 각각 비준(84.12.27.) 및 가입시(90.4.10.)에

유보한 바 있습니다.

　　2. 그러나、 남·녀 차별적 요소를 수정한 개정민법이 1991·1·1·부터

시행됨에 따라 상기조항에 대한 유보를 철회、 동 조항들은 91·3·15·부로

아국에 대하여 발효하였습니다.

0165

1505-25(2-1) 일(1)갑　　　/ 계 속 /
85. 9. 9. 승인　　"내가아낀 종이 한장 줄어나는 나라살림"

190mm×268mm 인쇄용지 2급 60g/㎡
가 40-41 1990. 3. 30

3. 동 유보철회와 관련、1991·2·7·자 국무회의 의결안 문서를 별첨과

같이 송부하오니 참고하시기 바랍니다··

첨부: 국무회의 의결안문서 2부· 끝·

0166

1505-25(2-2) 일(1)을
85. 9. 9. 승인　"내가아낀 종이 한장 늘어나는 나라살림"
190mm×268mm 인쇄용지 2급 60g /㎡
가 40-41 1988. 7. 11.

발 신 전 보

	분류번호	보존기간

번 호 : WUN-0540   910316 1419 DN 종별 : _____

수 신 : 주유엔   대사. 총영사

발 신 : 장 관 (법규)

제 목 : 인권관계 다자조약 유보철회

연 : 법규20420-6408

대 : UNW-529, 540

표제 유보철회는 91.3.15.자로 아국에 대하여 발효(국내공포조치)하였음.
(동일자로 공포조치)하였음.
(국제기구조약국장 문동석)

	91년 3월 16일	국제법규과	기안자 성명 정병화	과 장	심의관	국 장 전결	차 관	장 관		보안통제
앙고재										

외신과통제

0167

김

주 국 련 대 표 부

주국련 2031억2-330   1991. 5. 9.

수신 장관

참조 국제기구조약국장

제목 여성차별철폐협약 유보 철회

대 : WUN-0453

　　　유엔 사무총장은 당관앞 별첨 공한을 통하여 대호 아국

통보에 따라 표제협약 3개 조항 (16조 1항(c)(d)(f))   의 유보가

철회되고 91.3.15 부터 발효됨을 알려 왔는바 동 공한 사본을 별첨

송부합니다.

첨 부 : 사무총장 공한 사본 1부.   끝.

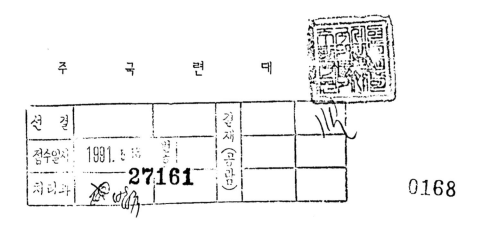

0168

UNITED NATIONS NATIONS UNIES

POSTAL ADDRESS—ADRESSE POSTALE: UNITED NATIONS, N.Y. 10017

CABLE ADDRESS—ADRESSE TELEGRAPHIQUE. UNATIONS NEWYORK

REFERENCE: LA 41 TR/221/1 (4-8)

The Secretary-General of the United Nations presents his compliments to the Permanent Observer of the Republic of Korea to the United Nations and has the honour to refer to the Permanent Observer's note KD/021/91 of 6 March 1991, notifying him that the Government of the Republic of Korea is withdrawing certain reservations made upon ratification, on 27 December 1984, to the Convention on the Elimination of all Forms of Discrimination against Women, adopted by the General Assembly of the United Nations on 18 December 1979.

Due note has been taken that the withdrawal concerns reservations to sub-paragraphs (c), (d) and (f) of paragraph 1 of article 16. The remaining reservations will now read as follows, the words appearing in square brackets having been withdrawn:

> "The Government of the Republic of Korea, having examined the said Convention, hereby ratifies the Convention considering itself not bound by the provisions of Article 9 and sub-paragraph[s (c), (d), (f) and] (g) of paragraph 1 of Article 16 of the Convention."

In accordance with paragraph 3, article 28, of the Convention, the above-mentioned notification took effect on the date of its receipt, i.e. on 15 March 1991.

The Centre for Social Development and Humanitarian Affairs (Division for the Advancement of Women) of the Secretariat in Vienna has been informed of the above and all interested States are being informed accordingly.

15 April 1991

0169

김   예

→ 대장관
승부
(글에대처?)

주 국 련 대 표 부

주국련 203142-403   1991. 5. 23.

수신 장관

참조 국제기구조약국장

제목 여성차별 철폐협약 유보철회

    아국 및 태국의 표제협약 유보철회 내용과 말타의 가입에 관한송
유엔 사무국측의 회람문서를 별첨 송부합니다.

첨 부 : C.N. 71, 1991 Treaties-2   끝.

            주   국   련   대

UNITED NATIONS NATIONS UNIES

POSTAL ADDRESS—ADRESSE POSTALE UNITED NATIONS, N.Y. 10017
CABLE ADDRESS—ADRESSE TELEGRAPHIQUE UNATIONS NEWYORK

REFERENCE: C.N.61.1991.TREATIES-2 (Depositary Notification)

CONVENTION ON THE ELIMINATION OF ALL FORMS OF
DISCRIMINATION AGAINST WOMEN
ADOPTED BY THE GENERAL ASSEMBLY OF THE UNITED NATIONS
ON 18 DECEMBER 1979

PARTIAL WITHDRAWAL OF RESERVATIONS MADE BY THAILAND
UPON ACCESSION

PARTIAL WITHDRAWAL OF RESERVATIONS MADE BY THE
REPUBLIC OF KOREA UPON RATIFICATION

ACCESSION BY MALTA

The Secretary-General of the United Nations, acting in his capacity as depositary, communicates the following:

I

On 25 January 1991, the Government of Thailand notified the Secretary-General of its decision to withdraw the reservations it had made upon accession to the Convention, as circulated by depositary notification C.N.223.1985.TREATIES-14 of 18 October 1985, to the extent that they apply to article 11, paragraph 1 (b), and article 15, paragraph 3. At the same time, the Government of Thailand reiterated the declaration it had also made upon accession, the contents of which remain unchanged. The remaining reservations will now read as follows, the words appearing in square brackets (in paragraphs 2 and 3) having been withdrawn:

(Original: English)

"1. In all matters which concern national security, maintenance of public order and service or employment in the military or paramilitary forces, the Royal Thai Government reserves its right to apply the provisions of the Convention on the Elimination of all Forms of Discrimination against Women, in particular Articles 7 and 10, only within the limits established by national laws, regulations and practices.

Attention: Treaty Services of Ministries of Foreign Affairs and of international organizations concerned

0171

2. With regard to Article 9, paragraph 2, [and Article 11, paragraph 1 (b), as far as night work of women and special protection of working women are concerned,] the Royal Thai Government considers that the application of the said provision[s] shall be subject to the limits and criteria established by national laws, regulations and practices.

3. The Royal Thai Government does not consider itself bound by the provisions of [Article 15, paragraph 3,] Article 16 and Article 29, paragraph 1, of the Convention."

In accordance with article 28, paragraph 3, of the Convention, the above-mentioned notification took effect on the date of its receipt, i.e. on 25 January 1991.

II

On 15 March 1991, the Government of the Republic of Korea notified the Secretary-General of its decision to withdraw the reservations it had made upon ratification of the Convention to the extent that they apply to sub-paragraphs (c), (d) and (f) of paragraph 1 of article 16, as circulated by depositary notification C.N.316.1984.TREATIES-12 of 11 January 1985. The reservation will now read as follows, the words appearing in square brackets having been withdrawn:

(Courtesy translation) (Original: Korean)

The Governemnt of the Republic of Korea, having examined the said Convention, hereby ratifies the Convention considering itself not bound by the provisions of Article 9 and sub-paragraph[s (c), (d), (f) and] (g) of paragraph 1 of Article 16 of the Convention.

In accordance with article 28, paragraph 3, of the Convention, the above-mentioned notification took effect on the date of its receipt, i.e. on 15 March 1991.

III

On 8 March 1991, the instrument of accession by the Government of Malta to the above-mentioned Convention was deposited with the Secretary-General.

The instrument of accession was accompanied by the following reservations:

0172

(Original: English)

"A. Article 11

The Government of Malta interprets paragraph 1 of Article II,
in the light of the provisions of paragraph 2 of Article 4,
as not precluding prohibitions, restrictions, or conditions
on the employment of women in certain areas, or the work
done by them, where this is considered necessary or   ·
desirable to protect the health and safety of women or the
human foetus, including such prohibitions, restrictions or
conditions imposed in consequence of other international
obligations of Malta.

"B. Article 13

(i) The Government of Malta reserves the right,
notwithstanding anything in the Convention, to continue
to apply its tax legislation which deems, in certain
circumstances, the income of a married woman to be the
income of her husband and taxable as such.

(ii) The Government of Malta reserves the right to
continue to apply its social security legislation which in
certain circumstances makes certain benefits payable to
the head of the household which is, by such legislation,
presumed to be the husband.

"C. Articles 13, 15, 16

While the Government of Malta is committed to remove, in
as far as possible, all aspects of family and property law
which may be considered as discriminatory to females, it
reserves the right to continue to apply present
legislation in that regard until such time as the law is
reformed and during such transitory period until those
laws are completely superceded.

"D. Article 16

The Government of Malta does not consider itself bound by
sub-paragraph (e) of paragraph (1) of Article 16 in so far
as the same may be interpreted as imposing an obligation
on Malta to legalise abortion."

In accordance with article 27 (2), the Convention entered into
force for Malta on the thirtieth day after the date of deposit of
the instrument, i.e. on 7 April 1991.

16 May 1991

0173

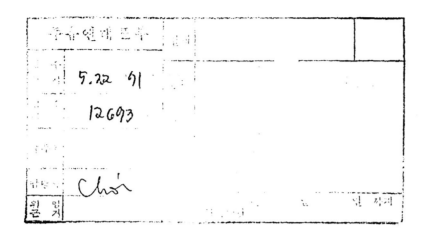

5.22 기

12693

Choi

0174

주 국 련 대 표 부

주국련   **465**

수신 장관

참조 국제기구조약국장

제목 인권규약 유보철회

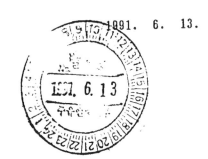

1991. 6. 13.

　　　91. 3. 아국정부가 유엔사무국에 통보한 시민적, 정치적 권리에 관한 국제규약 제23조 4항의 유보철회와 관련, 유엔 법률 담당 사무차장의 서한을 별첨 송부합니다.

　　　첨 부 : C. Fleischhauer 사무차장 서한 사본 1부.　끝.

선 결			결재	주	국	련	대　사
접수일시	1991.6 17						
처리과	33811						

0175

UNITED NATIONS ⊕ NATIONS UNIES

POSTAL ADDRESS—ADRESSE POSTALE UNITED NATIONS, N.Y. 10017
CABLE ADDRESS—ADRESSE TELEGRAPHIQUE: UNATIONS NEWYORK

REFERENCE: LA 41 TR/221/1 (4-4)   30 May 1991

Sir,

I have the honour, on behalf of the Secretary-General, to refer to the letter dated 27 February 1991 from the Minister of Foreign Affairs of the Republic of Korea, notifying the decision of the Government of the Republic of Korea to withdraw the reservation to paragraph 4 of article 23, made upon accession to the International Covenant on Civil and Political Rights, adopted by the General Assembly of the United Nations on 16 December 1966.

The withdrawal took effect on 15 March 1991, the date of the receipt of the above-mentioned letter.

All States concerned are being informed accordingly.

Carl-August Fleischhauer
The Legal Counsel

His Excellency
Mr. Chang Hee Roe
Ambassador Extraordinary and Plenipotentiary
Permanent Observer of
  the Republic of Korea
  to the United Nations
New York, N.Y. 10017

0176

정 리 보 존 문 서 목 록

기록물종류	일반공문서철	등록번호	2020020020	등록일자	2020-02-04
분류번호	734.24	국가코드		보존기간	준영구
명 칭	경제적, 사회적 및 문화적(A규약) 권리위원회, 1991				
생 산 과	국제연합2과	생산년도	1991~1991	담당그룹	
내용목차	* 제6차, 1991.11.27-29 - 북한의 A규약 최초 보고서 심의				

0001

주 제 네 바 대 표 부

74

제네(정) 2031-1020   1991. 11. 26.

수신 : 장관

참조 : 국제기구국장

제목 : 각국의 인권규약(A규약) 보고서 현황

91. 11. 2 9

1. 인권사무국이 작성한 경제적.사회적.문화적 권리에 관한 국제규약의 국별
    보고서 제출.심의 현황 관련 문건을 별첨 송부합니다.

2. 동 문건상에 북한은 최초 보고서(6-9조, 10-12조 및 13-15조)를 제출하였으나,
    동 보고서중 13-15조 관련 보고서에 대한 심의는 북한의 요청으로 연기 되고
    있으며, 6-9조 관련 2차 보고서 제출이 기한을 넘겨 지연되고 있는 것으로
    나와 있음을 첨언합니다.

    첨부 : E/C.12/1991/3 문서 2부.   끝.

주 제 네 바 대 사

접수일자 1991. 12. 2
처리과 2   68674

0002

Economic and Social Council

Distr.
GENERAL

E/C.12/1991/3
9 October 1991

Original: ENGLISH

COMMITTEE ON ECONOMIC, SOCIAL AND CULTURAL RIGHTS
Sixth session
Geneva
25 November-13 December 1991

STATES PARTIES TO THE INTERNATIONAL COVENANT ON ECONOMIC, SOCIAL
AND CULTURAL RIGHTS AND STATUS OF THE SUBMISSION OF REPORTS IN
ACCORDANCE WITH THE PROGRAMME ESTABLISHED BY THE ECONOMIC AND
SOCIAL COUNCIL IN RESOLUTIONS 1988 (LX) AND RULE 58 OF THE RULES
OF PROCEDURE OF THE COMMITTEE

Note by the Secretary-General

1. The International Covenant on Economic, Social and Cultural Rights, adopted by the General Assembly in resolution 2200 A (XXI) of 16 December 1966, entered into force on 3 January 1976, three months after the date of the deposit with the Secretary-General of the United Nations of the thirty-fifth instrument of ratification, as provided for in article 27 of the Covenant.

2. As at 1 October 1991, the Covenant had been ratified or acceded to by 100 States. A list of the States parties in the order in which the Covenant entered into force for each State, as well as information on the status of the submission of reports by States parties, is to be found in the annex to the present document.

Submission of initial reports concerning rights covered by articles 6 to 9 of the Covenant

3. In accordance with the programme established by the Economic and Social Council in resolution 1988 (LX) of 11 May 1976, initial reports concerning rights covered by articles 6 to 9 of the Covenant were due under the first

GE.91-17746/3864B

0003

cycle of the reporting procedure from 46 States parties by 1 September 1977
and initial reports concerning the same articles were due under the second
cycle of the reporting procedure from 32 States parties by 1 September 1983.
The Secretary-General, by a note verbale dated 1 June 1977, requested the
46 States parties for which the Covenant had entered into force by that date
to submit their initial reports concerning articles 6 to 9 of the Covenant by
1 September 1977 (see also E/1978/8). By a note verbale dated 1 March 1983,
the Secretary-General requested the 32 States parties for which the Covenant
entered into force subsequently to submit their initial reports concerning the
same articles of the Covenant by 1 September 1983. By another note verbale,
also dated 1 March 1983, the Secretary-General requested 16 States parties
which had not yet submitted their initial reports concerning those articles,
required under the first reporting cycle, to do so by 1 September 1983 (see
also E/1984/6, paras. 7-8).

4.   As at 1 October 1991, initial reports concerning rights covered by
articles 6 to 9 had been received from the following 49 States parties to the
Covenant: Afghanistan, Australia, Austria, Barbados, Bulgaria, Canada, Chile,
Colombia, Cyprus, Czech and Slovak Federal Republic, Democratic People's
Republic of Korea, Denmark, Ecuador, Finland, France, Germany, 1/ Hungary,
India, Iran (Islamic Republic of), 2/ Iraq, Italy, Jamaica, Japan, Jordan,
Madagascar, Mexico, Mongolia, Netherlands, Nicaragua, Norway, Panama, Peru,
Philippines, Poland, Portugal, 3/ Romania, Rwanda, Republic of Belarus, Spain,
Sweden, Syrian Arab Republic, Trinidad and Tobago, Tunisia, Ukraine,
Union of Soviet Socialist Republics, United Kingdom of Great Britain and
Northern Ireland, Venezuela, Yugoslavia and Zaire (see E/1978/8 and addenda
and E/1984/6 and addenda).

5.   The reports of Afghanistan (E/1984/6/Add.12) and Panama (E/1984/6/Add.19)
are pending consideration by the Committee on Economic, Social and Cultural
Rights. Consideration of those reports was postponed at the fifth session of
the Committee at the request of the Governments concerned.

<u>Submission of initial reports concerning rights covered by articles 10 to 12
of the Covenant</u>

6.   In accordance with the programme established by the Council in
resolution 1988 (LX), initial reports concerning rights covered by articles 10
to 12 of the Covenant were due under the first cycle of the reporting
procedure from 60 States parties by 1 September 1979 and initial reports
concerning the same articles were due under the second cycle of the reporting
procedure from 23 States parties by 1 September 1985. The Secretary-General,
by a note verbale dated 10 May 1979, requested the 60 States parties for which
the Covenant had entered into force by that date to submit their initial
reports concerning those articles by 1 September 1979 (see also E/1980/6). By
a note verbale dated 10 January 1985, the Secretary-General requested the
23 States parties for which the Covenant entered into force subsequently to
submit their initial reports concerning the same articles of the Covenant by
1 September 1985. By another note verbale, also dated 10 January 1985, the
Secretary-General requested 25 States parties which had not yet submitted
their initial reports concerning those articles, required under the first
reporting cycle, to do so by 1 September 1985 (see also E/1986/3).

0004

7.   As at 1 October 1991, initial reports concerning rights covered by articles 10 to 12 had been received from the following 49 States parties to the Covenant: Australia, Austria, Barbados, Bulgaria, Cameroon, Canada, Chile, Colombia, Cyprus, Czech and Slovak Federal Republic, Denmark, Democratic People's Republic of Korea, Ecuador, Finland, France, Germany, 1/ Hungary, India, Iraq, Italy, Jamaica, Japan, Jordan, Madagascar, Mexico, Mongolia, Netherlands, Nicaragua, Norway, Panama, Poland, Portugal, Republic of Belarus, Romania, Rwanda, Senegal, Spain, Sweden, Syrian Arab Republic, Trinidad and Tobago, Tunisia, Ukraine, Union of Soviet Socialist Republics, United Kingdom of Great Britain and Northern Ireland, United Republic of Tanzania, Venezuela, Yugoslavia, Zaire and Zambia (see E/1980/6 and addenda and E/1986/3 and addenda).

8.   The report of Nicaragua (E/1986/3/Add.15) is pending consideration by the Committee on Economic, Social and Cultural Rights.

Submission of initial reports concerning rights covered by articles 13 to 15 of the Covenant

9.   In accordance with the programme established by the Council in resolution 1988 (LX), initial reports concerning rights covered by articles 13 to 15 of the Covenant were due under the first cycle of the reporting procedure from 69 States parties by 1 September 1981 and initial reports concerning the same articles were due under the second cycle of the reporting procedure from 21 States parties by 1 September 1987. The Secretary-General, by a note verbale dated 25 March 1981, requested the 69 States parties for which the Covenant had entered into force by that date to submit their initial reports concerning those articles by 1 September 1981 (see also E/1982/3). By a note verbale dated 9 February 1987, the Secretary-General requested the 21 States parties for which the Covenant entered into force subsequently to submit their initial reports concerning articles 13 to 15 of the Covenant by 1 September 1987. By another note verbale, also dated 9 February 1987, the Secretary-General requested 29 States parties which had not yet submitted their initial reports concerning those articles, required under the first reporting cycle, to do so by 1 September 1987 (see E/1988/5).

10. As at 1 October 1991, initial reports concerning rights covered by articles 13 to 15 had been received from the following 47 States parties to the Covenant: Argentina, Australia, Austria, Barbados, Bulgaria, Canada, Chile, Colombia, Cyprus, Czech and Slovak Federal Republic, Democratic People's Republic of Korea, Denmark, Ecuador, Finland, France, Germany, 1/ Guyana, Hungary, India, Iran (Islamic Republic of), Iraq, Jamaica, Japan, Jordan, Libyan Arab Jamahiriya, Mexico, Mongolia, Netherlands, Nicaragua, Norway, Panama, Philippines, Poland, Portugal, Republic of Belarus, Romania, Rwanda, Senegal, Spain, Sweden, Trinidad and Tobago, Ukraine, Union of Soviet Socialist Republics, United Kingdom of Great Britain and Northern Ireland, Venezuela, Yugoslavia and Zaire (see E/1982/3 and addenda and E/1988/5 and addenda).

11. The reports of the Democratic People's Republic of Korea (E/1988/5/Add.6) and Panama (E/1988/5/Add.9) are pending consideration by the Committee on Economic, Social and Cultural Rights. Consideration of those reports was postponed at the fifth session of the Committee at the request of the Governments concerned.

0005

Submission of second periodic reports concerning rights covered by articles 6 to 9 of the Covenant

12. In accordance with the programme established by the Council in resolution 1988 (LX), second periodic reports concerning rights covered by articles 6 to 9 of the Covenant were due under the second cycle of the reporting procedure by 1 September 1983. The Secretary-General, by a note verbale dated 1 March 1983, requested the 31 States parties which had submitted initial reports under the first reporting cycle to submit their second periodic reports concerning those articles by 1 September 1983 (see also E/1984/7).

13. As at 1 October 1991, second periodic reports concerning rights covered by articles 6 to 9 had been received from the following 27 States parties to the Covenant: Australia, Bulgaria, Canada, Chile, Colombia, Cyprus, Czech and Slovak Federal Republic, Denmark, Ecuador, Finland, Germany, 1/ Hungary, Jamaica, Madagascar, Mongolia, Norway, Philippines, Poland, Republic of Belarus, Romania, Rwanda, Spain, Sweden, Ukraine, Union of Soviet Socialist Republics, United Kingdom of Great Britain and Northern Ireland and Yugoslavia (see E/1984/7 and addenda).

Submission of second periodic reports concerning rights covered by articles 10 to 12 of the Covenant

14. In accordance with the programme established by the Council in resolution 1988 (LX), second periodic reports concerning rights covered by articles 10 to 12 of the Covenant were due under the second cycle of the reporting procedure by 1 September 1985. The Secretary-General, by a note verbale dated 10 January 1985, requested the 35 States parties which had submitted initial reports under the first reporting cycle to submit their second periodic reports concerning those articles by 1 September 1985 (see also E/1986/4).

15. By its decision 1985/132 of 28 May 1985, the Council decided, while maintaining the current programme of biennial reports for the first cycle of the reporting procedure under article 16 of the Covenant, to prolong by one year the periodicity of reporting under the second and subsequent cycles. Accordingly, in a note verbale dated 21 October 1985, the Secretary-General informed those States parties which had not yet submitted their second periodic report on the rights covered by articles 10 to 12 of the Covenant that their reports would be due on 1 September 1986.

16. As at 1 October 1991, second periodic reports concerning rights covered by articles 10 to 12 had been received from the following 24 States parties to the Covenant: Australia, Austria, Bulgaria, Chile, Colombia, Cyprus, Czech and Slovak Federal Republic, Denmark, Finland, Germany, 1/ Hungary, Iraq, Mongolia, Netherlands, Norway, Panama, Poland, Republic of Belarus, Romania, Spain, Sweden, Ukraine, Union of Soviet Socialist Republics, United Kingdom of Great Britain and Northern Ireland (see E/1986/4 and addenda).

0006

17. The second periodic report of Panama (E/1986/4/Add.22) is pending consideration by the Committee on Economic, Social and Cultural Rights. Consideration of that report was postponed at the fifth session of the Committee at the request of the Government concerned.

Submission of second periodic reports concerning rights covered by articles 13 to 15 of the Covenant

18. In accordance with the programme established by the Council in resolution 1988 (LX), second periodic reports concerning rights covered by articles 13 to 15 of the Covenant were due under the second cycle of the reporting procedure by 1 September 1987.

19. By its decision 1985/132 of 28 May 1985, the Council decided, while maintaining the current programme of biennial reports for the first cycle of the reporting procedure under article 16 of the Covenant, to prolong by one year the periodicity of the reporting under the second and subsequent cycles. Accordingly, in a note verbale dated 18 May 1989, the Secretary-General requested the 21 States parties which had submitted initial reports on the rights covered by articles 13 to 15 of the Covenant under the first reporting cycle to submit their second periodic reports concerning those articles by 1 September 1989.

20. As at 1 October 1991, second periodic reports concerning rights covered by articles 13 to 15 had been received from the following 11 States parties to the Covenant: Colombia, Czech and Slovak Federal Republic, Finland, Hungary, Norway, Poland, Republic of Belarus, Sweden, Spain, Ukraine, Union of Soviet Socialist Republics.

21. Those second periodic reports, of Colombia (E/1990/7/Add.4), Czech and Slovak Federal Republic (E/1990/7/Add.6), Finland (E/1990/7/Add.1), Hungary (E/1990/7/Add.10), Norway (E/1990/7/Add.7), Poland (E/1990/7/Add.9), Republic of Belarus (E/1990/7/Add.5), Sweden (E/1990/7/Add.2), Spain (E/1990/7/Add.3), Ukraine (E/1990/7/Add.11) and Union of Soviet Socialist Republics (E/1990/7/Add.8), are pending consideration by the Committee on Economic, Social and Cultural Rights.

Submission of global reports concerning rights covered by articles 1 to 15 of the Covenant

22. As provided for under article 17 of the Covenant, the Economic and Social Council, by resolution 1988/4 of 24 May 1988, decided to revise its earlier programme of reporting by States parties established in its resolution 1988 (LX) of 11 May 1976 and endorsed the recommendation made by the Committee on Economic, Social and Cultural Rights at its second session (E/1988/14, para. 351) that States parties be requested to submit a single initial report within two years of the entry into force of the Covenant for the State party concerned and thereafter periodic reports at five-year intervals.

23. In a note verbale dated 30 September 1988, the Secretary-General informed States parties to the Covenant of this decision.

24. As at 1 October 1991, initial reports on articles 1 to 15 of the Covenant, submitted in accordance with Council resolution 1988/4, had been received from Afghanistan, Costa Rica, the Dominican Republic, Iceland, Luxembourg, New Zealand, and Uruguay; a second periodic report on articles 1 to 15 of the Covenant had been received from Italy and the Syrian Arab Republic.

25. As at 1 October 1991, the following 28 States parties to the Covenant had not yet submitted any reports at all since their ratification of, or accession to, the Covenant: Belgium, Bolivia, Central African Republic, Congo, Egypt, Equatorial Guinea, El Salvador, Gabon, Gambia, Greece, Guatemala, Guinea, Honduras, Kenya, Lebanon, Mali, Mauritius, Morocco, Niger, Saint Vincent and the Grenadines, San Marino, Solomon Islands, Sri Lanka, Sudan, Suriname, Togo, Uganda and Viet Nam. In accordance with the relevant decisions adopted by the Committee on Economic, Social and Cultural Rights at its third session (see E/1989/22, para. 337), the Secretary-General, in a note verbale dated 24 May 1989, informed the above-mentioned States parties that their initial reports on articles 1 to 15 of the Covenant should be submitted in one consolidated document by 30 June 1990 and their periodic reports at five-year intervals thereafter.

26. Zimbabwe, Nepal, and Grenada acceded to the Covenant on 13 May 1991, 14 May 1991 and 6 September 1991 respectively. Their initial reports on articles 1 to 15 of the Covenant are to be submitted by 30 June 1993 and their periodic reports at five-year intervals thereafter.

27. The initial reports submitted by the States parties listed in paragraphs 24, 25 and 26 above will be issued as addenda to document E/1990/5. The second periodic reports submitted by those States parties will be issued as addenda to document E/1990/6.

28. The initial reports of New Zealand (E/1990/5/Add.5), Iceland (E/1990/5/Add.6), Uruguay (E/1990/5/Add.7) and Afghanistan (E/1990/5/Add.8), as well as the second periodic reports of the Syrian Arab Republic (E/1990/6/Add.1) and Italy (E/1990/6/Add.2) are pending consideration by the Committee on Economic, Social and Cultural Rights. Consideration of the report of the Syrian Arab Republic was postponed at the fifth session of the Committee at the request of the Government concerned.

Notes

1/ Through the accession of the German Democratic Republic to the Federal Republic of Germany with effect from 3 October 1990, the two German States have united to form one sovereign State. As from the date of unification, the Federal Republic of Germany acts in the United Nations under the designation of "Germany". The former German Democratic Republic ratified the Covenant on 3 January 1976.

2/ The Group of Experts was informed at its 1980 session that the Government of the Islamic Republic of Iran had withdrawn the report concerning rights covered by articles 6 to 9 of the Covenant (see E/1980/60, para. 14).

3/ Not yet issued for technical reasons, in consultation with the reporting State.

Annex

STATES PARTIES TO THE COVENANT AND STATUS OF SUBMISSION OF REPORTS IN ACCORDANCE WITH THE PROGRAMME ESTABLISHED BY
ECONOMIC AND SOCIAL COUNCIL RESOLUTION 1988 (LX), DECISION 1985/132 AND RESOLUTION 1988/4

(As of 1 October 1991)

State party	Date of entry into force	INITIAL REPORTS			SECOND PERIODIC REPORTS		
		Articles 6-9 Due 1/9/77 or 1/9/83 a/	Articles 10-12 Due 1/9/79 or 1/9/85 a/	Articles 13-15 Due 1/9/81 or 1/9/87 a/	Articles 6-9 Second periodic reports due 1/9/83	Articles 10-12 Second periodic reports due 1/9/86 b/	Articles 13-15 Second periodic reports due 1/9/89 b/
		(Summary records of consideration of reports)			(Summary records of consideration of reports)		
1. Afghanistan	24 April 1983	E/1984/6/Add.12 (Pending consideration)	E/1990/5/Add.8 (Pending consideration)	E/1990/5/Add.8 (Pending consideration)	-	-	-
2. Algeria	12 December 1989	c/	c/	c/	-	-	-
3. Argentina	8 November 1986	Overdue	Overdue	E/1988/5/Add.4 E/1988/5/Add.8 (E/C.12/1990/SR.18-20)	-	-	-
4. Australia	10 March 1976	E/1978/8/Add.15 (E/1980/WG.1/SR.12-13)	E/1980/6/Add.22 (E/1981/WG.1/SR.18)	E/1982/3/Add.9 (E/1982/WG.1/SR.13-14)	E/1984/7/Add.22 (E/1985/WG.1/SR.17, 18 and 21)	E/1986/4/Add.7 (E/1986/WG.1/SR.10, 11, 13 and 14)	Overdue
5. Austria	10 December 1978	E/1984/6/Add.17 (E/C.12/1988/SR.3-4)	E/1980/6/Add.19 (E/1981/WG.1/SR.8)	E/1982/3/Add.37 (E/C.12/1988/SR.3)	-	E/1986/4/Add.8 and Corr.1 (E/1986/WG.1/SR.4 and 7)	Overdue
6. Barbados	3 January 1976	E/1978/8/Add.33 (E/1982/WG.1/SR.3)	E/1980/6/Add.27 (E/1982/WG.1/SR.6-7)	E/1982/3/Add.24 (E/1983/WG.1/SR.14-15)	Overdue	Overdue	Overdue
7. Belarus, Republic of	3 January 1976	E/1978/8/Add.19 (E/1980/WG.1/SR.16)	E/1980/6/Add.18 (E/1981/WG.1/SR.16)	E/1982/3/Add.3 (E/1982/WG.1/SR.9-10)	E/1984/7/Add.8 (E/1984/WG.1/SR.13-15)	E/1986/4/Add.19 (E/C.12/1988/SR.10-12)	E/1990/7/Add.5 (Pending consideration)
8. Belgium	21 July 1983	Overdue	Overdue	Overdue	Overdue	-	-
9. Bolivia	12 November 1982	Overdue	Overdue	Overdue	Overdue	-	-

Annex (continued)

State party	Date of entry into force	INITIAL REPORTS			SECOND PERIODIC REPORTS		
		Articles 6-9 Due 1/9/77 or 1/9/83 a/	Articles 10-12 Due 1/9/79 or 1/9/85 a/	Articles 13-15 Due 1/9/81 or 1/9/87 a/	Articles 6-9 Second periodic reports due 1/9/83	Articles 10-12 Second periodic reports due 1/9/86 b/	Articles 13-15 Second periodic reports due 1/9/89 b/
		(Summary records of consideration of reports)			(Summary records of consideration of reports)		
10. Bulgaria	3 January 1976	E/1978/8/Add.24 (E/1980/WG.1/SR.12)	E/1980/6/Add.29 (E/1982/WG.1/SR.8)	E/1982/3/Add.23 (E/1983/WG.1/SR.11-13)	E/1984/7/Add.18 (E/1985/WG.1/SR.9 and 11)	E/1986/4/Add.20 (E/C.12/1988/SR.17-19)	Overdue
11. Burundi	9 August 1990	c/	c/	c/	-	-	-
12. Cameroon	27 September 1984	Overdue	E/1986/3/Add.8 (E/C.12/1989/SR.6-7)	Overdue	-	-	-
13. Canada	19 August 1976	E/1978/8/Add.32 (E/1982/WG.1/SR.1-2)	E/1980/6/Add.32 (E/1984/WG.1/SR.4 and 6)	E/1982/3/Add.34 (E/1986/WG.1/SR.13, 15 and 16)	E/1984/7/Add.28 (E/C.12/1989/SR.8 and 11)	Overdue	Overdue
14. Central African Republic	8 August 1981	Overdue	Overdue	Overdue	-	-	Overdue
15. Chile	3 January 1976	E/1978/8/Add.10 and 28 (E/1980/WG.1/SR.8-9)	E/1980/6/Add.4 (E/1981/WG.1/SR.7)	E/1982/3/Add.40 (E/C.12/1988/SR.12-13 and 16)	E/1984/7/Add.1 (E/1984/WG.1/SR.11-12)	E/1986/4/Add.18 (E/C.12/1988/SR.12-13 and 16)	Overdue
16. Colombia	3 January 1976	E/1978/8/Add.17 (E/1980/WG.1/SR.15)	E/1986/3/Add.3 (E/1986/WG.1/SR.6 and 9)	E/1982/3/Add.36 (E/1986/WG.1/SR.15, 21 and 22)	E/1984/7/Add.21/Rev.1 (E/1986/WG.1/SR.22 and 25)	E/1986/4/Add.25 (E/C.12/1990/SR.12-14 and 17)	E/1990/7/Add.4 (Pending consideration)
17. Congo	5 January 1984	Overdue	Overdue	Overdue	-	-	-
18. Costa Rica	3 January 1976	E/1990/5/Add.3 (E/C.12/1991/SR.38, 40, 41 and 43)			Overdue	Overdue	Overdue
19. Cyprus	3 January 1976	E/1978/8/Add.21 (E/1980/WG.1/SR.17)	E/1980/6/Add.3 (E/1981/WG.1/SR.6)	E/1982/3/Add.19 (E/1983/WG.1/SR.7-8)	E/1984/7/Add.13 (E/1984/WG.1/SR.18 and 22)	E/1986/4/Add.2 and 26 (E/C.12/1990/SR.2, 3 and 5)	Overdue

0010

Annex (continued)

State party	Date of entry into force	INITIAL REPORTS			SECOND PERIODIC REPORTS		
		Articles 6-9 Due 1/9/77 or 1/9/83 a/	Articles 10-12 Due 1/9/79 or 1/9/85 a/	Articles 13-15 Due 1/9/81 or 1/9/87 a/	Articles 6-9 Second periodic reports due 1/9/83	Articles 10-12 Second periodic reports due 1/9/86 b/	Articles 13-15 Second periodic reports due 1/9/89 b/
		(Summary records of consideration of reports)			(Summary records of consideration of reports)		
20. Czech and Slovak Federal Republic	23 March 1976	E/1978/8/Add.18 (E/1981/WG.1/ SR.1-2)	E/1980/6/Add.21 (E/1981/WG.1/SR.3)	E/1982/3/Add.18 (E/1983/WG.1/ SR.6-7)	E/1984/7/Add.25 (E/C.12/1987/ SR.12-15)	E/1986/4/Add.15 (E/C.12/1987/ SR.12-15)	E/1990/7/Add.6 (Pending consideration)
21. Democratic People's Republic of Korea	14 December 1981	E/1984/6/Add.7 (E/C.12/1987/ SR.21-22)	E/1986/3/Add.5 (E/C.12/1987/ SR.21-22)	E/1988/5/Add.6 (Pending consideration)	Overdue	–	–
22. Denmark	3 January 1976	E/1978/8/Add.13 (E/1980/WG.1/ SR.10)	E/1980/6/Add.15 (E/1981/WG.1/ SR.12)	E/1982/3/Add.20 (E/1983/WG.1/ SR.8-9)	E/1984/7/Add.11 (E/1984/WG.1/ SR.17 and 21)	E/1986/4/Add.16 (E/C.12/1988/ SR.8-9)	Overdue
23. Dominican Republic	4 April 1978	E/1990/5/Add.4 (E/C.12/1991/SR.43-45 and 47)			–	Overdue	Overdue
24. Ecuador	3 January 1976	E/1978/8/Add.1 (E/1980/WG.1/ SR.4-5)	E/1986/3/Add.14 (E/C.12/1991/SR.37-39 and 42)	E/1988/5/Add.7	E/1984/7/Add.12 (E/1984/WG.1/ SR.20 and 22)	Overdue	Overdue
25. Egypt	14 April 1982	Overdue	Overdue	Overdue	Overdue	–	–
26. El Salvador	29 February 1980	Overdue	Overdue	Overdue	–	–	Overdue
27. Equatorial Guinea	25 December 1987	Overdue	Overdue	c/	–	–	–
28. Finland	3 January 1976	E/1978/8/Add.14 (E/1980/WG.1/SR.6)	E/1980/6/Add.11 (E/1981/WG.1/ SR.10)	E/1982/3/Add.28 (E/1984/WG.1/ SR.7-8)	E/1984/7/Add.14 (E/1984/WG.1/ SR.17-18)	E/1986/4/Add.4 (E/1986/WG.1 SR.8-9 and 11)	E/1990/7/Add.1 (Pending consideration)
29. France	4 February 1981	E/1984/6/Add.11 (E/1986/WG.1/ SR.18-19 and 21)	E/1986/3/Add.10 (E/C.12/1989/ SR.12-13)	E/1982/3/Add.30 and Corr.1 (E/1985/WG.1/ SR.5 and 7)	–	–	–
30. Gabon	21 April 1983	Overdue	Overdue	Overdue	Overdue	–	–
31. Gambia	29 March 1979	Overdue	Overdue	Overdue	Overdue	Overdue	Overdue

0012

Annex (continued)

State party	Date of entry into force	INITIAL REPORTS			SECOND PERIODIC REPORTS		
		Articles 6-9 Due 1/9/77 or 1/9/83 a/	Articles 10-12 Due 1/9/79 or 1/9/85 a/	Articles 13-15 Due 1/9/81 or 1/9/87 a/	Articles 6-9 Second periodic reports due 1/9/83	Articles 10-12 Second periodic reports due 1/9/86 b/	Articles 13-15 Second periodic reports due 1/9/89 b/
		(Summary records of consideration of reports)			(Summary records of consideration of reports)		
32. Germany d/	3 January 1976	E/1978/8/Add.8 and Corr.1 (E/1980/WG.1/SR.8) E/1978/8/Add.11 (E/1980/WG.1/SR.10)	E/1980/6/Add.6 (E/1980/WG.1/SR.8) E/1980/6/Add.10 (E/1981/WG.1/SR.10)	E/1982/3/Add.15 and Corr.1 (E/1983/WG.1/SR.5-6) E/1982/3/Add.14 (E/1982/WG.1/SR.17-18)	E/1984/7/Add.3 and 23 (E/1985/WG.1/SR.12 and 16) E/1984/7/Add.24 and Corr.1 (E/1986/WG.1/SR.22-23 and 25)	E/1986/4/Add.11 (E/C.12/1987/SR.11, 12 and 14) E/1986/4/Add.10 (E/C.12/1987/SR.19-20)	Overdue
33. Greece	16 August 1985	Overdue	c/	Overdue	-	-	-
34. Guatemala	19 August 1988	c/ Overdue	c/	c/	-	-	-
35. Guinea	24 April 1978	Overdue	Overdue	Overdue	-	Overdue	-
36. Guyana	15 May 1977	Overdue	Overdue	E/1982/3/Add.5, 29 and 32 (E/1984/WG.1/SR.20 and 22 and E/1985/WG.1/SR.6)	Overdue	Overdue	Overdue
37. Honduras	17 May 1981	Overdue	Overdue	Overdue	-	-	-
38. Hungary	3 January 1976	E/1978/8/Add.7 (E/1980/WG.1/SR.7)	E/1989/6/Add.37 (E/1986/WG.1/SR.6-7 and 9)	E/1982/3/Add.10 (E/1982/WG.1/SR.14)	E/1984/7/Add.15 (E/1984/WG.1/SR.19 and 21)	E/1986/4/Add.1 (E/1986/WG.1/SR.6-7 and 9)	E/1990/7/Add.10 (Pending consideration)
39. Iceland	22 November 1979	E/1990/5/Add.6 (Pending consideration)	E/1990/5/Add.6 (Pending consideration)	E/1990/5/Add.6 (Pending consideration)	-	-	Overdue
40. India	10 July 1979	E/1984/6/Add.13 (E/1986/WG.1/SR.20 and 24)	E/1980/6/Add.34 (E/1984/WG.1/SR.6 and 8)	E/1988/5/Add.5 (E/C.12/1990/SR.16-17 and 19)	Overdue	Overdue	Overdue
41. Iran (Islamic Republic of)	3 January 1976	E/1978/8/Add.2 e/	Overdue	E/1982/3/Add.43 (E/C.12/1991/SR.42, 43 and 45)	Overdue	Overdue	Overdue

0013

Annex (continued)

State party	Date of entry into force	INITIAL REPORTS			SECOND PERIODIC REPORTS		
		Articles 6-9 Due 1/9/77 or 1/9/83 a/	Articles 10-12 Due 1/9/79 or 1/9/85 a/	Articles 13-15 Due 1/9/81 or 1/9/87 a/	Articles 6-9 Second periodic reports due 1/9/83	Articles 10-12 Second periodic reports due 1/9/86 b/	Articles 13-15 Second periodic reports due 1/9/89 b/
		(Summary records of consideration of reports)			(Summary records of consideration of reports)		
42. Iraq	3 January 1976	E/1984/6/Add.3 and 8 (E/1985/WG.1/SR.8 and 11)	E/1980/6/Add.14 (E/1981/WG.1/SR.12)	E/1982/3/Add.26 (E/1985/WG.1/SR.3-4)	Overdue	E/1986/4/Add.3 (E/1986/WG.1/SR.8 and 11)	Overdue
43. Ireland	8 March 1990	c/	c/	c/	-	-	-
44. Italy	15 December 1978	E/1978/8/Add.34 (E/1982/WG.1/SR.3-4)	E/1980/6/Add.31 and 36 (E/1984/WG.1/SR.3 and 5)	Overdue	E/1990/6/Add.2 (Pending consideration)	E/1990/6/Add.2 (Pending consideration)	E/1990/6/Add.2 (Pending consideration)
45. Jamaica	3 January 1976	E/1978/8/Add.27 (E/1980/WG.1/SR.20)	E/1986/3/Add.12 (E/C.12/1990/SR.10-12 and 15)	E/1988/5/Add.3 (E/C.12/1990/SR.10-12 and 15)	E/1984/7/Add.30 (E/C.12/1990/SR.10-12 and 15)	Overdue	Overdue
46. Japan	21 September 1979	E/1984/6/Add.6 and Corr.1 (E/1984/WG.1/SR.9-10)	E/1986/3/Add.4 and Corr.1 (E/1986/WG.1/SR.20-21 and 23)	E/1982/3/Add.7 (E/1982/WG.1/SR.12-13)	-		-
47. Jordan	3 January 1976	E/1984/6/Add.15 (E/C.12/1987/SR.6-8)	E/1986/3/Add.6 (E/C.12/1987/SR.8)	E/1982/3/Add.38/Rev.1 (E/C.12/1991/SR.30-32)	Overdue	Overdue	Overdue
48. Kenya	3 January 1976	Overdue	Overdue	Overdue	Overdue	Overdue	Overdue
49. Rep. of Korea	10 July 1990	c/	c/	c/	-	-	-
50. Lebanon	3 January 1976	Overdue	Overdue	Overdue	Overdue	Overdue	Overdue
51. Libyan Arab Jamahiriya	3 January 1976	Overdue	Overdue	E/1982/3/Add.6 and 25 (E/1983/WG.1/SR.16-17)	Overdue	Overdue	Overdue

0014

Annex (continued)

State party	Date of entry into force	INITIAL REPORTS			SECOND PERIODIC REPORTS		
		Articles 6-9 Due 1/9/77 or 1/9/83 a/	Articles 10-12 Due 1/9/79 or 1/9/85 a/	Articles 13-15 Due 1/9/81 or 1/9/87 a/	Articles 6-9 Second periodic reports due 1/9/83	Articles 10-12 Second periodic reports due 1/9/86 b/	Articles 13-15 Second periodic reports due 1/9/89 b/
		(Summary records of consideration of reports)			(Summary records of consideration of reports)		
52. Luxembourg	18 November 1983	E/1990/5/Add.1 (E/C.12/1990/SR.33-36)			Overdue	-	-
53. Madagascar	3 January 1976	E/1978/8/Add.29 (E/1981/WG.1/ SR.2)	E/1980/6/Add.39 (E/1986/WG.1/ SR.2-3 and 5)	Overdue	E/1984/7/Add.19 (E/1985/WG.1/ SR.14 and 18)	Overdue	Overdue
54. Mali	3 January 1976	Overdue	Overdue	Overdue	Overdue	Overdue	Overdue
55. Malta	13 December 1990	c/	c/	c/	-	-	-
56. Mauritius	3 January 1976	Overdue	Overdue	Overdue	Overdue	Overdue	Overdue
57. Mexico	23 June 1981	E/1984/6/Add.2 and 10 (E/1986/WG.1/ SR.24, 26 and 28)	E/1986/3/Add.13 (E/C.12/1990/ SR.6, 7 and 9)	E/1982/3/Add.8 (E/1982/WG.1/ SR.14-15)	-		
58. Mongolia	3 January 1976	E/1978/8/Add.6 (E/1980/WG.1/ SR.7)	E/1980/6/Add.7 (E/1981/WG.1/ SR.8-9)	E/1982/3/Add.11 (E/1982/WG.1/ SR.15-16)	E/1984/7/Add.6 (E/1984/WG.1/ SR.16 and 18)	E/1986/4/Add.9 (E/C.12/1988/ SR.5 and 7)	Overdue
59. Morocco	3 August 1979	Overdue	Overdue	Overdue	-	Overdue	Overdue
60. Nepal	14 August 1991	c/	c/	c/	-	-	-
61. Netherlands	11 March 1979	E/1984/6/Add.14 and 20 (E/C.12/1987/ SR.5-6) (E/C.12/1989/ SR.14-15)	E/1980/6/Add.33 (E/1984/WG.1/ SR.4-6 and 8)	E/1982/3/Add.35 and 44 (E/1986/WG.1/ SR.14 and 18) (E/C.12/1989/ SR.14-15)	-	E/1986/4/Add.24 (E/C.12/1989/ SR.14-15)	Overdue
62. New Zealand	28 March 1979	E/1990/5/Add.5 (Pending consideration)	E/1990/5/Add.5 (Pending consideration)	E/1990/5/Add.5 (Pending consideration)	-		Overdue

Annex (continued)

State party	Date of entry into force	INITIAL REPORTS			SECOND PERIODIC REPORTS		
		Articles 6-9 Due 1/9/77 or 1/9/83 a/	Articles 10-12 Due 1/9/79 or 1/9/85 a/	Articles 13-15 Due 1/9/81 or 1/9/87 a/	Articles 6-9 Second periodic reports due 1/9/83	Articles 10-12 Second periodic reports due 1/9/86 b/	Articles 13-15 Second periodic reports due 1/9/89 b/
		(Summary records of consideration of reports)			(Summary records of consideration of reports)		
63. Nicaragua	12 June 1980	E/1984/6/Add.9 (E/1986/WG.1/ SR.16-17 and 19)	E/1986/3/Add.15 (Pending consideration)	E/1982/3/Add.31 and Corr.1 (E/1985/WG.1/ SR.15)	-	-	-
64. Niger	7 June 1986	Overdue	c/	Overdue	-	-	-
65. Norway	3 January 1976	E/1978/8/Add.12 (E/1980/WG.1/ SR.5)	E/1980/6/Add.5 (E/1981/WG.1/ SR.14)	E/1982/3/Add.12 (E/1982/WG.1/ SR.16)	E/1984/7/Add.16 (E/1984/WG.1/ SR.19 and 22)	E/1986/4/Add.21 (E/C.12/1988/ SR.14-15)	E/1990/7/Add.7 (Pending consideration)
66. Panama	8 June 1977	E/1984/6/Add.19 (Pending consideration)	E/1980/6/Add.20 and 23 (E/1982/WG.1/ SR.5)	E/1988/5/Add.9 (Pending consideration)	Overdue	E/1986/4/Add.22 (Pending consideration)	Overdue
67. Peru	28 July 1978	E/1984/6/Add.5 (E/1984/WG.1/ SR.11 and 18)	Overdue	Overdue	-	Overdue	Overdue
68. Philippines	3 January 1976	E/1978/8/Add.4 (E/1980/WG.1/ SR.11)	Overdue	E/1988/5/Add.2 (E/C.12/1990/ SR.8-9 and 11)	E/1984/7/Add.4 (E/1984/WG.1/ SR.15 and 20)	Overdue	Overdue
69. Poland	18 June 1977	E/1978/8/Add.23 (E/1980/WG.1/ SR.18-19)	E/1980/6/Add.12 (E/1981/WG.1/ SR.11)	E/1982/3/Add.21 (E/1983/WG.1/ SR.9-10)	E/1984/7/Add.26 and 27 (E/1986/WG.1/ SR.25-27)	E/1986/4/Add.12 (E/C.12/1989/ SR.5-6)	E/1990/7/Add.9 (Pending consideration)
70. Portugal	31 October 1978	E/1984/6/ Add.16 f/	E/1980/6/Add.35/ Rev.1 (E/1985/WG.1/ SR.2 and 4)	E/1982/3/Add.27/ Rev.1 (E/1985/WG.1/ SR.6 and 9)	Overdue	Overdue	Overdue
71. Romania	3 January 1976	E/1978/8/Add.20 (E/1980/WG.1/ SR.16-17)	E/1980/6/Add.1 (E/1981/WG.1/ SR.5)	E/1982/3/Add.13 (E/1982/WG.1/ SR.17-18)	E/1984/7/Add.17 (E/1985/WG.1/ SR.10 and 13)	E/1986/4/Add.17 (E/C.12/1988/ SR.6)	Overdue

Annex (continued)

State party	Date of entry into force	INITIAL REPORTS (Summary records of consideration of reports)			SECOND PERIODIC REPORTS (Summary records of consideration of reports)		
		Articles 6-9 Due 1/9/77 or 1/9/83 a/	Articles 10-12 Due 1/9/79 or 1/9/85 a/	Articles 13-15 Due 1/9/81 or 1/9/87 a/	Articles 6-9 Second periodic reports due 1/9/83	Articles 10-12 Second periodic reports due 1/9/86 b/	Articles 13-15 Second periodic reports due 1/9/89 b/
72. Rwanda	3 January 1976	E/1984/6/Add.4 (E/1984/WG.1/ SR.10 and 12)	E/1986/3/Add.1 (E/1986/WG.1/ SR.16 and 19)	E/1982/3/Add.42 (E/C.12/1989/ SR.10-12)	E/1984/7/Add.29 (E/C.12/1989/ SR.10-12)	Overdue	Overdue
73. Saint Vincent and the Grenadines	9 February 1982	Overdue	Overdue	Overdue	Overdue	-	-
74. San Marino	18 January 1986	Overdue	c/	Overdue	-	-	-
75. Senegal	13 May 1978	Overdue	E/1980/6/Add.13/ Rev.1 (E/1981/WG.1/ SR.11)	E/1982/3/Add.17 (E/1983/WG.1/ SR.14-16)	-	Overdue	Overdue
76. Solomon Islands	17 March 1982	Overdue	Overdue	Overdue c/	Overdue	-	-
77. Somalia	24 April 1990	c/	c/	c/	-	-	-
78. Spain	27 July 1977	E/1978/8/Add.26 (E/1980/WG.1/ SR.20)	E/1980/6/Add.28 (E/1982/WG.1/ SR.7)	E/1982/3/Add.22 (E/1983/WG.1/ SR.10-11)	E/1984/7/Add.2 (E/1984/WG.1/ SR.12 and 14)	E/1986/4/Add.6 (E/1986/WG.1/ SR.10 and 13)	E/1990/7/Add.3 (Pending consideration)
79. Sri Lanka	11 September 1980	Overdue	Overdue	Overdue	-	-	Overdue
80. Sudan	18 June 1986	Overdue	c/	Overdue	-	-	-
81. Suriname	28 March 1977	Overdue	Overdue	Overdue	Overdue	Overdue	Overdue
82. Sweden	3 January 1976	E/1978/8/Add.5 (E/1980/WG.1/ SR.15)	E/1980/6/Add.8 (E/1981/WG.1/ SR.9)	E/1982/3/Add.2 (E/1982/WG.1/ SR.19-20)	E/1984/7/Add.5 (E/1984/WG.1/ SR.14 and 16)	E/1986/4/Add.13 (E/C.12/1988/ SR.10-11)	E/1990/7/Add.2 (Pending consideration)
83. Syrian Arab Republic	3 January 1976	E/1978/8/Add.25 and 31 (E/1983/WG.1/ SR.2)	E/1980/6/Add.9 (E/1981/WG.1/ SR.4)	-	E/1990/6/Add.1 (Pending consideration)	E/1990/6/Add.1 (Pending consideration)	E/1990/6/Add.1 (Pending consideration)
84. Togo	24 August 1984	Overdue	Overdue	Overdue	-	-	-

0017

Annex (continued)

State party	Date of entry into force	INITIAL REPORTS			SECOND PERIODIC REPORTS		
		Articles 6-9 Due 1/9/77 or 1/9/83 a/	Articles 10-12 Due 1/9/79 or 1/9/85 a/	Articles 13-15 Due 1/9/81 or 1/9/87 a/	Articles 6-9 Second periodic reports due 1/9/83	Articles 10-12 Second periodic reports due 1/9/86 b/	Articles 13-15 Second periodic reports due 1/9/89 b/
		(Summary records of consideration of reports)			(Summary records of consideration of reports)		
85. Trinidad and Tobago	8 March 1979	E/1984/6/Add.21 (E/C.12/1989/ SR.17-19)	E/1986/3/Add.11 (E/C.12/1989/ SR.17-19)	E/1988/5/Add.1 (E/C.12/1989/ SR.17-19)	–	Overdue	Overdue
86. Tunisia	3 January 1976	E/1978/8/Add.3 (E/1980/WG.1/ SR.5-6)	E/1986/3/Add.9 (E/C.12/1989/ SR.9)	Overdue	Overdue	Overdue	Overdue
87. Uganda	21 April 1987	Overdue	c/	Overdue	–	–	–
88. Ukraine	3 January 1976	E/1978/8/Add.22 (E/1980/WG.1/ SR.18)	E/1980/6/Add.24 (E/1982/WG.1/ SR.5-6)	E/1982/3/Add.4 (E/1982/WG.1/ SR.11-12)	E/1984/7/Add.9 (E/1984/WG.1/ SR.13-15)	E/1986/4/Add.5 (E/C.12/1987/ SR.9-11)	E/1990/7/Add.11 (Pending consideration)
89. Union of Soviet Socialist Republics	3 January 1976	E/1978/8/Add.16 (E/1980/WG.1/ SR.14)	E/1980/6/Add.17 (E/1981/WG.1/ SR.14-15)	E/1982/3/Add.1 (E/1982/WG.1/ SR.11-12)	E/1984/7/Add.7 (E/1984/WG.1/ SR.9-10)	E/1986/4/Add.14 (E/C.12/1987/ SR.16-18)	E/1990/7/Add.8 (Pending consideration)
90. United Kingdom of Great Britain and Northern Ireland	20 August 1976	E/1978/8/Add.9 and 30 (E/1980/WG.1/ SR.19 and E/1982/WG.1/ SR.1)	E/1980/6/Add.16 and Corr.1, Add.25 and Corr.1 and Add.26 (E/1981/WG.1/ SR.16-17)	E/1982/3/Add.16 (E/1982/WG.1/ SR.19-21)	E/1984/7/Add.20 (E/1985/WG.1/ SR.14 and 17)	E/1986/4/Add.23 (E/C.12/1989/ SR.16-17)	Overdue
91. United Republic of Tanzania	11 September 1976	Overdue	E/1980/6/Add.2 (E/1980/WG.1/ SR.5)	Overdue	Overdue	Overdue	Overdue
92. Uruguay	3 January 1976	E/1990/5/Add.7 (Pending consideration)	E/1990/5/Add.7 (Pending consideration)	E/1990/7/Add.7 (Pending consideration)	Overdue	Overdue	Overdue
93. Venezuela	10 August 1978	E/1984/6/Add.1 (E/1984/WG.1/ SR.7-8 and 10)	E/1980/6/Add.38 (E/1986/WG.1/ SR.2 and 5)	E/1982/3/Add.33 (E/1986/WG.1/ SR.12, 17 and 18)	Overdue	Overdue	Overdue
94. Viet Nam	24 December 1982	Overdue	Overdue	Overdue	Overdue	–	–

Annex (continued)

State party	Date of entry into force	INITIAL REPORTS			SECOND PERIODIC REPORTS		
		Articles 6-9 Due 1/9/77 or 1/9/83 a/	Articles 10-12 Due 1/9/79 or 1/9/85 a/	Articles 13-15 Due 1/9/81 or 1/9/87 a/	Articles 6-9 Second periodic reports due 1/9/83	Articles 10-12 Second periodic reports due 1/9/86 b/	Articles 13-15 Second periodic reports due 1/9/89 b/
		(Summary records of consideration of reports)			(Summary records of consideration of reports)		
95. Yemen g/	9 May 1987	-	-	-	-	-	-
96. Yugoslavia	3 January 1976	E/1978/8/Add.35 (E/1982/WG.1/ SR.4-5)	E/1980/6/Add.30 (E/1983/WG.1/ SR.3)	E/1982/3/Add.39 (E/C.12/1988/ SR.14-15)	E/1984/7/Add.10 (E/1984/WG.1/ SR.16 and 18)	Overdue	Overdue
97. Zaire	1 February 1977	E/1984/6/Add.18 (E/C.12/1988/ SR.16-19)	E/1986/3/Add.7 (E/C.12/1988/ SR.16-19)	E/1982/3/Add.41 (E/C.12/1988 SR.16-19)	Overdue	Overdue	Overdue
98. Zambia	10 July 1984	Overdue	E/1986/3/Add.2 (E/1986/WG.1/ SR.4-5 and 7)	Overdue	-	-	-
99. Zimbabwe	13 August 1991	c/	-	c/	-	-	-

a/   Depending on date of entry into force.

b/   See Economic and Social Council decision 1985/132 of 28 May 1985.

c/   Not yet due.

d/   Through the accession of the German Democratic Republic to the Federal Republic of Germany with effect from 3 October 1990, the two German States have united to form one sovereign State. As from the date of unification, the Federal Republic of Germany will act in the United Nations under the designation of "Germany". The former German Democratic Republic ratified the Covenant on 3 January 1976.

e/   Withdrawn.

f/   Not yet issued for technical reasons, in consultation with the reporting State.

g/   As of 22 May 1990 the People's Democratic Republic of Yemen and the Yemen Arab Republic merged into a single sovereign State, the Republic of Yemen, with Sana'a as its capital. The People's Democratic Republic of Yemen had acceded to the Covenant on 9 May 1977. The Yemen Arab Republic was not a State party to the Covenant.

0018

주 제 네 바 대 표 부   김

제네(정) 2031-1025   1991. 11. 28.

수신 : 장관

참조 : 국제기구국장, 법무부장관

제목 : 일본의 경제적.사회적.문화적 권리에 관한 국제규약

(seal) 91. 11. 29

　　　일본의 인권규약(A 규약) 최초 보고서와 심의기록을 별첨 송부하오니,
아국 최초 보고서 준비에 참고 하시기 바랍니다.

첨부 : 일본의 최초 보고서 및 심의기록 각 1부.   끝.

주 제 네 바 대 사

선결			결재(공람)		
접수일시 1991. 12. 6					
처리과 2과 68677					

0019

관리	91
번호	ㅡ/72

<table>
<tr><td></td><td>분류번호</td><td>보존기간</td></tr>
<tr><td></td><td></td><td></td></tr>
</table>

발 신 전 보

WGV-1755　911204 1434　FL

번　　호 :　　　　　　　　　　　　　　종별 : 지 급

수　　신 :　주　　　제네바　　　대사. ♣♣♣♣♣

발　　신 :　장　관 (연이)

제　　목 :　제6차 경제.사회.문화적 권리위원회

　　　12.3자 제네바발 로이타 통신은 지난주 개최된 경제.사회.문화적

권리위원회에서의 북한 보고서 심의시 소련, 몽골등 동구권국가 위원들이

북한의 문화적 권리보장문제를 집중 제기하였다고 보도하였는바, 상기

북한 보고서 심의내용을 파악, 관련 Press Release와 함께 지급 보고바람. 끝.

(국제기구국장　문동석)

일반문서로 재분류(1991 .12.31.)

<table>
<tr><td></td><td></td><td>보 안
통 제</td><td></td></tr>
</table>

<table>
<tr><td rowspan="3">앙
고
재</td><td rowspan="3">91
년
12
월
4
일</td><td rowspan="3">유민
2
과</td><td>기안자
성 명</td><td></td><td>과 장</td><td>심의관</td><td>국 장</td><td></td><td>차 관</td><td>장 관</td></tr>
<tr><td rowspan="2">기동술</td><td></td><td></td><td></td><td></td><td></td><td></td><td></td></tr>
<tr><td></td><td></td><td></td><td></td><td></td><td></td><td></td></tr>
</table>

외신과통제

0020

FORMER COMMUNIST ALLIES GRILL NORTH KOREA ON HUMAN RIGHTS
    By Robert Evans
    GENEVA, Dec 3, Reuter - North Korea, one of the world's few
remaining Marxist states, has undergone tough grilling on human
rights from former communist countries that were once its close
allies, according to documents released on Tuesday.
    The often clearly hostile cross-examination took place
during a session of the Economic, Social and Cultural Rights
Committee (CESCR) of the United Nations Commission on Human
Rights in Geneva last week, the documents showed.
    Joining the offensive were representatives of the Soviet
Union, Mongolia, Bulgaria and Poland -- all of whom in the past
could have been expected to resist any attempt to pillory a
fellow communist government.
    Officials from the four, and from several developing
countries and Germany, closely questioned Pyongyang's top
diplomat in Geneva on educational and cultural freedoms he had
told them the North Korean people fully enjoyed.
    According to an account released by the CESCR, Soviet
delegate Valery Kuznetsov said members of the committee knew
there was no country in the world without problems including
North Korea, and asked to be told what they were.
    Mongolia's woman delegate asked the Pyongyang official, Ri
Cheul, if it was possible for anyone to publish his work if it
did not conform to the line of the ruling Workers' Party of
President Kim Il-Sung or to government policies.
    Were there any structures other than the Party or the state
which controlled the country's cultural life, she demanded,
according to the paraphrased account of the session issued by
the CESCR.
    "It was a clear illustration of how things have changed at
the United Nations with the end of the Cold War and the collapse
of the Communist bloc," said one Geneva diplomat.
    "Here you had former communist countries not only taking
part in the attack on human rights issues, but in effect leading
it, and against a one-time ally."
    At annual sessions, the CESCR hears reports from countries
which signed a 1976 U.N. covenant on economic, social and
cultural rights -- covering areas ranging from education to the
role of women -- on how they are implementing it.
    For years Western countries argued that hearings in U.N.
human rights bodies were weighted in favour of communist states
and left-wing regimes in developing countries whose delegates
worked together to prevent discussion of their record.
    The questioning of the North Korean delegate came after he
told the committee his country was guided by Kim Il-Sung's
"juche" -- self-reliance -- philosophy which had found "perfect
solutions" and put human beings "at the centre of all concerns".
    Polish delegate Wladyslaw Neneman noted that an earlier
North Korean report had begun with the phrase: "In a socialist
paradise, everybody lives happily" and that the latest one had
declared everyone in the country enjoyed freedom.
    If this were so, he asked, could anyone go or work anywhere
he wanted, or could he say anything he wanted and preach
anything he chose?
    Bulgaria's Vassil Mrachkov asked the Pyongyang diplomat to
explain the meaning of the "monolithic educational system" Ri
Cheul had told the CESCR was in place in his country.
    Such a system, declared Mrachkov, did not appear to take
into account the inherent differences between children.
    REUTER RJE BM   4
    Reut14:55 03-12   0021

Former Communist Allies Grill NK on Human Rights

GENEVA (Reuter) — North Korea, one of the world's few remaining Marxist states, has undergone tough grilling on human rights from former communist countries that were once its close allies, according to documents released on Tuesday.

The often clearly hostile cross-examination took place during a session of the Economic, Social and Cultural Rights Committee (CESCR) of the United Nations Commission on Human Rights in Geneva last week, the documents showed.

Joining the offensive were represen-tatives of the Soviet Union, Mongolia, Bulgaria and Poland — all of whom in the past could have been expected to resist any attempt to pillory a fellow communist government.

Officials from the four, and from several developing countries and Germany, closely questioned Pyongyang's top diplomat in Geneva on educational and cultural freedoms he had told them the North Korean people fully enjoyed.

According to an account released by the CESCR, Soviet delegate Valery Kuznetsov said members of the committee knew there was no country in the world without problems including North Korea, and asked to be told what they were.

Mongolia's woman delegate asked the Pyongyang official, Ri Che-ul, if it was possible for anyone to publish his work if it did not conform to the line of the ruling Workers' Party of President Kim Il-sung or to government policies.

Were there any structures other than the Party or the state which controlled the country's cultural life, she demanded, according to the paraphrased account of the session issued by the CESCR.

"It was a clear illustration of how things have changed at the United Nations with the end of the Cold War and the collapse of the communist bloc," said one Geneva diplomat.

The questioning of the North Korean delegate came after he told the committee his country was guided by Kim Il-sung's "Juche" — self-reliance — philosophy which had found "perfect solutions" and put human beings "at the center of all concerns."

0022

北韓인권 집중거론 _{유엔小委}

蘇등·前맹방국들 적대적 질문공세

【제네바=聯合】북한은 지난주 제네바에서 열린 유엔인권위원회 경제 사회및 문화

적 권리소위원회(CESCR)에서 북한의 前공산맹방들로 부터 북한내 인권문제와 관련, 노골적으로 적대적인 질문공세를 받은 것으로 3일 공개된 유엔문서에서 밝혀졌다.

이 문서에 따르면 지난 76년 유엔 교육 사회 문화적 권리협약 서명국들로 부터 그 실천방안에 대한

국제회의에서 소련을 위시한 그들의 前공산맹방들을 비롯한 국제회의에서 북한은 완전한 해결방안을 제시하고 인간을 모든 事物의 중심에 두는 金日成의 주체사상에 의해 영도되고 있다는 북한대표 李철의 보고가 있은 직후 소련 몽골 불가리아 폴란드등의 대표들이 "종종 분명히 적대적인 반대신문을 던진 것으로 밝혀졌다.

보고를 청취하기 위해 지난 주 제네바에서 열린 한 주제네바에서 소련을 한국 국제회의에서 소련

소련등 이들 4개국과 독일, 그리고 일부 개발도상 국 대표들은 회의석상에서 李에게 북한이 100%향 유하고 있다고 주장하는 교육및 문화분야에서의 자유실태에 대해 상세한 질문을 던졌는데, 특히 소련대표 발레리 쿠즈네쵸프는 각국 대표들에게 아무런 문제도 없다면서 만약 그런 나라를 북한을 포함하여 한 나라도 없는 이 세상에서 북한을 본 적이 있는지를 반문하기조차 했다.

北인권실태 중점거론 유엔인권小委 연례회의

【제네바=朝鮮】北韓은 지난 주 제네바에서 열린 한국 주제네바에서 蘇聯을 비롯한 제회의에서 그들의 前공산맹방들로부터 북한내 인권문제와 관 력, 적대적인 질문공세를

받은것으로 3일 공개된 유엔문서에서 밝혀졌다.

이 문서에 따르면 지난주 제네바에서 열린 유엔인권 위원회 경제 사회및 문화 권리소위원회(CESCR)에 서는 金日成의 「주체사상」에 의해 영도되고 있다는 북 한대표 李철의 보고가 있 은 직후 소련 몽골 불가리 아 폴란드등의 대표들이 「분명히 적대적인」 반대신 문을 던진 것으로 밝혀졌 다.

「北韓 인권」에 집중화살

蘇·몽골등 UN인권위 小委서 힐난

"黨이념 어긋나는 책 못봤다"

[제네바=聯合] 북한은지 난주 제네바에서 열린 한 국제회의에서 소련을 위시 한 그들의 前 공산맹방들 로부터 북한내 인권문제와 관련, 굴욕적으로 적대적인 질문공세를 받았던것으로 3 일 공개된 유엔문서에서 밝혀졌다.

이 문서에 따르면 교육에 서부터 여성의역할에 이르 기까지 광범한분야에 관한 지난 76년 유엔 교육·사회· 문화적 권리협약 서명국들 로부터 그 「실천상」에 대한 보고를 청취하기위해 지난 주 제네바에서열린 유엔인 권위원회 경제·사회문화 관리 소위원회(CESCR) 연례회의에서 북한은완전 히 해결방안)을 제시하고 간을 모든사물의「주체사상」에의 노선이나 정부정책에 부합 되지않은 저술을 발간하는 일이 가능한가고 질문에 답변되고있었다는 북한대 표季章철의 보고가 있은직후

소련·몽골·불가리아·폴란 드등의 대표들이 「敵意」분 명히 적대적인 반대질문을 을 던진것으로 밝혀졌다. 소련등 이들 4개국과

독일 대표들은 회의석상에 서 향유하고 있다고 주장 하는 교육및 문화분야에서 의 자유 실태에 대해, 상세 한 질문을 던졌는데, 특히 소련대표 발레리 쿠즈네 초프는 각국 대표들에게 아무런 문제도 없는 나라 는 이 세상에서 북한뿐이 라함으로 北韓의 과장된 %서 향유에게 북한이 1백 상 李章철로 밝혔다.

만약 그런 나라들이 있 어 변적이 있는지를 방문 하기조차 했으며 「%만의여 성대표는 李章철에게 북한에 서 누구라도 북한당국의

외 무 부

종   별 :

번   호 : GVW-2559   일   시 : 91 1205 1500

수   신 : 장관(연이,기정동문) 사본: 주유엔대사(본부중계필)

발   신 : 주 제네바대사

제   목 : 제 6차 경제.사회.문화적 권리위원회

　　대: WGV-1755

　　1. 표제회의는 11.27-29 간 A 규약 제 13-15 조(교육 및 문화 예술활동) 관련 북한이 제출한 최초 보고서를 심의한바, 인권위 사무국으로 부터 파악한 동 결과를 아래 보고함.

　　가. 회의진행 및 참석

　　- 북한 보고서는 11.27-29 3 일간에 걸쳐 심의되었으나 실제 심의시간은 5-6시간 정도 소요(매일 오후 SESSION 에서만 다루어졌고, 동 SESSION 에서는 여타국 보고서도 함께 심의)

　　- 11.27 이철대사의 보고서 소개 및 위원질문에 이어 11.28 북한측의 답변 및 추가질문이 있었고 11.29 에는 COUCLUDING OBSERVATION 이 있었음.

　　- 북한에서는 이철대사, 국가교육위원회 채양일, 참사관 박덕훈, 이태준등이 참석

　　나. 북한 보고서 구성 및 내용 요지

　　- 서론부 및 상기 조항별 보고 부분으로 구성(총 11 페이지)

　　- 서론부에서는 일제 식민통치, 국토분단, 6.25. 전쟁등 어려움에도 불구 북한 정권은 해방직후부터 교육, 과학, 기술 및 문화 예술 창달을 중시해 왔다고주장

　　- 13,14 조(교육) 관련 부분에서는 김일성의 "사회주의 교육 테제"에 따른 무상, 의무교육, 직장교육, 학교선택의 자유등을 언급

　　- 15 조(과학, 기술연구 및 문화 예술활동) 관련 부분에서는 해당분야 권리보장 및 지원에 관한 당과 정부의 역할, 해당분야 활동현황, 저작권 및 과학기술연구 및 창조활동 자유보장을 언급

　　3. 의원질문 및 북측 답변

　　- 교육관련 부분에서는 김일성의 "사회주의 교육 테제"가 교육관련 모든 이론직

국기국	장관	차관	1차보	2차보	외정실	분석관	청와대	안기부
중계								

외신 2과　통제관 FM

0025

현실문제에 대한 완벽한 해결책을 제시하고 있다는 북측 보고 내용 및 북한의 단일(MONOLITHIC) 교육 체제 및 유일 주체사상등과 관련, 학교선택권, 교육선택의 자유등이 보장될 수 있는지의 여부등에 대해 질문이 집중됨.(폴란드, 세네갈, 불가리아, 독일등)

- 연구 및 문화 예술활동 부분에 대해서도 역시 유일사항 하에서 동 활동에 대한 진정한 자유가 보장될 수 있는지 의문이 폴란드, 필리핀등 다수위원들로부터 제기되었고, 특히 창작 및 출판 검열위원회(SCREENING COMMITTEE)에 의한동 활동자유 저해 위험성이 집중 추궁됨. 이에 대해 북한은 타국(서방국가 지칭)에도 동종의 심사위원회가 있음을 강변하였으나 일부위원(독일등) 들로 부터 서방국가에는 사법적 재심제도가 있으므로 북한과는 사정이 다르다는 반론이 있었고, 이에따라 CONCLUDING OBSERVATION 에 예술, 문화 작품 심사를 위한 제도가 표현의 자유를 부적절하게 보호하는 결과를 초래하고 있다는 우려 표명 문안이포함됨.

- 또한 루안다 위원은 북한의 보고서가 법률적 이론적 측면만 부가시키고 북한내 현실적 상황에 관한 구체적 진술을 결여하고 있다는 평가를 하였으며 북한이 교육에 대한 참여를 확대하는등 제도를 개선하려는 노력을 계속하도록 고무하여야 한다고 언급한바, 이는 그대로 CONCLUDING OBSERVATION 에 반영됨.

- 기타 교과내용 결정과정에 대한 학부형, 교사등의 참여 가능성, 교사의 봉급수준, 사립학교 설치 자유유무, 외국영화의 상영여부, 외국출판물에의 접근허용, 인권교육실시 여부등에 관한 질문이 있었다고 함.

2. 관련 PRESS RELEASE(CONCLUDING OBSEVATION 포함)는 별전 FAX 송부하며,현재 사무국에서 인쇄 과정에 있는 SUMMARY RECORD 는 입수되는대로 북한이 제출한 보고서(E/1988/5/ADD.6)와 함께 파편 송부 예정임.

첨부: 상기 PRESS RELEASE 3 건(GVW(F)-0579). 끝

(대사 박수길-국장)

예고:91.12.31. 까지

일반 문서로 재분류 (1991. 12.31 .)

PAGE 2

0026

주 제 네 바 대 표 부

번 호 : GVW(F) - 57/   년월일 : 1205   시간 : 1800

수 신 : 장 관 (연이, 기정)

발 신 : 주제네바대사

제 목 :

"첨부물"

총 17 매 (표지포함)

보안 통제	
외신과 통제	

0027

57/- 17-1

NATIONS UNIES · UNITED NATIONS

SERVICE DE L'INFORMATION · OFFICE DES NATIONS UNIES A GENÈVE
INFORMATION SERVICE   ·   *UNITED NATIONS OFFICE AT GENEVA*

Press Release HR/2973
27 November 1991 (Afternoon)

ECONOMIC, SOCIAL AND CULTURAL RIGHTS COMMITTEE TAKES UP

DEMOCRATIC PEOPLE'S REPUBLIC OF KOREA REPORT

Concludes Discussion of Afghanistan Report

The Committee on Economic, Social and Cultural Rights this afternoon focused on how the Democratic People's Republic of Korea was meeting its obligations under the International Covenant on Economic, Social and Cultural Rights, in particular with regard to the rights to education and to take part in cultural life.

Introducing the initial report of his Government, Ri Tcheul, Permanent Representative of the Democratic People's Republic of Korea to the United Nations Office at Geneva stated that from the first days after liberation from Japanese domination, the Government had considered that education, science, technology and culture is integral to the building of a new society.

Many of the experts acknowledged the achievements of the country, especially in the priority given to education. However, concern was expressed over the implications of the "monolithic system of education", the heavy emphasis on physical education, and whether the people had access to the masterpieces of world culture.

Several experts found disturbing the statement in the report that the "Theses on Socialist Education" of President Kim Il Sung gave "perfect answers to all theoretical and practical problems arising in education". They noted, in this regard, that nobody and no system was perfect and that education theories and practices were constantly developing and changing. One speaker said it was not clear to him how people could freely exercise genuine freedoms if all policies of a State were based on one idea.

(more)

0028

Press Release HR/2975
Page 2

Taking part in the debate were the experts from Poland, the Philippines, the Soviet Union, Bulgaria, Senegal, Mongolia, Guinea, Cyprus, Mexico, Ecuador, Jamaica, Germany and Spain.

Prior to taking up this item, the Committee concluded discussion on the initial report of Afghanistan, hearing the rest of the replies of the delegation to the questions posed earlier this morning Committee members.

The experts of Peru, Mexico, Rwanda asked additional questions.

The Committee will meet again at 10:00 a.m. Thursday, 28 November, to begin examination of the second periodic report of Syria.

MOHAMMAD ANWAR WAHIDI, Vice-Minister of Justice of Afghanistan, said basic rights and freedoms recognized in the Constitution of Afghanistan were in full conformity with the international human rights Covenants and with the Koran, the Muslim holy book. Legislative organs were bound to observe Islam, the religion of the Republic. The Constitution stipulated that no law could run counter to Islam.

Regarding marriage and divorce, men could marry at the age of 18, women at the age of 16. If the marriage contract was dissolved, any party could remarry after a specified period of time. Some 99.9 per cent of the population was Muslim: 80 per cent were Sunni; and 18 per cent Shiite.

There was a State organ in charge of building homes, the delegate added. Land was also distributed for those who wanted to build homes. A State bank provided housing loans and the Government provided interest-free housing credits. The Government also assisted those who rented their dwellings. A Ministry of Reconstruction and Development had been established to rebuild the country. Immigrants were looked after by a Government agency.

There were no cases of AIDS in the country, he went on. A study group was looking at the problem very carefully. The law on investment had been recently revised with the help of the United Nations. Minority foreign buildings were permitted.

MOHAMMAD NABI AMANI (Afghanistan) added that national sovereignty was exercised through the Assembly and the Parliament. The Government had embarked on a policy of reconciliation. As for the policy with respect to refugees, even before the events of 1978 there had been one million Afghans working outside the country. In addition, 2 million Afghan nomads had been trapped outside the country's borders once war broke out. The problem of refugees was not one that could be discussed in a simple, straightforward manner. The Government had done much to resettle refugees. Returning refugees were entitled to regain their property and their employment. Each time there had been an influx of refugees, obstacles had been imposed by the opposition.

As for the Islamization of Afghanistan, he reiterated that 99 per cent of the population was Muslim. There was a Ministry of Islamic Affairs. There were more than 16,000 mosques in the country, with over 2,000 of them built in the last few years. All Muslims had freedom of religion.

(more)

0029

57P - 17-3

Additional Questions

JUAN ALVAREZ VITA (Peru) said he was grateful for the replies given by the delegation to their questions. Recalling what had been said here and elsewhere on the situation of the 5 million refugees from Afghanistan, he said it would be very useful to hear the views of the Government of Afghanistan on the right to self-determination.

JAVIER WIMER ZAMBRANO (Mexico) asked what the legal status of the King of Aghanistan was and whether he could return to the country.

ALEXANDRE MUTERAHEJURU (Rwanda) noted that not everything he had asked had been covered; in particular, what the difference in treatment for boys and girls in families in matters of inheritance was, how much was spent on public education, what the causes of and remedies for discrimination between towns and cities and between schools for boys and girls were.

MR. AMANI replied that the Committee had heard of the Secretary-General's five-point peace plan, which called for free elections in Afghanistan. The country had signed the Geneva accords with Pakistan on the return of refugees. There were obstacles from other countries intervening in the affairs of Afghanistan. The King was welcome to come back to aid in the peace process. The people of Afghanistan would decide what his status should be after their will had been expressed in free elections under the auspices of the United Nations.

Mr. WAHIDI, stated that Afghanistan observed the Islamic Religion. On that basis, daughters enjoyed half the inheritance rights of sons. There was no fundamental difference between schools for boys or for girls; both had the same subjects and curricula. Moreover, most schools were coeducational. The curricula for city and rural area schools were also the same, he added.

Democratic Peoples' Republic of Korea Report

The Committee's list of issues relating to the initial report of the Democratic Peoples' Republic of Korea on articles 13 to 15 of the International Covenant (document E/1988/5/Add.6) focused on the general framework in which the Convention was implemented; the right to education; and the right to take part in cultural life and to enjoy the benefits of material interests resulting from any author's production.

With regard to the first area, the delegation was requested to inform the Committee of any developments since the report was prepared, giving both general information and details of action taken to ensure full exercise of each right referred to, and to provide a brief outline of Juche philosophy. It was also asked to indicate the extent to which these rights were guaranteed to non-nationals and the extent to which they were guaranteed equally to men and women.

As for the right to education, the Committee wished to know, among other things, about measures taken to ensure full exercise of the right of everyone to education so as to strengthen respect for human rights and fundamental freedoms; the percentage share of budget allocations for education and culture; and what difficulties the State was encountering in fulfilling its obligations under articles 13 to 15.

(more)

0030

Press Release HR/2975
Page 4

        Furthermore, the delegation was asked what success there had been in
implementing the goal enshrined in the Constitution of "universal compulsory
10-year education". The Committee also wondered what steps had been taken to
further the access of particular disadvantaged groups to education, whether
parents had the right and opportunity to choose the school their children
attended, and what measures had been adopted or proposed to further the right
of parents to ensure the religious and moral education of their children in
conformity with their own beliefs.

        Other areas for additional clarification related to the "financial
and material assistance" given to pupils of "regular educational institutions
of higher learning"; the nature of State expenditure on students'
"extracurricular activities"; why the State spent the same amount on a child
in a crèche as it did on a student graduating from university; and the
correlation between education proper and productive labour.

        Information was also requested on the proportion of time spent on
physical training in the schools; on the school building provided for
pupils; the number of pupils per class; what practical steps had been taken
to prevent interference with the freedom of individuals and bodies to
establish and direct educational institutions.

        Data was asked on teacher's wages and pensions and how they related
to the minimum living wage, the principal instruments intended to improve the
material conditions of teachers, and the part teachers and their organizations
played in drawing up curricula and in preparing teaching equipment and
programmes.

        Concerning the right to take part in cultural life and to enjoy the
benefits of scientific progress, the Committee wondered whether under the
Constitution, literature, art, science and technology, which were not based on
Juche ideas were illegal. If not, what laws protected freedom of creative
activity and artistic production and what limitations or restrictions were
imposed on this freedom?

        Information was requested concerning the number of theatres and
cinemas in the country; whether ticket prices were affordable and foreign
films and plays shown; and statistics regarding publication and the
availability of books.

        The Committee also wished to know about the steps taken to enable
everyone to benefit from the applications of scientific progress and to
promote the spread of information on scientific progress and to prevent its
use for purposes contrary to the enjoyment of all human rights; any
restrictions on exercise of this right; how the rights of authors and
performing artists were protected by the law; and the opportunities for
Korean scientists to learn about "modern scientific achievements realized in
other countries".

                              (more)

                                                        0031

                        51P- 17-5

Press Release HR/2975
Page 5

Introduction of Report

Introducing the report, RI TCHEUL (Democratic Peoples' Republic of Korea) to the United Nations Office at Geneva, said the population of his country was about 20 million people. The Korean people had lived as a homogeneous nation for 5,000 years in harmony on the Korean Peninsula. However, the Korean nation had suffered 30 years of Japanese colonial domination. Under the leadership of President Kim Il Sung, the Korean people had conducted a revolutionary struggle for independence. Although the country had been liberated in 1945, it had inherited a cultural backwardness due to colonialism. Furthermore, the division of the country by foreign forces had placed obstacles on the path of national progress. In these difficult conditions, the Government had considered from the first days of liberation that education, science, technology and culture as integral to the building of a new society.

The right to education was guaranteed by the socialist construction and relevant provisions of the legislation, Mr. TCHEUL went on. Education was free and mandatory. In the short time since liberation, the State had set up a system of public education. Since 1972, the State had started full and compulsory education for children over an 11-year period. There was a system of education in work, introduced at the same time. The right to education was enjoyed by foreigners as well. Although the people still could not be said to live in opulence, the State allocated 18 per cent of its budget to education and culture.

The State also provided all necessary equipment and conditions for learning, he continued. In general education each class had 30 to 35 pupils; the number was 20 in higher education. School annexes had been established for children in distant villages. Parents had always shown the greatest interest in the education of their children. They had the full right to select the schools their children attended. Citizens had the right to practise the religion of their choice. Parents could send their children to the theology school run by a religious association or to the Religious Studies section of Kim Il Sung University. Students were permitted to consolidate their theoretical knowledge with practical experience. After school, children could perform scientific, athletic and artistic activities in facilities provided by the State. During holidays there were no formal activities, but activities were organized for those students who wanted to take part.

Regarding article 15, the delegate said all citizens were equal before the law. They enjoyed the freedom to pursue scientific, literary and artistic activities. Copyrights and patents were protected under the law. The Government developed education as much as science, technology and culture taking the Juche ideal as the guiding principle. This idea placed human beings at the centre of all concerns. The implantation of the Juche meant the solving of all the problems of the revolution in conformity with the reality of the country. It was the principle to keep so that the popular masses could enjoy their rights and the freedom to pursue scientific research and cultural and literary activities. This did not mean, however, that the exercise of the rights and freedoms of citizens was limited, nor that the science, technology or culture of other countries were rejected.

(more)

0032

Press Release HR/2975
Page 6

According to Mr. TCHEUL, the Ministry of Culture was charged with the organization and direction of works of artistic and literary creation, to which mass organizations contributed. There were 35 theaters and 5,121 cinemas in the country. The price of a theater ticket was two wons, one-fiftieth of the average salary. Foreign films were screened mostly by the television stations. Through cultural exchange programmes an average 10 foreign artistic troupes visited the country each year and the country's artistic troupe visited some 20 countries per year.

There were several dozen publishing houses, he said, putting out about one billion publications a year. More than 180 cooperation accords in the fields of science and education had been signed with 68 countries. The country was informed of scientific progress through exchange seminars and courses organized by international economic and technical entities.

Additional Questions

WLADYSLAW NENEMAN (Poland) expressed gratitude to the delegation for coming in force and giving the Committee such an interesting presentation. He recalled that the previous report had started with the phrase that "In a socialist paradise, everybody lives happily ...". Since the present report stated that everyone enjoyed freedom in the country, the expert wondered whether anyone could go or work anywhere he wanted, and whether anyone could say whatever he wanted or preach anything he chose. Noting that the report indicated that "perfect answers" had been found in the field of education, he asked, as nobody was perfect, whether teacher weres able to learn or benefit from developments and progress made elsewhere in education? How did people acquire the goods they needed? There did not seem to be many shops in the North Korean capital, he recalled.

The expert said he found the "sweeping generalizations" in the report disturbing. There was an impressive number of theatres and cinemas in the country, but what was being shown there? Were world classics or American films being shown, for example? One sometimes had difficulty in grasping the way things were done in the country, he concluded.

VIRGINIA BONOAN-DANDAM (Philippines) said she felt she was looking at a world which was beyond her grasp. The amount of financial support provided by the Government was truly fantastic. Since physical education was such a major subject, what were disabled children doing? What were the "family responsibilities of girls" and what were "women's occupations"? Were foreign publications available and was foreign artwork exhibited?. Could Korean children study in foreign schools and vice versa? The expert wished to know how the curricula were monitored and by whom, and asked for clarification of the term "cultural backwardness" as used by the delegate.

VALERI KOUZNETSOV (Soviet Union) said they were all well aware that there was no country in the world without problems, including the one they were now considering. He said he would like the delegation to share its experience in this regard, to tell the Committee what problems they had and how they had overcome them.

(more)

0033

57P-17-1

Press Release HR/2975
Page 7

VASSIL MRATCHKOV (Bulgaria) requested additional details on practical implementation of the Covenant, in particular the meaning of the phrase in the Constitution referring to "educating the community". Did the commitment of the State to compulsory education not risk damaging aspects of the right to education? He requested clarification of the phrase "monolithic educational system", as stated in the report, which appeared to him inadequately to take into account the inherent diferences between children. How were students admitted to university? Finally, he requested more information on the criteria for grants and on the working conditions of teachers.

SAMBA COR KONATE (Senegal) said article 13 of the Covenant stipulated that the goals of education should enable all persons to participate effectively in a free society, promote understanding, tolerance and friendship among all nations and all racial, ethnic or religious groups, and further the activities of the United Nations for the maintenance of peace. Was the Juche idea compatible with this article? Was there freedom to promote culture other than that advanced by the Party and State? With reference to Mr. Neneman's question, he asked whether African films were screened in the country.

LUVSANDANZANGIIN IDER (Mongolia) said it was evident that quite visible results had been achieved by that country. She asked whether it was possible to establish private schools and if not, whether people were interested in having such schools established. Who decided upon the programmes and curricula of primary and secondary schools and universities and under what procedure? What was the ratio of males to females in educational institutions and were there any restrictions on the training of women at the higher institutions? She also wished to know how world culture was reflected in the textbooks and curricula of the schools. Was it possible for any person to publish his work if it was not in line with the Party or the Government? Were there any structures other than the Party or the State which ran the country's cultural life?

MOHAMED LAMINE FOFANA (Guinea) wanted to know whether education was also provided by private institutions. He requested more information regarding the claim that illiteracy had been eliminated.

MIKIS DEMETRIOU SPARSIS (Cyprus) joined the other experts in extending their thanks both for a lucid report and presentation. He wished to know whether the monolithic education system was ever revised and, if so, by whom. In addition, did objective criteria for admission to university exist, by whom were they applied, and was appeal possible? Who else participated in the development of the school system — the parents, the students, religious groups or even the parents themselves? Or did the State determine everything in the light of what it considered best for all concerned?

JAVIER WIMER ZAMBRANO (Mexico) asked for information regarding the way ethnic minorities were dealt with in the educational and cultural fields.

JAIME MARCHAN ROMERO (Ecuador) asked whether any legislation indicated the working age. Roughly, in United States dollars, how much was spent per child for education? He also requested clarification with regard to military service and education.

(more)

0034

57P-17-8

Press Release HR/2975
Page 8

KENNETH OSBORNE RATTRAY (Jamaica) said it was quite evident that significant advances had been made in the Democratic Peoples' Republic of Korea in relation to education and the rights recognized. Questions had been raised regarding freedom of choice in relation to the right to education. Freedom was essentially an expression of the people's will. The question was whether the education system was part of this free expression. Could one express dissenting ideas with regard to the education system? Was there a prohibition on the establishment of independent schools? Was there freedom in cultural activities? Was there religious education?

BRUNO SIMMA (Germany) said it was not clear to him how people could freely exercise genuine freedoms if all policies of a State were based on one idea. Furthermore, the ideas of Kim Il Sung gave "perfect answers to all theoretical and practical problems arising in education". What exactly were the restrictions on freedom of religious education?

MARIA JIMENEZ BUITRAGUENO (Spain) asked when higher education started, given that students in the country were obliged to study for 11 years. In light of the situation in many countries in the world, she wanted to know whether the education system had undergone any liberalization or opening up. Was there any teaching of human rights in the schools of the Democratic People's Republic of Korea?

* *** *

0035

57P-17-P

NATIONS UNIES · UNITED NATIONS

SERVICE DE L'INFORMATION · OFFICE DES NATIONS UNIES A GENÈVE
INFORMATION SERVICE · UNITED NATIONS OFFICE AT GENEVA

Press Release HR/2977
28 November 1991 (Afternoon)

ECONOMIC, SOCIAL AND CULTURAL RIGHTS COMMITTEE MAKES FINAL OBSERVATIONS

ON PANAMA AND AFGHANISTAN REPORTS

CONCLUDES DISCUSSION OF REPORT BY DEMOCRATIC PEOPLES' REPUBLIC OF KOREA

The Committee on Economic, Social and Cultural Rights this afternoon found information provided by Panama on forced evictions following the United States military intevention unsatisfactory and it expressed concerns over the situation of the 5 million refugees from Afghanistan.

These conclusions came at the end of the Committee's examination of reports from those two countries on how they implemented the International Covenant on Economic, Social and Cultural Rights. The 18-member treaty body then moved on to examine a report by the Government of the Democratic Peoples' Republic of Korea. Discussion on that report focused on how the right to take part in cultural life and to enjoy the benefits of scientific progress was assured. A major focus was the issue of artistic freedom. One of the highlights in this area according to the delegation, was the holding last year of the Pan-national unification concerts in which Koreans from the north and the south as well as from many other parts of the world participated.

The Committee will make concluding observations on that report tomorrow at 3.00 p.m.

The experts from Germany, Poland, the Philippines, Senegal and Jamaica asked further questions.

The Committee will meet again at 10.00 a.m. on Friday, 29 November, to resume consideration of the second periodic report of Syria.

(more)

0036

Press Release HR/2977
Page 2

Concluding Observations on Panama Report

The members of the Committee noted that the report of Panama was presented against the background of the extraordinary circumstances in the country resulting from political turmoil and the aftermath of the United States invasion of 1989. This had created great disorder in all sectors throughout the country with serious consequences for the enjoyment of economic, social and cultural rights. Against this background, it was gratifying that the Government of Panama was prepared to establish a dialogue with the Committee.

The report was too general and legalistic in nature. Members of the Committee noted that the indigenous peoples were among the least privileged in the society, and that the rate of illiteracy among them was quite high despite the provisions for compulsory education. The view was also expressed that the restrictions placed on the participation of foreigners in the executive committees of trade unions were not in conformity with article 8 of the Covenant. Concern was also expressed regarding the unequal distribution of household income.

The Committee concluded that the information provided by the delegation regarding forced evictions was unsatisfactory. Firstly, the Government's claim that 3,000 persons were affected by the bombing of El Chorrillo differed substantially from all other sources available on this issue, which placed the figure between 12,500 and 20,000 persons. Secondly, the responses to questions concerning the current living conditions of residents of El Chorrillo made homeless by the bombing differed substantially from other information available to the Committee. Moreover, two years after the invasion, a large number of persons had yet to be rehoused. Thirdly, the justification for the actions carried out by Panamanian and United States forces in early 1990 which affected over 5,000 persons was unacceptable as a ground for forcibly removing people from their homes, under the terms of the Covenant. No drugs or arms were found during these three actions. However, a large number of houses were demolished, in spite of the affected persons having lived in the area concerned for more than two years.

OSVALDO VELASQUEZ (Panama) said the Government would send the information requested in writing. He asked that the concluding observations be sent to the Government in writing.

Concluding Observations on Afghanistan Report

The Committee observed that there were two kinds of problems reflected in the Afghanistan report, some of which were short-term, due to the war, others were long-term and structural, for example, the situation of women in Afghan society. The Committee thanked the Government for submitting a report at this session and expressed satisfaction that a dialogue had begun. It found the report legalistic but thanked the delegation for responding to the many questions raised. Although the delegation gave useful information, some questions did not receive satisfactory replies.

(more)

0037

Concern remained over the situation of the political prisoners, and of the 5 million refugees who had sought shelter outside the country. The rules of Islamic law, including ancestral customs, might prevent implementation of the right to equality of the sexes, including within the family and outside. With regard to the status of women, a full answer was requested to questions 8 and 9 put forward by the pre-sessional Working Group. The first question sought information on women's participation in political, social and trade union activity and their position in work and professional activities, particularly at the senior level. The second question asked whether full equality of rights between men and women had been achieved in all fields of law and, if so, to indicate the discrepancies which existed and the measures planned to eliminate them. Concern also remained with regard to trade union rights.

MOHAMMAD ANWAR WAHIDI, Vice-Minister of Justice of Afghanistan thanked the Committee for their accurate, scientific evaluation and judgement and said he was sincerely happy with its evaluation.

Examination of Democratic Peoples' Republic of Korea Report

CHAE RYANG IL, Director of International Affairs of the State Education Commission of the Democratic Peoples' Republic of Korea, responded to questions posed yesterday by Committee members regarding the implementation of articles 13 to 15 of the Covenant on the rights to education and to participate in cultural activities. He said there had been many difficulties in building the education system in the country after liberation. Eighty per cent of the population was illiterate. The Government had called on all Koreans to help build a new society.

After the Korean war, the country again faced a very difficult situation, he went on. The division of Korea by foreign forces was a great obstacle to the development of the nation, not to mention to education. One difficulty faced today was in the learning of foreign languages, which in itself resulted in difficulties in adapting scientific and technological experience from abroad.

Parents could select the school they wanted their children to attend, declared Mr. CHAE. Parents could send their children to religious institutions or to Kim Il Sung University to study religion. Parents could also send their children to creches and kindergartens if they so desired. The introduction of compulsory one-year pre-school education did not affect the parents' right to choose. The State guaranteed the freedom of activities of social organizations and individuals. Such organizations could set up schools. No one individual was so rich that he or she could set up a school on their own. So far, no one was willing to set up private schools. Many schools had been set up by religious and social organizations such as the Women's Union and the Farmers' Union.

Concerning admission to institutions of higher learning, he said this was done through objective and impartial competitive examinations. Some 195,000 students had entered university in 1990. Forty-two per cent of university students were female. In some institutions, most of the students were women, such as at the University of Education. The role of mothers in social education was very important.

(more)

0038

Press Release HR/2977
Page 4

As for questions concerning the "monolithic" character of education, he affirmed that the State strove to provide the same level of knowledge to students studying the same subjects in different areas of the country. The term "monolithic" had been a mistranslation; the report should have said "unified".

Professors and teachers went to foreign countries frequently, he went on. In 1990, 180 professors had gone abroad and 166 foreign lecturers had come to the People's Republic. Cooperation with the United Nations Educational, Scientific and Cultural Organization (UNESCO) and the United Nations Children's Fund (UNICEF) was increasing. In 1990 there were some 800 students abroad, while 400 studied in the People's Republic. In order to foster international understanding and peace, students were taught about the history and literature of other countries. Besides this, world literature had been translated. Human rights was not taught as a separate subject, but children were given human rights education. The Convention on the Rights of the Child, the International Covenant on Economic, Social and Cultural Rights and the Universal Declaration of Human Rights were available in schools and libraries. On World Human Rights Day, additional lectures were given to children about human rights.

Not only scholars but teachers were widely involved in the entire process of drafting the curricula and editing textbooks, he went on. Parents also participated in the education process through regular contact with their children's teachers and schools. A State scholarship system had been introduced covering many different categories. In addition, students of higher-learning received many other benefits including free room, free medical care and half prices on books and other school necessities. Uniforms were provided at a very low price and, in some cases, free of charge.

Physical culture education had no objectives other than the usual ones connected with this training, he added. Special programmes were also offered for the physically disabled in this regard. The delegate then indicated the relative salaries received by teachers and other workers and noted that salaries more than adequately covered a person's needs in view of the economic system in place in the country.

Korea was an homogenous nation with one culture, so there was no ethnic minority in the country, he stated. He then described how the problem of illiteracy was eliminated since the liberation of Korea in 1945. Illiteracy at that time was about 80 per cent. Literacy was made a priority goal, accorded the necessary facilities and large numbers of teachers. A literacy crusade was launched in 1947 on a nationwide scale, a measure which eliminated much illiteracy in a short time. The speaker stressed the importance of enlisting the participation and enthusiasm of the masses in this regard. Everyone who could read and write contributed to the effort, which solved the critical problem of the teacher shortage. It seemed as if the whole country had turned into a huge school. As a result, less than four years after independence, some 2 million persons were no longer illiterate, thereby beginning to shake off the cultural backwardness which was the heritage of colonial rule.

(more)

0039

PAK DOK HUN (Democratic Peoples' Republic of Korea) added, with regard to the difficulties in realizing the right to participate in cultural activity, that at the time of liberation in 1945 many national relics had been taken away by the colonial rulers. Many others had been destroyed during the Korean war. The traditional national arts were restricted before liberation. Many people looked down on their own culture while admiring that of other countries. Another difficulty had arisen from the 46-year division imposed on the country.

In the development of art and literature the Party and the State put forward directives according to the desire of the working people, Mr. PAK went on. Literature and art had to be nationalist in form and socialist in contents. This did not mean that any artistic work deviating from these directions could not be disseminated. There were numerous films that criticized leading figures and cadres in the country. Anyone could write books and create artistic works. Whether their works were publicly disseminated was another matter. An examination committee ruled on the suitability of artistic works. Artistic works advocating violence or war were restricted. Artistic or literary works designed for the entertainment of the masses and for which they had to pay had to go through the examination committee. There were no private publishing houses, film studios, theaters or cinemas. Freedom of the press was recognized, but as far as he knew no one wanted to set up separate organs. Foreign films were regularly shown on television. The films were mostly from Egypt, India, the Soviet Union, Algeria and China. Several United States films, such as "Roots" and "Gone with the Wind", had been shown in the country. A Pan National Unification Concert had been held last year in Pyongyang and Seoul bringing together Koreans from both sides of the Peninsula and from abroad.

The Juche idea, he went on, was a man-centred philosophy. It meant that man was the master of his own destiny. This idea had come out of the analysis of reality conducted by the movement of national liberation to counter the tendency to admire ideas from other, bigger countries. It was true that there were problems in the development of the country, he concluded. Although the situation was tense, Koreans enjoyed the right to choose their jobs as well as freedom of movement, except near the Military Demarcation Line.

Additional Questions from Committee

BRUNO SIMMA (Germany) said a few points were still not entirely clear to him, first as regards the average incomes of civil servants, teachers and workers. In response, the delegate said what he had meant was that, in general, teachers' salaries were higher than for ordinary and office workers. Nevertheless, the prices of all the essential goods - food, clothing and housing - were kept intentionally low by the Government. Medical treatment was free, housing was nearly free. This was the policy whereby the Government tried to ensure that everyone shared in the benefits of society.

Mr. SIMMA (Germany) wondered when the "Western" paintings which were considered to be a problem to be done away with in 1945 had entered Korea. In response, Mr. PAK stated that these paintings were introduced during colonial rule.

(more)

0040

Press Release HR/2977
Page 6

WLADYSLAW NENEMAN (Poland) said he was grateful for the many answers provided by the delegation. Some questions, however, had not been answered such as those on the theses of educational theory of Kim Il Sung. He asked whether free artistic expression was allowed in the Peoples' Republic.

Mr. CHAE said that on the basis of the directives given in the educational theses, a discussion had been started on how to change the educational system. There was a long-standing committee on educational guidance comprising Government officials, educational authorities, teachers and social organizations. The committee met once a month to register and discuss all issues raised by teachers, students or parents. The theses on education indicated the principal direction for the development of education.

Mr. PAK added that as mentioned before, the directive put forward by the State and the Party was the guideline to follow. This did not mean that works which deviated from this could not be created.

VIRGINIA BONOAN-DANDAM (Philippines) asked whether there was freedom for the viewer of art to appreciate a work of artistic freedom, and if that person would be able to benefit from the imagination or creation of an artist whose work was not deemed to be according to the taste of the masses.

In response, Mr. PAK said it was that there was an examination commitee which determined which works should be published or performed. However, if a work did not pass through this committee, that person could still share his creative work with colleagues and friends. He added that it was very rare for a work to be rejected.

SAMBA COR KONATE (Senegal) said he wondered how the statement in the report to the effect that the educational theses of President Kim Il Sung had provided "perfect answers to all theoretical and practical questions arising in education" fit with the theory of historical matrialism, which held that things change and evolve.

KENNETH OSBORNE RATTRAY (Jamaica) said the discussion on freedom of artistic work had provoked him - and confronted him with a dilemma. It was well-known that even in Western countries boards were established to pass on films and problems of obscenity existed.

Mr. PAK agreed with the statement just made that every country had some kind of system to pass judgement on the morality of artistic work.

Committee Chairman PHILIP ALSTON (Australia) said the discussion on artistic freedom pointed to the problem the Committee faced in the absence of general comments dealing with specific articles. There were no benchmarks to indicate what the Covenant meant in specific articles.

* **** *

0041

57P-17-15

NATIONS UNIES · UNITED NATIONS ·

SERVICE DE L'INFORMATION · OFFICE DES NATIONS UNIES A GENÈVE
INFORMATION SERVICE · UNITED NATIONS OFFICE AT GENEVA

Press Release HR/2979
29 November 1991 (Afternoon)

ECONOMIC, SOCIAL AND CULTURAL RIGHTS COMMITTEE CONCLUDES

EXAMINATION OF DEMOCRATIC PEOPLES' REPUBLIC OF KOREA REPORT

Expresses Concern over Freedom of Artistic Expression

The Committee on Economic, Social and Cultural Rights this afternoon, considered that the right to culture and to education had been to a certain extent guaranteed to the citizens of the Democratic People's Republic of Korea, despite the inherent difficulties of the country. It expressed concern, however, that the machinery in place for the examination of works of art and literature for publication could result in inadequate protection of freedom of expression.

These were among the concluding observations adopted by the Committee in ending its consideration of the second periodic report by the People's Republic on how it gave effect to the International Covenant on Economic, Social and Cultural Rights.

The Committee then discussed its methods of work, focusing among other things, on the work of the pre-sessional Working Group which draws up the lists of issues to be taken up in connection with the consideration of the reports; the urgent need for the Centre for Human Rights to make available a "resource room" for the collection of information for the benefit of all the human rights treaty bodies; and more effective questioning procedures in order to achieve a genuine dialogue with the Government concerned. The time needed for the various stages of examination of reports was also raised, including, in particular, how to improve the process of drafting the concluding observations.

Other issues related to confidentiality of concluding observations; bringing to the attention of States parties the Committee's guidelines for drawing up the reports; and the use of other resources of information such as the news media.

(more)

0042

Press Release HR/2979
Page 2

On Monday, 2 December, at 10.00 a.m. the Committee is scheduled to conclude consideration of the report of Syria and to take up a report by Finland.

Concluding Observations on Report

The Committee expressed its thanks to the Government of the Democratic People's Republic of Korea for the goodwill it displayed in continuing the dialogue through the regular presentation of reports. It noted with satisfaction that that Government had made efforts to ensure that its citizens enjoyed the rights provided by articles 13 to 15 of the Covenant.

It considered that the right to culture and to education had been to a certain extent guaranteed to the citizens, despite the inherent difficulties of the country. However, the experts had found the report to be legalistic and theoretical, and that concrete situations reflecting the reality had not been given enough attention.

The Committee encouraged the Government of the People's Republic to continue its efforts to promote a system of teaching which would encourage participation in this field. That would better enable citizens to exercise their freedom to choose the educational institutions in conformity with the Convention.

With regard to the right to take part in cultural life, the Committee expressed concern that the machinery in place for the examination of works of art and literature for the purpose of publication could result in inadequate protection of freedom of expression.

* *** *

주 제 네 바 대 표 부

제네(정) 2031-52   1991. 12. 11.

수신 : 장   관

참조 : 국제기구국장

제목 : 북한의 A규약 심의

연 : GVW-2559

북한의 A 규약 (13조-15조) 보고서와 동 심의 관련 Summany Record 및
A 규약 위원명단을 별첨 송부합니다.

첨부 : 상기 문건 3건. 끝.

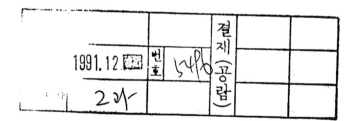

주 제 네 바 대   사

0044

UNITED
NATIONS

 Economic and Social
Council

Distr.
GENERAL

E/1988/5/Add.6
14 April 1989

Original: ENGLISH

First regular session of 1989

IMPLEMENTATION OF THE INTERNATIONAL COVENANT ON
ECONOMIC, SOCIAL AND CULTURAL RIGHTS

Initial reports submitted by States parties to the Covenant,
concerning rights covered by articles 13-15, in accordance
with the third stage of the programme established by Economic
and Social Council resolution 1988 (LX)

Addendum

THE DEMOCRATIC PEOPLE'S REPUBLIC OF KOREA

[14 January 1989]

GE.89-16079/0666B

0045

1.   All policies of the Democratic People's Republic of Korea are based on the Juche idea, a man-centred philosophical outlook on the world created by the respected leader Comrade Kim Il Sung, President of the Democratic People's Republic of Korea.

2.   In the Democratic People's Republic of Korea the working masses directly participate in the realization of a State power and management of the State and freely exercise the genuine freedom and right to political activity as the master of State and society.

3.   They enjoy equal rights in all spheres of the State and social life irrespective of sex, nationality, occupation, length of residence, property status, education, party affiliation, political views and religion.

4.   Below are the achievements and steps taken by the Democratic People's Republic of Korea in the implementation of articles 13-15 of the Covenant.

Article 13

Right to Education

5.   Since the first day of its foundation, the Government of the Democratic People's Republic of Korea has given priority to education, considering it as a serious question decisive of the destiny of the country's future.

6.   The great leader Comrade Kim Il Sung, President of the Democratic People's Republic of Korea, made public the immortal classic works titled "Theses on Socialist Education" at the fourth Session of the 5th Plenary Meeting of the Central Committee of the Workers' Party of Korea on 5 September 1977.

7.   The theses gives perfect answers to all theoretical and practical problems arising in education: content and method of education; fundamental principle of socialist pedagogy; establishment of the socialist education system; task and role of the educational institutions and guidance and assistance on education.

8.   During the last period the effort has been made to carry out the thesis on education, and thus the socialist educational system has been further consolidated and developed and great success scored in people's education and training of national cadres.

9.   The right to education is legally guaranteed by the Democratic People's Republic of Korea.

10. The Socialist Constitution of the Democratic People's Republic of Korea prescribes as follows:

> "Article 40. The State is giving precedence to public education and the training of cadres for the nation and is combining general education with technological education, and education with productive labour."

> "Article 41. The State provides universal compulsory ten-year education which includes senior middle school training for all young people under working age. 'The State provides education to all pupils and students free of charge.'"

0046

"Article 42. The State trains competent technicians and experts by developing the regular educational system as well as different forms of studying while working."

"Article 43. The State provides all children with a compulsory one-year pre-school education."

"The State maintains all children of pre-school age in crèches and kindergartens at State and public expense."

I. **Right to Primary and Secondary Education**

11. The Democratic People's Republic of Korea established the principle of giving education to the entire people and young generation and pursues the policy to enrol all working people in the certain educational system for compulsory education while compulsorily educating the young generation in regular schools.

12. During the last period the State established stage by stage the universal free and compulsory educational system on the basis of the development of revolution and construction and the sound foundation of the country's economy.

13. In 1956, the hard post-war period of rehabilitation, the State abolished the tuition-fee system enforcing universal primary education and in 1958 effected with flying colours the universal secondary compulsory education.

14. Since 1959 all educational institutions across the country have been under the universal free educational system and run at State expense.

15. Since April 1967, the universal 9-year compulsory technical education has been successfully enforced and an advanced educational system which requires a close combination of general education with elementary technical education and education with productive labour; since September 1972, 11-year compulsory higher-level education has been enforced to give complete secondary education to all new generations.

16. The universal 11-year compulsory education includes one year pre-school education and compulsory 10-year school education. Under this educational system children from age 5 to 16 receive pre-school education and primary or secondary education free of charge.

17. Under this compulsory educational system all new generations study the same subjects in line with a monolithic educational system and according to a unified educational programme at primary and senior middle schools.

18. In the course of the 11-year compulsory education system every pupil receives the same complete secondary general education and after finishing the course, he or she is eligible for higher schools up to university according to his or her wishes and talents.

II. **Right to Higher Education**

19. The State has carried out with flying colours the grand task set forth by the 5th Congress of the Party held on August 1975 to increase the rank of competent technicians and experts by more than a million by increasing the

higher educational institutions and ceaselessly improving the quality of education. As a result, our country has 1.31 million technicians and experts as of 1987.

20. In the Democratic People's Republic of Korea all working people including young people who finished the 11-year compulsory education are eligible for higher education according to their hopes, talent and temperament.

21. The State established the system of studying on the job along with the regular educational system, thus all the working people are included in the educational system of higher learning.

22. As a result they have acquired living knowledge closely associated with production and theory through factory college, farm college, fishing college and broadcasting college by correspondence courses.

23. The pupils of regular educational institutions of higher learning study free of charge and even on scholarships. The working people who study on the job receive financial and material assistance so as to be freed from any worries about their livelihood because they receive the treatment according to the ranks in the whole course of their study.

III. Free Education

24. Our educational system is substantial and popular and is firmly guaranteed by universal free education.

25. The State is entirely responsible for all expenses needed for educating the children of the working people.

26. The State provides all pupils and students with school uniforms in every season and sells dirt cheap textbooks, notebooks and various school things to say nothing of exemption from tuition fees.

27. The State bears the expenses for the pupils and students' extracurricular activities, inspection of factories and enterprises and camping.

28. Model pupils of specialized schools and students receive monthly a honourable "Kim Il Sung scholarship" and various other kinds of scholarships.

29. Those pupils of senior middle schools who live on islands but study on the mainland also enjoy the benefit of scholarships.

30. The State pays 15,800 won for one child who graduates from a university having passed through a crèche, a kindergarten and a primary school.

IV. Content and Method of Education

31. The State has advanced the policy of giving adequate general rudimentary knowledge through general middle-school education and of combining it properly with fundamental technical knowledge and it has been thoroughly implemented.

32. At the stage of primary and high-school education pupils are taught systematically the general concept and essence of things and phenomena and the rudimentary knowledge on the law governing their change and development.

0048

33. Efforts are being made especially to teach in depth the general knowledge of fundamental scientific fields such as mathematics, physics, chemistry and biology.

34. At senior middle schools stress is put on fundamental technical education so that all pupils possess the fundamental technical knowledge needed in production, having been taught more than one technical subject and the know how to handle skilfully a lorry, a tractor and the mechanical equipment widely used in production and construction.

35. The basic principles, the basis of production techniques are commonly taught as well at all schools.

36. Depending on geographical conditions the content varies in towns and workers' districts, pupils are taught how to handle a lorry and a machine tool, whereas in rural areas they are taught how to drive a tractor and Juche farming methods.

37. Besides, girl pupils are taught systematically the elementary knowledge and techniques needed with regard to their family responsibilities and women's occupations.

38. Theoretical and practical education programmes are closely combined with productive labour to teach all pupils useful knowledge and foster their abilities.

39. Lectures, experiments and practice are properly combined, and productive labour well organized for school education so that the pupils may master what they are taught and skilfully apply it to practical activities.

40. Pupils are systematically educated in physics and art at schools pursuant to the Party's policy to push ahead with intellectual, moral and physical education in a co-ordinated way.

41. Physical training is defined as a major subject in the educational programme at primary school and senior middle school and is conducted systematically.

42. In order to raise the quality of physical education and successfully provide extracurricular courses in physical education, teachers specialized in physical training are dispatched to senior middle schools and universities and even to primary schools where one teacher is in charge of all subjects.

43. It is an important policy of the Government of our Republic to make physical training a popular habit.

44. Pursuant to this policy, collective physical activities are included in the daily routine of a school or everyday life.

45. Pupils begin their daily routine by group running at school, and all of them take exercise on a playground during breaks after two or three lessons.

46. After lessons they enjoy daily extracurricular physical activity for more than one hour under the teacher's direction.

47. Such activity continues without let up even during the period of vacation.

48. Group physical activities such as climbing, trips and hiking are also conducted frequently at schools.

49. To popularize physical culture at schools, the testing of the people's physical strength is organized and all pupils throughout the country participate.

50. All generations are growing into talented men with high cultural attainments, a sense of the aesthetic and artistic ability with the result that the policy of the Government of the Republic to intensify art education was successfully implemented at schools.

V. Development of School System

51. The State directs the lion's share of the yearly increasing State budget earmarked for education to school construction and provides its powerful backing.

52. The State gives priority to the building of schools whenever it designs a new dwelling district or residential area.

53. The State mobilizes the internal reserves of local areas to the maximum and concentrates building materials, funds and manpower on the construction of schools and kindergartens.

54. The State pays deep attention to equipping a school with educational facilities and teaching aids.

55. It has built numerous factories in the capital and provinces to produce a variety of substantial teaching aids and experimental equipment for practice as well as notebooks, desks and chairs necessary for educational work.

56. In order to ensure that all pupils acquire more than one technique during the period of compulsory education, the State has established a system under which equipment and materials for educational purposes such as lorries, tractors and communication components are produced and supplied as priority items.

57. As of 1987 there are 244 universities, 499 special schools, 4,820 senior middle schools and 4,779 primary schools, all of which were built by the State.

VI. Improvement of the Material Conditions for Teaching Staff

58. After setting up the teacher-training centres under the regular teacher education system the State is looking to the future and is training the teachers needed to provide native technical cadres.

59. Today the country's teacher-training system consists of teachers' training colleges, universities of education, post-graduate courses and institutes offering doctorates, etc.

60. Every Province has universities of education and teachers' training colleges; and post-graduate courses and institutes offering doctorates are in the main universities including the Kim Il Sung University.

0050

61. The high-grade State decorations and the honorary titles such as People's Teacher and Merited Teacher are awarded to teachers for special achievements in their services.

62. The "Pension of the respected and beloved leader Comrade Kim Il Sung" is also awarded to those teachers who have devoted their all to education for a generation serving for more than 20 years in the primary schools.

63. The teachers are also awarded the title of professor and associate professor according to their achievements in their instructional and educational work; and the scientific and academic degrees of academician, doctor and associate doctor are awarded on the basis of their talents and ability.

64. Teachers are provided with stable and good living conditions by the State.

65. Higher salaries are paid to teachers and houses are provided to them before anyone else.

66. They go on regular paid leave every year and take recuperation and recreation at State expense.

67. In particular special care is given to the female teachers to provide them with adequate working and living conditions.

68. In order to reduce the working hours of female teachers more teachers are allocated to the schools which have many female teachers and sub-crêches are attached to the schools which have more than five female teachers with babies.

69. Besides, weekly nurseries and monthly nurseries are arranged for the female teachers to reduce their burdens in bringing up their children and help them concentrate their energies on the instructional and educational work and social activities.

VII. Right to Elementary Education

70. The State completely eradicated over 2.3 million illiterates in only three years or so after liberation.

71. After the eradication of illiteracy, emphasis was given to adult education thus continuously raising the cultural and technical level of the working people in conformity with actual development.

72. As a result, all members of society have acquired a level of education higher than that of secondary school graduates.

73. The aim of adult education is to ensure that all the working people have general knowledge higher than that of senior school graduate level and in more than one technical subject.

74. According to the "Rules on Working People's Senior Middle School" announced as decision No. 128 of the Administration Council of the Democratic People's Republic of Korea in May 1958, working people's senior middle schools were set up to give the working people middle-school education.

0051

Article 14

Principle of Free and Compulsory Education

75. As mentioned in Article 13 of the Rule free and compulsory education has already been provided successfully in the Democratic People's Republic of Korea.

Article 15

Guarantee of Cultural Life, Benefit from Scientific Development and Authors' Rights

76. The working people of the Democratic People's Republic of Korea are provided with better cultural and material conditions through the vigorous struggle to implement the three revolutions - ideological, technical and cultural.

77. On the development of literature and art and science and technology the Socialist Constitution of the Democratic People's Republic of Korea stipulates under:

"Article 44. The State accelerates the nation's scientific and technological progress by establishing Juche in scientific research and by strengthening creative co-operation between scientists and producers."

"Article 45. The State is developing a Juche-oriented, revolutionary literature and art, national in form and socialist in content."

"The State encourages the creative activities of writers and artists and draws the broad masses of workers, farmers and other working people into literary and artistic activities."

I. Right to Cultural Life

78. The Party and State are enforcing the policy of making the arts and literature popular among the masses of people and enabling them to appreciate and enjoy them to their hearts' content at any place.

79. A solid material base has been laid for the creation and spread of art and literature and a regular propaganda system has been established with the newly-built and expanded facilities and supplies of art and literature that serve the masses in every part of the country.

80. The number of theatres and cinemas reaches 5,156 as of 1987.

81. The State advertises properly all cultural facilities - theatres, cinemas and libraries - in cities and provinces and sets up cultural centres and houses for democratic propaganda everywhere in cities and in the countryside, and, by centralizing them, fosters cultural activities.

82. The working people can participate in the creative work of art and literature at any place - cities, countryside, forest and fishing villages - as they wish and get assistance at any time from the experts specialized in popular literature, because standing bodies have been set up to guide the creative work of popular art and literature in the capital and provinces.

83. It is of special importance as regards the Government's popular cultural policy to note that art and literature groups have been organized everywhere the working people work and live and embrace the broad masses in their activities.

84. Art and literature groups can be organized in any region, neither occupation nor standing is a criterion for participation, and the broad masses can be drawn into art and literature activities. The increase in group membership makes it possible to involve more working masses in art and literature activities.

85. Therefore, the Party and State organize art and literature groups everywhere people work and live and make them standardize their activities so that the members of society at large - workers, peasants, officials and youth and students - can take an active part in art and literature activities.

86. New generations are taught the elementary knowledge necessary for appreciating art and literature and writing works from childhood and are embued with the skills and rich emotion necessary for playing more than one musical instrument.

87. Besides, the youth and students participate in various extracurricular activities in all schools from a primary school to a college after class and thus bring their artistic temperament, skill and joy of youth into full display.

88. This extracurricular art activities include all aspects of art and literature - literature, music, dance and the fine arts, and all the youth and students, whether in the city or countryside, lowland or mountainous areas, take part in such activities.

89. They also contribute greatly to improving their artistic temperament and writing ability and to popularizing art and literature through a literary prize contest among teachers and students and an art festival and art contests among the youth and students and at kindergarten level.

90. The popular art activity being fostered actively among the youth and students, has become a reservoir for ceaseless efflorescence and development of the Juche-oriented art and literature of our country and many famous singers, players and actors have passed through the stage of youth and students' art festivals.

91. The State not only popularizes art and literature activities but also systematically selects and educates children with special art talent and temperament.

92. In the capital there are a music and dance university, a film university and a fine arts university and each province has a specialized art school.

0053

93. The State concentrates to the maximum the collective efforts and wisdom of all members concerned in creating one production which gives full rein to the creative ability and wisdom of individual actors.

94. In this way, the State solves all the problems arising in the process of creating art and literature and fosters a ceaseless renewal in creative art.

95. The policy of popularizing art and literature is being put into effect more brilliantly through the mass media including TV and radio networks.

96. The central broadcasting station airs music (symphony and opera included) and literary works 47 per cent and 6 per cent of its time respectively; and the central TV Station telecasts 10 per cent music, 45 per cent films and 8 per cent literary works.

97. There are libraries, bookshops and reading rooms in the capital and provinces and in institutions and enterprises and the working people read to their hearts' content various publications including newspapers and magazines.

98. Today, workers, youth and students are contributing greatly to pushing ahead with the revolution and construction by constantly increasing their knowledge of science and technology and the level of culture through libraries.

99. Historic relics and remains are well preserved and dealt with in accordance with the "provision on preservation of the historic relics and remains adopted as decision No. 6 of the Administration Council of the Democratic People's Republic of Korea in February 1976.

100. Districts have been set up for the preservation and protection of relics and remains of historical value and have been converted into recreation centres for educating the working people in national pride and honour.

II. Protection of Copyright

101. In accordance with the "provision on copyright of publication" adopted as decision No. 55 of the Administration Council of the Democratic People's Republic of Korea in August 1980, writers' copyright is legally protected.

III. Freedom of Scientific Research and Creative Activity

102. Scientistis are provided by the State with all the material conditions for their activities and devote their wisdom and energy to scientific research on up-to-date research bases without any worry.

103. Before the liberation our country had no single university or scientific research institute in the northern half of the Republic and had only a small supply of native technicians.

104. But, today, we have many scientific research organs such as the Academy of Agricultural Science and Academy of Medical Science which facilitate research work for the improvement of the standard of living and the national economy.

105. Scientists are carrying out scientific research work utilizing well-equipped libraries, laboratories and modern experimental facilities.

0054

106. The State provides scientists with all living conditions - food, clothing, housing.

107. In order to keep scientists up to date in science and technology without delay and popularize the successes in scientific research, the State intensifies publishing projects.

108. Several publishing organs to publish scientific and technical treaties have been set up to issue academic magazines and books covering various scientific spheres, translate and publish various kinds of scientific books and thus provides our scientists with the conditions necessary not only for the broad popularization of their successes but also for assimilating modern scientific achievements realized in other countries.

0055

Economic and Social Council

Distr.
GENERAL

E/C.12/1991/SR.8
3 December 1991

Original: ENGLISH

COMMITTEE ON ECONOMIC, SOCIAL AND CULTURAL RIGHTS

Sixth session

SUMMARY RECORD OF THE 8th MEETING

Held at the Palais des Nations, Geneva,
on Thursday, 28 November 1991, at 3 p.m.

Chairman: Mr. ALSTON

CONTENTS

Organization of work (continued)

Consideration of reports

(a) Reports submitted by States parties in accordance with articles 16 and 17
of the Covenant (continued)

   Panama (continued)

   Afghanistan (continued)

   Democratic People's Republic of Korea (continued)

Organization of work (continued)

This record is subject to correction.

Corrections should be submitted in one of the working languages. They
should be set forth in a memorandum and also incorporated in a copy of the
record. They should be sent within one week of the date of this document to
the Official Records Editing Section, room E.4108, Palais des Nations, Geneva.

Any corrections to the records of the meetings of the Committee at this
session will be consolidated in a single corrigendum, to be issued shortly
after the end of the session.

GE.91-18693/3984B

<u>The meeting was called to order at 3.05 p.m.</u>

ORGANIZATION OF WORK (<u>continued</u>)

1.   The <u>CHAIRMAN</u> reminded members that the Committee had pioneered the procedure of adopting concluding observations as the final phase in its consideration of reports. He noted that other treaty bodies, such as the Committee against Torture and the Human Rights Committee, had recently adopted similar procedures, with a view to securing a clear, concise and unified response to reports. The Committee on Economic, Social and Cultural Rights was thus no longer alone in adopting that approach, which had become common practice. He stressed the need for the widest possible informal consultations among members during preparation of the concluding observations.

CONSIDERATION OF REPORTS (agenda item 7)

(a)   REPORTS SUBMITTED BY STATES PARTIES IN ACCORDANCE WITH ARTICLES 16 AND 17
      OF THE COVENANT (<u>continued</u>)

<u>Panama</u> (E/1984/6/Add.19, E/1986/4/Add.22, E/1988/5/Add.9, E/1989/5/Add.5)
(<u>continued</u>)

2.   <u>At the invitation of the Chairman, Mr. Ucros, Ms. Vallarino and
Mr. Velásquez (Panama) took places at the Committee table</u>.

3.   The <u>CHAIRMAN</u> invited Mr. Rattray to begin the concluding observations phase of the Committee's consideration of the report of Panama.

4.   Mr. <u>RATTRAY</u> said that members of the Committee had noted that the report by Panama had been presented against a background of the political turmoil resulting from the United States invasion, which had created great disorder in all sectors throughout the country, with serious consequences for the enjoyment of economic, social and cultural rights. Against that background, it was gratifying that the Government of Panama had been prepared to establish a dialogue with the Committee. The presence of the Panamanian delegation had enabled members to gain a clearer appreciation of the situation obtaining in that country.

5.   The report submitted by Panama had been too generalized and legalistic in nature, merely enumerating legislative decrees, rather than giving details of practical measures taken to secure implementation of the Covenant. The Committee therefore welcomed the further details given by the delegation of Panama in the oral presentation, although it noted that a number of questions raised by the pre-sessional working group remained unanswered.

6.   Concern had been expressed by some members of the Committee regarding forced evictions in the <u>barrios</u> and the need to ensure that such evictions did not deny the most vulnerable sectors of Panamanian society the right to adequate housing.

7.   Members of the Committee had noted that the indigenous peoples were among the less privileged in that society, and that the rate of illiteracy among them was quite high, despite the provisions for compulsory education. In that

regard, note had been taken of the fact that the indigenous populations lived on reservations, often in remote areas, and were determined to maintain their traditions, customs and laws.

8.   The question of the reported high incidence of drug abuse and drug trafficking had been raised. It had been noted that there was an alarmingly high rate of involvement of foreigners in those activities.

9.   The view had been expressed that the restrictions placed on the participation of foreigners in the Executive Committee of Trade Unions were not in conformity with article 8 of the Covenant. Concern had also been expressed regarding the unequal distribution of household income in Panama, and the Government of Panama was requested to indicate measures proposed to redress that situation.

10.   Mr. SIMMA fully endorsed Mr. Rattray's remarks as reflecting the view of the Committee. His only reservation concerned the question of forced evictions, regarding which he felt that a fuller and more strongly worded text was called for. He wished to submit to the Committee a text which he had drafted in consultation with Mr. Wimer Zambrano and Mrs. Jiménez Butragueño, and which the Committee might adopt as its concluding observation on the question of forced evictions in Panama. That text stated that several detailed questions had been asked concerning both housing rights and evictions in Panama. The information provided by the delegation of Panama was considered unsatisfactory by the Committee for three reasons.

11.   First, the Government's claim that 3,000 persons had been affected by the bombing of El Chorrillo differed substantially from all other estimates, which placed the figure at between 12,500 and 20,000. The absence of reliable census figures on the population of El Chorrillo prior to the bombing might account for the disparity in the estimates. The Committee viewed that disparity with alarm, in view of the obligations incumbent upon the Government under the Covenant.

12.   Secondly, the responses given to questions concerning the current living conditions of residents of El Chorrillo made homeless by the bombing differed substantially from other information made available to the Committee. The Committee had received information pointing to the many complaints made by residents who had been provided with alternative accommodation, regarding the distance they must now travel to and from places of employment by relatively expensive public transportation, and regarding the generally poor quality of the housing in the resettlement sites. Moreover, two years after the invasion, a large number of persons had still to be rehoused.

13.   Thirdly, under the terms of the Covenant, the justification provided for the actions carried out by Panamanian and United States forces in Tocumen, San Miguelito and Panamá Viejo in early 1990, which had affected over 5,000 persons, was unacceptable as a reason for forcibly removing people from their homes. Searches for drugs, arms and criminals were frequently cited as justification for evictions. According to information received by the Committee, no drugs or arms had been found during those three actions. However, a large number of houses had been demolished, in spite of the fact that the persons affected had lived in the area concerned for more than two

0058

years. Additionally, those evictions had not been accompanied by legal
eviction orders. The Committee was of the view that evictions carried out in
that way not only infringed the right to adequate housing, but also infringed
inhabitants' rights to privacy and security of the home.

14. Mr. VELASQUEZ (Panama) thanked members of the Committee for their
concluding observations, and requested that they should be submitted to his
delegation in writing.

15. The CHAIRMAN said that the Committee had concluded its consideration of
the report of Panama. He assured the Permanent Representative of Panama that
the concluding observations would be included in the Committee's report on its
sixth session, which would be forwarded to the Permanent Mission in due
course. He thanked the delegation of Panama for its participation in a
constructive dialogue with the Committee.

16. Mr. Ucros, Ms. Vallarino and Mr. Velásquez (Panama) withdrew.

The meeting was suspended at 3.25 p.m. and resumed at 3.30 p.m.

Afghanistan (E/1990/5/Add.8, E/1984/6/Add.12) (continued)

17. At the invitation of the Chairman, Mr. Amani, Mr. Damoon and Mr. Wahadi
(Afghanistan) took places at the Committee table.

18. The CHAIRMAN invited Mrs. Jiménez Butragueño to open the concluding
observations phase of the Committee's consideration of the report on
Afghanistan.

19. Mrs. JIMENEZ BUTRAGUEÑO noted that the Committee had thanked the
Government of Afghanistan for submitting its report on articles 1 to 15 of the
Covenant at the present session, and had expressed its satisfaction at the
initiation of a dialogue with Afghanistan as a State party. With regard to
the report, the Committee had considered it to be unduly legalistic, since it
did not provide data on practical implementation of the provisions of the
Covenant, or on the true situation in Afghanistan with regard to the enjoyment
of economic, social and cultural rights.

20. The Committee thanked the delegation of Afghanistan for replying to
the 36 questions put by the pre-sessional working group, and to the questions
put by members of the Committee. While the delegation of Afghanistan had
provided useful additional information, answers to some of the Committee's
questions and concerns had not been fully satisfactory. First, the Committee
had expressed its concern at the situation regarding guarantees of respect
for fundamental freedoms, and at the treatment of political prisoners. The
Committee had been particularly concerned at the problem of the 5 million
Afghan refugees, accounting for one third of all refugees in the world, and,
in particular, at the state of implementation of the decrees to facilitate
their return, referred to by the Special Rapporteur, Mr. Ermacora, in
paragraph 32 of document E/CN.4/1991/31. It had also expressed concern
regarding the victims of the war, especially children.

0059

21. Special consideration had been given to the situation of women, in view of the fact that, although the Government had lodged no reservation at the time of ratification, so that article 3 of the Covenant was fully applicable in Afghanistan, some provisions of Islamic law, and also ancestral customs predating Islam, might impede full application of that article and prevent full respect for the principle of equality of rights between the sexes.

22. Lastly, the Committee had noted with interest the situation regarding the principles of freedom to form and join trade unions, tripartism, collective bargaining and the right to strike, set forth in article 8 of the Covenant, which Afghanistan, as a State party, was obliged to respect. In the light of all those considerations, the Committee was requesting the Government of Afghanistan to submit additional information on those issues. With regard to the situation of women, the Committee requested full answers to the questions put by the pre-sessional working group regarding the situation of women in Afghan society (their participation in political, social and trade union activity and their position in the field of work and professional activities, both in private economic activity and in public service, particularly at the senior level, and developments in that situation during the past five years); and as to whether full equality of rights between men and women had been achieved in Afghanistan in all areas of law (in civil law, particularly family law, penal and labour law), with an indication of any discrepancies that still existed and the measures planned to eliminate them.

23. The CHAIRMAN said that the Committee had concluded its consideration of the report of Afghanistan. He thanked the Vice-Minister of Justice and the other members of the delegation of Afghanistan for their willingness to engage in a constructive dialogue with the Committee.

24. Mr. Amani, Mr. Damoon and Mr. Wahidi (Afghanistan) withdrew.

Democratic People's Republic of Korea (E/1988/5/Add.6) (continued)

25. At the invitation of the Chairman, Mr. Chae Ryang Il, Mr. Li Tae Jun and Mr. Pak Dok Hun (Democratic People's Republic of Korea) took places at the Committee table.

26. Mr. CHAE Ryang Il (Democratic People's Republic of Korea), replying to questions from the Committee, said that by 1953, there had been widespread destruction of both material and human resources. There was not a single university and only 43 secondary schools remained throughout the country. Teaching aids and scientific equipment for schools were lacking. There was also a shortage of teachers: furthermore the economic situation did not permit sufficient funds to be allocated to the development of education. In addition, the difficulties experienced by Koreans in learning foreign languages, especially English and French, proved a bar to the acquisition of foreign culture.

27. The Constitution provided for parental right of choice in education. Furthermore, article 54 of the Constitution guaranteed freedom of religion while article 53 authorized a variety of activities by social organizations. Accordingly, many schools had been established by religious foundations or by social organizations such as the women's or the farmers' unions to which

0060

parents could send their children if they chose. There were also special
schools for gifted children and a few private schools in particular sectors,
such as computer training. Very young children could attend crèches or
kindergarten if the parents so wished, thus facilitating the employment of
women. Emphasis was laid on the development of young children, particularly
on their physical education. Access to higher education was strictly regulated
by competitive examination. In 1990, the intake of university and college
students had been 195,000, with 100,000 coming directly from secondary schools
and 95,000 having completed a period of employment after leaving school. In
1989, girls had constituted 51 per cent of primary and secondary school pupils
and 42 per cent of university students. All universities were open to both
sexes without discrimination but there was a tendency for women to specialize
in education and men in scientific subjects. Parents, social organizations
and the State were all actively involved in improving education and in
promoting an atmosphere conducive to learning. Schools had parent-teacher
guidance committees which met regularly once a month. They could make
suggestions for changes: for example, a recommendation from the committees of
specialized technical schools that they should be upgraded to colleges had
been accepted by the State. Rural and city schools offered the same standards
and the same textbooks were used throughout the country. In that connection,
the use of the words "monolithic educational system", in paragraph 17 of the
country report (E/1988/5/Add.6) was a mistake of translation. The position
would be better described by a word such as "uniform". Efforts were made to
promote knowledge about the science and technology of other countries.
Article 65 of the Constitution provided for cultural exchanges and scientific
agreements with foreign countries. In 1990, 180 teachers went abroad and
166 foreign lecturers came to the Democratic People's Republic. In the same
year 800 students went abroad to Eastern Europe, Asia and Western Europe,
including France and Switzerland, and 400 foreign students came to the
country. His Government's cooperation with UNICEF and UNESCO was increasing
steadily: in September 1990, a workshop on preschool education had been
organized in cooperation with UNICEF.

28.   In order to further international understanding and peace, teachers were
trained to teach world history and world geography; world literature, music
and art were studied at universities. Selected world literature was published
in translation. Children's stories, which were highly popular, were also
published in translation. Human rights was not taught as a separate subject
in educational institutions, but information was given about the rights of the
child and the Covenants and translations of them were available in libraries
and schools. Human Rights Day was celebrated by special lectures. Teachers
were actively involved in editing text books and in organizing curricula for
final approval by the State Education Commission.

29.   In addition to scholarships of various kinds, schoolchildren and students
enjoyed many benefits: no fees were payable at boarding schools, they received
free medical care and they paid only 40 to 50 per cent of the normal price for
text books. Uniforms were provided cheaply through university shops. In
addition, the State spent 585 won per head every year on social activities for
students and schoolchildren. The main purpose was to train young people to be
competent future builders of society through their knowledge, their high morals
and their good health. The purpose of physical education was solely to ensure
a healthy rising generation.

30. Teachers received relatively higher salaries than other workers, who averaged 100 won per month, whereas the average for teachers was about 130 won. Such salaries were larger than they appeared because the people-centred policy of the State ensured that basic necessities such as food, clothing and housing were provided very cheaply; for example, the monthly rent for a four-bedroomed house, including electricity, heating and water was 10 won. There was no discrimination against women in teaching appointments and if they had more than two children they received the salary appropriate for an eight-hour day for six hours daily work. They received 150 days maternity leave on full pay in addition to the regular paid leave.

31. There was no problem of ethnic minorities, since all the people spoke a single language and had the same culture and customs; the nation had lived from time immemorial on the same territory.

32. Turning to the problem of the eradication of illiteracy, he recalled that in 1945, the time of the liberation of the country, there had been 2.3 million illiterates, accounting for nearly 80 per cent of the adult population. Accordingly, the literacy campaign had been assigned priority as a most important factor in the construction of a new society. It had been no easy task to eradicate illiteracy within a short period of time, since millions of adults were involved. A large number of teachers had to be provided, as well as great quantities of teaching material. Since most of those concerned were workers engaged in productive activities, it had been necessary to arrange for them to learn on the job without interrupting their productive work. At the same time, the task of building a new society had to go on unimpeded. The nationwide literacy campaign had been conducted under the State's unified plan of guidance, which set up State machinery for the control and guidance of the campaign, as well as a unit in the Education Department to ensure uniformity in the conduct of the literacy campaign; in addition, a special committee was set up, with the task of investigating the extent of illiteracy and ensuring that illiterate persons attended literacy classes.

33. In that connection, it should be remembered that State guidance could be fruitful only when the masses themselves were actively involved. The necessary zeal had had to be instilled into both learners and teachers. An awareness of the importance of the campaign had had to be propagated. Many persons had taken an active interest in learning but some - especially peasants and women - were not fully motivated because of ignorance due to the influence of the older society. That influence had produced a passive attitude on the part of those who said "What is the use of learning now?". It had been necessary to root out those ideas and to impress upon the working people that knowledge was power and ignorance was ruin. Accordingly, the slogan "Study, study and continue to study" had been posted everywhere in factories, farms and streets. Propaganda to promote literacy had also taken the form of lectures, talks and songs with literacy as the theme. All available teachers and university students, and indeed all literate persons, had been mobilized so that one person taught 10 other persons to read and write; those 10 persons, in their turn, taught 100 others to read and write. That method had proved decisive in securing the services of the large number of teachers needed. As for classrooms, the problem had been solved by using institutions, enterprises, dwelling houses and schools. In short, the nationwide campaign turned the

0062

whole country into one great school. By March 1949, in less than four years, 2.3 million persons had been made literate. That achievement represented the first victory of his people in the struggle against the backwardness left by the old society.

34. Mr. PAK Dok Hun, replying to the questions which had been raised, explained that the main difficulty encountered after liberation by his country with respect to the development of literature and the arts was the painful fact that numerous national relics had been taken away by foreigners during the 46 years of the colonial period. In addition, many such items forming part of the national cultural heritage had been destroyed during the 1950-1953 war. The main difficulty, however, was the fact that a large proportion of the adult population was illiterate. In addition, the traditional national arts had suffered terribly from the colonial policy of obliterating the national culture. Also, Western music and painting had attracted so much interest that the public tended to look down upon their own culture while admiring that of other countries.

35. A further difficulty arose from the fact that the country had been divided for 46 years, so that it was not possible to promote a uniform cultural development.

36. Furthermore, writers and artists at the outset of the construction of socialism had had a tendency to remain working at their desks without mixing with the people. That situation had produced artistic works which did not depict reality and which did not attract the interest of the masses. Lastly, amateur art groups had a tendency to professionalize their artistic work.

37. Those were the main difficulties encountered by his country in the matter. Article 60 of the Constitution stated: "Citizens are free to engage in scientific, literary and artistic pursuits". Replying to the question by some members of the Committee about the existence of organs or institutions to guide the development of artistic and literary work, he stressed that the Party and the State only provided guidance, in conformity with the feelings, desires and requirements of the working people. Consequently, the State directives in the matter promoted the creation of literary and artistic works which were national in form and socialist in content. The Ministry of Culture and the Ministry of Literature and the Arts directed and organized artistic and literary activities in conformity with that approach. Subordinated to those Ministries, there were creative literary organizations, film studios, dramatic art companies, film distribution centres and publication centres responsible for the creation and dissemination of writings and artistic works. He stressed that the guidance of the State was based on the tastes and interests of a working people; that approach, however, did not mean that works departing from the approved standards could not be created. He could give the example of a song which had become popular recently and the lyrics of which were based on a poem going back to the period before the revolution which depicted love between a boy and a girl. Also, many films were produced which criticized leading personalities.

38. Any citizen could write freely or create artistic works but the question whether the book would be published or the artistic work exhibited was another matter. For that to occur, it would have to be submitted to the National

0063

E/C.12/1991/SR.8
page 9

Examination Committee (an institution which existed in other countries as well) consisting of leading members of the Ministry of Literature and the Arts and of experienced professional artists. He stressed that no Party official was a member and that there was no interference from the Party with the work of the Committee. The Committee was responsible for ensuring that objectionable material dealing with war and violence was kept to a minimum. Much creative work in the matter of literature and art did not go through the Committee. However, literary and artistic works designed for entertainment on a nationwide scale had to be approved by the Committee before they were sold to the public or performed.

39. There were no private publishing houses in the country or private film studies or cinemas. Freedom of the press was guaranteed by article 53 of the Constitution. As far as he knew, however, there had been no request from any private organization to set up a publishing house.

40. Foreign films were shown regularly on television to large audiences on Saturday and Sunday. Most foreign films came from India, the Soviet Union, China, Egypt and Algeria. Moreover, although it was true that his country constantly called for the withdrawal of the United States from South Korea, there was no objection to benefiting from art and literature created by persons in the United States. Thus, such United States film classics as "Roots" and "Gone with the Wind" had been shown and Korean children enjoyed cartoon films from the United States.

41. Many foreign books had been translated as few people read and wrote foreign languages. Foreign books as well as foreign newspapers and magazines were available at the Grand People's Study Home with its 600 reading rooms. The libraries of the Ministry of Foreign Affairs and the Ministry of Foreign Trade, the many research institutions and universities, as well as foreign language schools, had a large stock of foreign books. At those institutions, there were regular showings of foreign films in their original versions. Pursuant to cultural exchange agreements with foreign countries and with individual companies abroad, foreign theatre companies visited the country and Korean companies toured abroad every year.

42. In 1990, a Pan-National Unification Concert had been held both at Pyongyang and at Seoul in South Korea with the participation of musicians and singers from north and south of the country as well as overseas Koreans from the Soviet Union, China, Japan and even the United States.

43. Turning to the question of the Juche philosophy, he stressed that it was essentially a people-centred philosophy which considered man to be the master of his own destiny and the decisive factor in transforming the world. That approach was based on the idea that man must display independence, creativity and consciousness. It served to combat the unfortunate tendency to look down upon one's own culture and admire that of the larger countries surrounding the Democratic People's Republic. That approach was fully consistent with article 14 of the Covenant. The promotion of the people's own creativity did not mean any opposition to the ideas and thoughts of other peoples.

0064

44. The overall development of the country was rendered difficult by its division. His Government, nevertheless, did its best to promote stable living conditions for the population. Its citizens enjoyed freedom of expression and freedom of movement over the whole of its territory except in the vicinity of the military zone.

45. In conclusion, he said that his delegation would attempt to answer any further questions put to it.

46. Mr. SIMMA said that he had understood from the government representative's statement that one of the problems encountered after the liberation of the Democratic People's Republic of Korea from Japanese colonial domination in 1945 had been the considerable number of Western paintings that had had to be done away with, and he asked when exactly such paintings had actually entered the country, since the Communist Party had taken over immediately after the liberation and he did not imagine that the Japanese authorities would have encouraged such painting.

47. Mr. PAK Dok Hun (Democratic People's Republic of Korea) said that Western painting had been introduced during the period of colonial rule between 1910 and 1945. He pointed out that his country had an age-old tradition of specifically Korean painting.

48. Mr. NENEMAN said that, although interesting answers had been given to many questions, some had remained unanswered, possibly for reasons beyond the delegation's control. A case in point had been the question raised about the affirmation that the President's theses gave perfect answers to all theoretical and practical problems arising in education.

49. He sought further clarification on some points. For instance, with reference to the statement that decisions concerning publication or performance of creative works were taken by a committee, he assumed that such decisions were based on the premise that such works should be socialist in content and nationalist in form, failing which they would probably be prohibited. To take a specific, if somewhat extreme, example, it could be assumed that portrayals of nudes in artistic works would not be allowed. He asked, therefore, whether there was free artistic expression or, on the contrary, strict rules based on very narrow criteria.

50. Mr. CHANG Ryang Il (Democratic People's Republic of Korea) said that the "Theses on Socialist Education" of President Kim Il Sung, published in 1977, had mapped out the direction which educational development should take. On the basis of those guidelines, the people, including educationists, teachers, students, parents and even religious bodies, had been actively involved in the debate on how the education system and educational content and methods should be reshaped and improved. The long-standing committee for educational guidance, which was composed of government officials, educational authorities, teachers, social organizations of all kinds, as well as parents, and met once a month, monitored progress in education and examined all problems and issues raised by teachers, students and other interested parties themselves, on an ongoing basis. The resolutions it adopted, which were thus an expression of the will of the people, subsequently had force of law after adoption by the Council of Ministers. It could thus be seen that the theses

laid down the basic direction that education should take, but the system itself was seen as an evolving process and was constantly updated, further developed and enriched to meet the needs of the people objectively. An example were the examinations set for admission to higher educational institutions.

51. Mr. PAK Dok Hun (Democratic People's Republic of Korea) said that the guidelines formulated by the State and the Party for the development of literature and the arts did not mean that all works contrary to those principles were prohibited. Feature films about all aspects of life, including life in foreign countries, were shown regularly, as were numerous foreign films, for instance at the film festival of the non-aligned countries. In response to the comment about nude paintings, he said that the traditional way of life in Korean society and the modesty of Korean women must be respected. To his knowledge, such portrayals were alien to the Korean tradition.

52. Mrs. BONOAN-DANDAM said that there was another facet to Mr. Neneman's pertinent question about freedom of artistic expression, namely the opportunity for any person to appreciate freely a work of art of his own choosing. If a group of people was assigned the task of determining which works were in conformity with the good of the people and, if not, banning it from public view, how could members of the public at large benefit fully from free creative expression?

53. Mr. PAK Dok Hun (Democratic People's Republic of Korea) said that works that had not passed the National Examination Committee could be enjoyed in private, but all works for publication or public viewing or performance were subject to the Committee's authorization. It was, however, very rare for the Committee to veto works submitted to it.

54. Mr. KONATE, commenting on the use of the word "immortal" in connection with President Kim Il Sung's theses on education, observed that, in accordance with the concept of historical materialism, developments in society - and hence theories - should surely be seen as a dialectical and dynamic process.

55. Mr. RATTRAY said that the discussion on freedom of artistic expression put him in an intellectual and cultural dilemma. Even in Western countries, films and other productions had to pass boards of censors, and works contrary to public morals might be banned. It was still not altogether clear to him whether the prohibition of certain works by the Korean authorities was based on the criterion that in their judgement they were contrary to public morals.

56. Mr. PAK Dok Hun (Democratic People's Republic of Korea) said that to his knowledge every country had some kind of system to check films before they were released to the public, and the Korean system was no exception. Artistic works and publications which constituted incitement to hatred, violence, crime and war, for instance, would not be passed, but the Committee would examine the content and give its opinions to the authors.

0066

57.   The CHAIRMAN thanked the representatives of the Democratic People's
Republic of Korea for their participation.

58.   Mr. Chae Ryang Il, Mr. Li Tae Jun and Mr. Pak Dok Hun (Democratic People's
Republic of Korea) withdrew.

ORGANIZATION OF WORK (continued)

59.   The CHAIRMAN said that the issue of artistic freedom, which had arisen
during the Committee's consideration of the previous report, seemed to be a
good example of the difficulties faced by the Committee in the absence of a
comprehensive range of bench-marks or established positions on issues raised
by the Covenant, and might usefully be the subject of a general comment.

60.   Mr. KONATE said that, with a view to drafting a general comment on
article 15, he would gladly take the lead in preparing some initial thoughts
on artistic freedom for discussion at the next session.

61.   The CHAIRMAN thanked Mr. Konate for his offer, which would be an important
first step towards drafting a general comment.

62.   Mr. WIMER ZAMBRANO expressed the view, which had also been expressed by
other members of the Committee on other occasions, that the approach adopted
by the Committee during the concluding observations phase of its consideration
of the reports of Panama and Afghanistan was not in fact the most appropriate
approach.   Some members felt strongly that the concluding observations phase
of the proceedings should take place in closed session.   He saw no advantage
in permitting representatives of State parties, who had already had an
opportunity to put their countries' views, to be present at those sessions.
Indeed, there was a danger that, if delegations were present, the proceedings
might end in acrimony.   He asked the Chairman to take note of his comments,
which, he hoped, would be borne in mind when, at some appropriate time,
the Committee came to review its work methods.

63.   The CHAIRMAN said that the matter raised by Mr. Wimer Zambrano was
clearly an issue on which some members felt strongly.   The possibility of
conducting the final phase of consideration of reports in closed session was
an option to which serious consideration should be given.

The meeting rose at 5.30 p.m.

MEMBERSHIP OF THE COMMITTEE ON ECONOMIC, SOCIAL AND CULTURAL RIGHTS

Name of member	Country of nationality	Term expires on 31 Dec.
Mr. Philip ALSTON	Australia	1994
Mr. Juan ALVAREZ VITA	Peru	1992
Mr. Abdel Halim BADAWI	Egypt	1994
Mrs. Virginia BONOAN-DANDAN	Philippines	1994
Mr. Mohamed Lamine FOFANA	Guinea	1992
Mrs. Luvsandanzangiin IDER	Mongolia	1994
Mrs. Maria de los Angeles JIMENEZ BUTRAGUENO	Spain	1992
Mr. Samba Cor KONATE	Senegal	1992
Mr. Valeri KOUZNETSOV	Union of Soviet Socialist Republics	1994
Mr. Jaime MARCHAN ROMERO	Ecuador	1994
Mr. Vassil MRATCHKOV	Bulgaria	1992
X Mr. Alexandre MUTERAHEJURU	Rwanda	1994
Mr. Wladyslaw NENEMAN	Poland	1992
Mr. Kenneth Osborne RATTRAY	Jamaica	1992
Mr. Bruno SIMMA	Germany,	1994
Mr. Mikis Demetriou SPARSIS	Cyprus	1992
Mr. Philippe TEXIER	France	1992
Mr. Javier WIMER ZAMBRANO	Mexico	1994

0068

북한의 A규약 보고서(개요)

o 북한은 주체사상에 입각, 아래와 같이 동규약을 이행하고 있음.

제 13 조 (교육권)

o 북한의 교육은 김일성이 1977년 제5차 노동당 중앙위 4차 회기에서 발표한 "사회주의 교육에 관한 테제"에 근거

o 헌법상 관련조항
   - 제40조 : 공교육과 국가기관 요원양성에 우선
   - 제41조 : 10년간의 무상 의무교육
   - 제42조 : 정규교육제도를 통한 기술자 및 전문가 양성
   - 제43조 : 모든 취학전 아동에 1년간 의무교육

I. 초등 및 중등교육권

   o 1956년부터 무상 초등교육 실시
   o 1958년부터 무상 중등교육 실시
   o 1967년부터 9년간의 보통의무기술교육 실시
   o 1972년부터 11년간의 보통의무교육(1년간의 취학전 교육포함) 실시

II. 고등교육권

   o 11년간의 의무교육을 이수한 자는 희망, 재능, 적성에 따라 고등교육을 받을 자격이 있음.
   o 고등교육의 실시로 131만명의 기술자 및 전문가 양성
   o 현장교육제도의 확립으로 공장대학, 농장대학, 어촌대학, 방송대학을 통한 생활지식 교육

1

Ⅲ. 무상교육

   o 국가가 근로인민아동의 모든 교육비용을 부담

   o 교복, 학용품, 특별활동비등도 부담

   o 모범학생에 대한 "김일성 장학금" 수여

Ⅳ. 교육의 내용 및 방법

   o 수학, 물리, 화학등 기본과학분야의 일반지식

   o 생산에 필요한 기본적 기술교육(지역, 성별에 따라 상이)

   o 체육교육, 특히 집단체육활동 중시

Ⅴ. 학교제도의 발전

   o 국가는 학교건립, 교육시설, 기타 교육지원을 위해 예산등 각종 지원

   o 87년 현재, 대학교 244개, 특수학교 499개, 중.고등학교 4820개,
      국민학교 4779개

Ⅵ. 교사요원의 물적조건 향상

   o 교사교육제도에는 교사교육대학, 사범대학, 대학원 과정, 자격증 수여
      연구원이 있음.

   o 특별한 성과나 능력등에 따라 "인민교사", "우수교사" 또는 "교수",
      "조교수"의 호칭부여

   o 여교사에 대한 특별보호

Ⅶ. 기초교육권

   o 해방이후 3년만에 2백 30여만의 문맹퇴치

   o 성인교육은 모든 근로인민의 중등교육 이상을 목표

제 14 조 (무상.의무교육의 원칙)

제 15 조 (문화생활, 과학발전의 이익, 저술권의 보장)

o 관련 헌법조항

 - 제44조 : 과학연구의 주체확립과 협력강화를 통한 과학.기술의
          진보 촉진

 - 제45조 : 주체적 혁명문학과 예술 개발

I . 문화적 생활권

 o 예술과 문학을 인민에게 대중화시켜 최대한 향유할수 있도록 노력

 o 극장, 도서관 및 각종 문화시설을 설치

 o 예술 및 문학그룹의 조직, 아동 및 학생들에 대한 문화특별활동 실시

II . 저작권 보호

III . 과학연구와 창조활동의 자유

 o 농업과학원, 의학원등 과학연구기관 설치

 o 기타 과학자의 연구활동을 위한 각종 지원

3

0071

북한의 인권규약 보고서 제출 및 심의

1. 경제적, 사회적, 문화적 권리에 관한 국제규약(A규약)

o 발효일자 : 81.12.14.

o 최초보고서 제출 및 심의

- 제1부 : 84년 제출, 87년 심의

- 제2부 : 86년 제출, 87년 심의

- 제3부 : 88년 제출, 91년 심의

o 제2차 보고서 제출

- 83.9.1까지 제출시한인 2차 보고서 제1부를 아직 제출치 않고 있음.

* 최초보고서 제3부 심의내용(91.11.27-29)

- 보고서 내용

. 해방직후부터 교육, 과학, 기술 및 문화예술 창달 노력 주장

. 교육관련, 김일성의 "사회주의 교육 테제"에 따른 무상, 의무교육, 직장교육, 학교선택의 자유등을 기술

. 과학, 기술연구 및 문화예술활동 관련, 당과 정부의 역할, 저작권 및 과학기술 연구, 창조활동 자유보장을 기술

- 위원 질문내용

. 북한의 단일(monolithic) 교육체제 및 유일 주체사상의 영향하에서 학교선택권, 교육선택의 자유가 보장될수 있는지 여부

. 또한 유일사상하에서 연구 및 문화예술 활동이 보장될수 있는지, 특히 창작 및 출판검열위원회에 의한 활동자유 침해 위험성이 집중 제기됨.

. 보고서가 법률적, 이론적 측면만 부각되고 현실적 상황에 관한 구체적 진술이 결여됨.

0072

2. 시민적, 정치적 권리에 관한 국제규약(B규약)

o 발효일자 : 81.12.14.

o 최초보고서 제출 및 심의

　- 83.10.23, 84.4.2. 제출

　- 84.4월 심의

o 제2차 보고서 제출

　- 87.12.13. 제출시한이나 아직 미제출

0073

외교문서 비밀해제: 한국 인권문제 17
한국 인권문제 민주화 관련 기타 자료 2

초판인쇄 2024년 03월 15일
초판발행 2024년 03월 15일

지은이 한국학술정보(주)
펴낸이 채종준
펴낸곳 한국학술정보(주)
주 소 경기도 파주시 회동길 230(문발동)
전 화 031-908-3181(대표)
팩 스 031-908-3189
홈페이지 http://ebook.kstudy.com
E-mail 출판사업부 publish@kstudy.com
등 록 제일산-115호(2000. 6. 19)

ISBN 979-11-7217-071-4 94340
     979-11-7217-054-7 94340 (set)